(DSDP, Leg 26). In: T.A. Davies, B.P. Luyendyk, et al., Initial Reports of the Deep Sea Drilling Project, 26. U.S. Govt. Printing Office, Washington, D.C., pp.675—741.

Boltovskoy, E., in prep. Neogene deep water benthonic foraminifera of the Indian Ocean.

Burmistrova, I.I., 1974. Raspredelenie glubokovodnykh bentosnykh foraminifer v Bengal'skom zalive i na severnom sklone thentral'nogo basseina Indijskogo Okeana (in Russian, with English abstract). In: Mikropaleontologia Okeanov i morej. Nauka, Moscow, pp.130—137.

Davies, T.A. and Luyendyk, B.P., 1974. Site reports. In: T.A. Davies, B.P. Luyendyk et al., Initial Reports of the Deep Sea Drilling Project, 26. U.S. Govt. Printing Office, Washington, D.C., pp.3—414.

Douglas, R.G., 1973. Benthonic foraminiferal biostratigraphy in the Central North Pacific, Leg 17, DSDP. In: E.L. Winterer, J.L. Ewing et al., Initial Reports of the Deep Sea Drilling Project, 17. U.S. Govt. Printing Office, Washington, D.C., pp.607—671.

Loeblich, A.R. and Tappan, H., 1964. Sarcodina, Chiefly "Thecamoebians" and Foraminiferida, part C. In: R. Moore (Editor), Treatise on Invertebrate Paleontology. Geological Society of America and University of Kansas, 900 pp.

McGowran, B., 1974. Foraminifera. In: C.C. von der Borch, J.G. Sclater et al., Initial Reports of the Deep Sea Drilling Project, 22. U.S. Govt. Printing Office, Washington, D.C., pp.609—627.

Parker, F.L., 1964. Foraminifera from the experimental Mohole drilling near Guadelupe island, Mexico. J.Paleontol., 38: pp.1507—1532.

Todd, R., 1965. The foraminifera of the Tropical Pacific collections of the "Albatross", 1899—1900, part 4. Rotaliform families and planktonic families. U.S. Nat.Mus., Bull., 161(part 4): pp.1—139.

Von der Borch, C.C. and Sclater, J.G., 1974. Site reports. In: C.C. von der Borch, J.G. Sclater et al., Initial Reports of the Deep Sea Drilling Project, 22. U.S. Govt. Printing Office, Washington, D.C., pp.1—348.

SCIENCE AND RELIGION

one world - changing perspectives on reality

SCIENCE AND RELIGION

one world - changing perspectives on reality

Papers presented at the
Second European Conference on Science and Religion
March 10-13, 1988

University of Twente

edited by
Jan Fennema and Iain Paul

KLUWER ACADEMIC PUBLISHERS
DORDRECHT / BOSTON / LONDON

ISBN 0-7923-0731-3 (HB)

Published by Kluwer Academic Publishers,
P.O. Box 17, 3300 AA Dordrecht, The Netherlands.

Kluwer Academic Publishers incorporates
the publishing programmes of
D. Reidel, Martinus Nijhoff, Dr W. Junk and MTP Press.

Sold and distributed in the U.S.A. and Canada
by Kluwer Academic Publishers,
101 Philip Drive, Norwell, MA 02061, U.S.A.

In all other countries, sold and distributed
by Kluwer Academic Publishers Group,
P.O. Box 322, 3300 AH Dordrecht, The Netherlands.

Paperback available from:
EUR. CONF. ON SCIENCE AND RELIGION
c/o J.W.R. Fennema CS
Postbus 665,
1200 AR Hilversum, The Netherlands
ISBN 90-365-0324-8 (PB)

Cover and lay-out:
Videac, University of Twente,
Enschede, The Netherlands

Printed on acid-free paper

Printed in the Netherlands

Contents

Statement of Intention   p.   8
Preface (Jan Fennema, Iain Paul)   p.   9
An encounter between science and religion;
preliminary observations (Jan Fennema)   p. 13

Part I   Lectures in full sessions

Epitome of Part I   p. 26

Introduction to the conference theme
   A.G.M. van Melsen, *Science and religion*   p. 27
   T.F. Torrance, *Fundamental issues in theology and science*   p. 35
   M. Bloemendal, *Science and religion - the Jewish position*   p. 47

Reconciling developments in the natural sciences - the question of scientism
   A. Gierer, *Physics, life and mind*   p. 61
   W. Weidlich, *Reconciling concepts between natural science and theology*   p. 73
   J.C. Polkinghorne F.R.S., *A revived natural theology*   p. 87

Reconciling developments in theology - the question of dogmatism
   W.B. Drees, *Theology and cosmology beyond the Big Bang theory*   p. 99
   J. Van der Veken, *God's world and man becoming:*
how can science possibly help us transcend dogmatism?   p. 131

The divorce of science and religion - a process in retrospect
   O. Pedersen, *Historical interaction between science and religion*   p. 139
   J.R. Durant, *Is there a role for theology in an age of secular science?*   p. 161

Science and religion studies today and tomorrow
   J. Hübner, *Science and religion coming across*   p. 173
   G. Vahanian, *Creation and Big Bang: the word as space of creation*   p. 183

Part II   Contributions in sectional meetings

J.A. Mawuli Awudza, *Science and religion: a Ghanaian perspective*   p. 194
R. Becerra-Acevedo, *The mystical ideal and the humanistic ideal*
    within the world of ideals in the sciences   p. 195
G.J. Béné, *Scientific truth and religious truth*   p. 196
P.W. Böckmann, *Two approaches and one reality*:
    on religion and the perception of the Cosmos   p. 197
S.L. Bonting, *Man and the high-technology society*   p. 198
M.E. Carvallo, *On David Bohm's theory of wholeness and implicate order*:
    provisional notes, some of which with special regard
    to the possible applications to the philosophy of religion   p. 199
A. Drago, *A. Koyré and the metaphysics of modern science*   p. 200
H. van Erkelens, *The unus mundus (One World)*
    as meeting ground of science and religion   p. 201
A.D. Fokker, *The play that is going on in the cosmic scenery*   p. 202
B. Gaál, *A report from the Reformed College of Debrecen*   p. 203
G. Gaizler, *Interdisciplinary lectures at 6 o' clock*   p. 204
M. Głódź, *Beyond the alternative: divorce or methodological chaos*   p. 205
H. Hafner, *Neither divorce nor reconciliation*:
    is there a gospel for the sciences?   p. 206
M. Heller, *The experience of limits: new physics and new theology*   p. 207
I. Hofmann, *Evolution and progressive revelation*:
    the Bahá'i approach to a converging reality   p. 208
J. Wentzel V. van Huyssteen,
    Beyond dogmatism: rationality in theology and science   p. 209
R. Kirby, *Spirituality and science: summary of purpose and proceedings*   p. 210
P.P. Kirschenmann, M.A. Maurice and A.W. Musschenga,
    The unchanged relationship of theology and science   p. 211
R. Koltermann S.J., *The concept of evolution*:
    its reception in philosophy and theology   p. 212
U. Krolzik, *Secularization of nature during the early Enlightenment*:
    conceptions of water circulation as an impulse for secularization   p. 213
G. Lepoutre, *The scientific mind and personal faith*   p. 214
G. Medgyesi, *The views of a Hungarian catholic scholar on evolution*
    at the end of the nineteenth century   p. 215
C. Ouafo Moghomaye, *Traditional religion and Christianity*   p. 216
L. Morren, *A generalized principle of complementarity - seen as a sign*   p. 217
W. Noodt, *Evolution and future of human possibilities of gaining knowledge*   p. 219
K.H. Reich, *The relation between science and theology*:
    the case for complementarity revisited   p. 220
J. Scheer, *Base the science-religion dialogue on facts, not on doctrines!*   p. 221

M. Siciński, *The reconciliation of social science and theology:*
    is it still not possible?   p. 222
G.J. Stavenga, *A new perspective on reality*   p. 223
J. Szél, *Humanitas ecologica*   p. 224
C. Wassermann, *On a relativistic structure in theology*   p. 225
H.J. Winkler, *The Academy of Research of the Evangelical Church of the Union,*
    German Democratic Republic, a research report   p. 226
J. Życiński, *The split between science and religion*
    and the doctrine of God's immanence in nature   p. 227

Part III   **List of names and addresses**   p. 230

Statement of intention

In December 1986, the Organizing Committee issued a statement of intention, the text being:

It is the aim of the organizers of the European Conferences on Science and Religion to provide a forum for discussing this fundamental theme of Western culture in an interdisciplinary way. Science is a dominant factor of present day society, and so is religion in its many forms, both inside and outside the traditional institutions.
Scientific points of view and expectations need to be in dialogue with religious forms of understanding - and religious traditions need to take account of the new scientific perspectives on the world and the ethical problems generated by science, medicine and technology. Thus the organizers hope to provide an opportunity for a balanced exchange fruitful for both 'science' and 'religion', and for the benefit of society as a whole.

Preface

The world is increasingly becoming one. It is, at the same time, one endangered ecosystem and one thriving market place with material and spiritual goods on competitive display. And the good and evil things of life cannot easily be sorted out. The world is becoming one also in the sense that it is better understood today than it was in earlier times, that the material good and the spiritual good, though seemingly belonging to different realms of fact defined by their respective modes of existence, together constitute effectively one and the same reality: the modern world of science, technology, computerized administration and power, that calls upon humankind to struggle for a 'just, participatory and sustainable society'*, and to strive for a society of the future that will be the world over both long-lived and worth living. The Second European Conference on Science and Religion, held on 10-13th. March, 1988, on the campus of the Universiteit Twente, Enschede, The Netherlands, was meant to be a modest market place, a forum, where standpoints and opinions could be presented and criticized. It was meant to offer an opportunity to meet and to make acquaintances in the expectation that the exchange of thoughts would lead to new conceptual horizons that would challenge what so far had been considered as hard fact or what until now had been looked upon as a distinctive feature of a well-established view either of the kingdom of the sciences or of the realm of religion.

The decision to organize the Second European Conference on Science and Religion was taken by the International Committee, at the time consisting of the following members:

Prof. Dr. S. Andersen, theologian, Aarhus Universitet, Aarhus

Dr. J. W. R. Fennema, physicist, NWO/FOM, Universiteit Twente, Enschede

Dr. H. May, theologian, Evangelische Akademie Loccum, Rehburg-Loccum

Dr. A. R. Peacocke, physical-biochemist and theologian, Ian Ramsey Centre, St. Cross College, Oxford

Prof. Dr. K. Schmitz-Moormann, theologian and anthropologist, Fachhochschule, Dortmund

Dr. M. Striegnitz, physicist, Evangelische Akademie Loccum, Rehburg-Loccum.

---

* World Council of Churches terminology; see e.g. Charles Birch et al, *Faith, Science and the Future*, Church and Society, WCC, Geneva 1978.

The first meeting of this Committee followed the closing of the First European Conference on Science and Religion, which was held in the Evangelische Akademie Loccum, 10-13th. March, 1986. The theme of the Second Conference was chosen and details of its programme were arranged in conformity with the wishes expressed by the participants during the closing session of the First Conference. In order to organize the new Conference properly, an Organizing Committee was formed consisting of the members of the International Committee and representatives of four institutions in The Netherlands that are active in the field of 'science' and 'religion'. The names of these institutions and of their representatives are given below.

The theme of the Conference was: 'One world - changing perspectives on reality'. The Organizing Committee invited twelve speakers to address the conference participants in full session. Moreover thirty three papers were submitted for discussion in sectional meetings.

Part I of the present book contains the texts of the lectures that were delivered by the invited speakers; due to unfortunate circumstances one lecture could not be delivered at the Conference. The texts are given following the pattern of the Conference programme. After introductions to the Conference theme from different angles, surveys are given of developments that are taking place in the natural sciences and in theology; next come the lectures that consider in retrospect the traditional dichotomy between science and religion, and, finally, there are those lectures that enlarge upon expectations for the future.

Part II contains the summaries of contributions made by participants in the sectional meetings, although two of them, those by J.A. Mawuli Awudza and by C. Ouafo Moghomaye, were presented in a full session; five contributions, those intended by A. Drago, G. Gaizler, J. Scheer, J. Szél and H.J. Winkler, were not presented for a variety of reasons, such as delayed arrival or ill-health. All summaries are in English but, at the Conference itself, many papers were read in French or German. The summaries have been placed in the alphabetical order of the authors' names, an arrangement that seemed much less contrived in the present context than the six original groupings of the Conference programme. The summaries reflect a wide variety of opinion and approach, dealing with all kinds of questions. We suggest that the reader interested in a particular text should correspond with the author(s). All texts edited by us have been returned to their authors for a final check. In some cases, we have not received a reply (in good time). This circumstance is indicated by the sign '(eds.)', appearing at the end of the given text.

Part III concludes the book with a list of names and addresses. At the Conference desk we registered one hundred and forty seven participants, including speakers, but the list also contains the names of those who showed their interest in other ways.

We asserted earlier that the Conference was a market place. These words may be taken as an apology for the absence of a report on the discussions that took place in full session. In principle, ample time was allowed for the exchange of thoughts among the participants on questions relating to the Conference as a whole. A case in point is the discussion, which remained open-ended, concerning the name of future conferences: Are they to be called 'conferences on science and religion' or 'conferences on science and theology'? Times are changing. And the name does make a difference: the right name makes an auspicous start in creating a programme!

Some explanatory words about religious confessions seem to be in order. In addition to typical Jewish and Christian points of view, more or less implicitly taken as a framework for many discussions or conversations, Islamic and Bahá'i convictions were expressed, as well as the persuasions of many participants who had obviously no particular religious affiliation. It was, indeed, a great pleasure for the Organizers to find so much evidence of a 'pluriformity' of expression regarding religion. In fact, traditions that appear to be well-established and that have been hallowed through the centuries should be open to criticism and dialogue, from the bottom up rather than from the top down. They should be challenged to make their positions clear and secure in modern - and post-modern - times, and to this momentous end they should be questioned at the grass roots by those who profess entirely different things, whether religious or irreligious.

Finally, though probably superfluously, we wish to stipulate that the responsibility for any of the texts published in this book rests with the author of that text.

The Conference has received considerable financial support from several sources. During the preparation of this book, further support was obtained to enable its publication at a reasonable price and promote its distribution. We acknowledge gratefully the generosity bestowed upon us. Listed alphabetically, the supporting institutions are:

Euregio
Evangelische Akademie Loccum
Faculteit der Wijsbegeerte en Maatschappijwetenschappen, Universiteit Twente
Haella Stichting
Kirchenkanzlei der Evangelischen Kirche der Union, Berlin
Koninklijke Nederlandse Akademie van Wetenschappen
Ministerie van Onderwijs en Wetenschappen
Sormanifonds
Stichting Universiteitsfonds Twente
Vereniging voor Christelijk Wetenschappenlijk Onderwijs.

Moreover, three donations were received from private sources in France and in The Netherlands.

The host of the Conference was the Universiteit Twente (the University of Twente), and the participants were welcomed by its Rector Magnificus, Prof. Dr. Ir. H.H. van den Kroonenberg.

While organizing the Conference in the University's conference and study centre, Drienerburght, institutional support, again listed in alphabetical order, was graciously given by: Atomium (Prof. Dr. H.W. de Knijff; Dr. P. van Dijk)
Bezinningscentrum Vrije Universiteit (Prof. Dr. A.W. Mussschenga; Drs. W. Haan)
Katholiek Studiecentrum Katholieke Universiteit Nijmegen
(Prof. Dr. J.C.F. Nuchelmans; Drs. G.P.A. Dierick)
Multidisciplinair Centrum voor Kerk en Samenleving (Dr. Mady A. Thung);

and by the
Secretariaat Wijsbegeerte, and other departments, Universiteit Twente
Directors and Staff Drienerburght, Logica and Bastille.
In addition, there was fruitful co-operation with:
Evangelische Akademie Loccum
Raad van Kerken in Nederland.
The Organizers could also rely on recommendations given by (emeritus) members of the following universities:
Katholieke Universiteit Nijmegen (Prof. Dr. P. Bennema, physicist)
Rijksuniversiteit Leiden (Prof. Dr. P. van Duijn, biologist; Prof. Dr. A.A. Verveen, physiologist)
Rijksuniversiteit Utrecht (Prof. Dr. H.M. de Knijff, theologian;
Prof. Dr. H.M. de Lange, economist)
Vrije Universiteit Amsterdam (Prof. Dr. M.A. Maurice, mathematician;
Prof. Dr. P.P. Kirschenmann, philosopher)
Universiteit Twente (Prof. Dr. D. Feil, chemical-physicist).
The Organizers felt honoured that the VHS-Kammerorchester, Ahaus, and the Euregio-trio, Enschede, both conducted by Mrs. M. Lindeboom, were willing to grace one of the Conference evenings by giving a concert, that was greatly appreciated.

It is a pleasure for us to acknowledge the co-operation of Videac and Centrale Repro-afdeling, Universiteit Twente, of Fit-to-Print, and of Kluwer Academic Publishers, in matters of publication: posters, the Conference programme and, finally, this book.
Last but by no means least, the organization of the Conference would have been impossible without the gentle(wo)men's agreement with Mrs. M. Schmand (Drienerburght) and Drs. F.S. Verschoor (Universiteit Twente) at an early stage of the preparations, and it still would have come to nothing if Anja, Lila and Roel had not been there to assist us so ably no matter the nature of the task that had to be tackled during those hectic days.
Working in the field of 'science' and 'religion' is a life long undertaking that can only be invigorated by those who awaken joy and enthusiasm in creativity and knowledge. The editors, therefore, are pleased to acknowledge gratefully their great indebtedness to the institutions for interdisciplinary research in which they were active: Atomium (Enschede) and the Center of Theological Inquiry (Princeton), respectively.

Jan Fennema,
Universiteit Twente,
Faculteit der Wijsbegeerte en
Maatschappijwetenschappen,
Enschede,
The Netherlands.

Iain Paul, S.O.Sc.
Craigneuk and Belhaven
Parish Church,
Wishaw (Lanarkshire),
Scotland.

An encounter between science and religion
preliminary observations

Jan Fennema

'Η Παρθένος σήμερον
τὸν ὑπερούσιον τίκτει,
καὶ ἡ γῆ τὸ Σπήλαιον
τῷ ἀπροσίτῳ προσάγει...

(Κοντάκιον. Δεκέμβριους κε')*

It is appropriate to introduce the present volume by explaining what was in our minds as we planned the organization of this Conference on Science and Religion. In order to avoid any misunderstanding it is emphasized at the outset that these 'preliminary observations' do *not* constitute a synoptic attempt to introduce the articles and summaries contained in this book. In this respect the reader is confidently left to his or her resources. Besides, although the pronouns 'we', 'us' and 'our' are used frequently, the observations made and developed in the paragraphs which follow are presented by one person only, who is solely responsible for their contents. The intention is to describe what was seen and experienced at the point where all the letters and telephone calls met, where they heightened or lowered existing tensions, depressions and expectations, and where they required urgent (new) decisions to be taken. In fact, the organization of this Conference, which truly exacted great industry, was particularly gratifying in the many ways that it established and extended personal contacts. And it was a pleasure to receive so many letters in which participants expressed their thanks for what had proved to be for them an unexpectedly rewarding encounter!

These preliminary observations have been divided into four short sections followed by acknowledgements. This division is not strict. Some overlapping derives from the original order in which things occurred, for here we strive to do justice to 'history'. Three main points are raised; they concern respectively, (1) the global setting of the Conference, (2) the reason for reproducing the portrait of Erasmus on Conference publications, and (3) the question of an adequate anthropology, (4) a question that leads us back to Erasmus.

---

*　　See footnote 25

1. A European conference and a global setting

The Conference was called 'European' for practical reasons. For, although it is questionable whether something like a 'European culture' exists, it cannot be denied that our continent with all its differences has a long history of its peoples living together - in times of peace and war. And in the long run many a conflict creates understanding; it builds a common substratum and fosters the growth of a common identity. Thus, on the European scene, there is certainly cultural coherence which, however, needs expression and explanation through a continued exchange of thoughts. The Conference in Enschede, like its predecessor[1] and those that will follow, are expected to further this exchange.

Clearly, as organized, the Conference was meant to be an exploration of the world of ideas, a spiritual and intellectual world. In contradistinction to the realm of scholarly learning, the science and technology of today constitute, in the eyes of many people, a world of hard facts and of power that may be used 'to the glory of God and the benefit of the human race', as the Puritan adage says[2], but that, nevertheless, are so often misused. In this connection it seems appropriate to recall the famous maxim that we owe to Archimedes: 'Give me a place to stand, and I will move the earth'. These words, which in fact mark pur sang imperialism and principally proclaim the right of the strongest, are now turning their edge against man himself, against even the most privileged! For, to a large extent, the developments that are taking place appear to be 'autonomous', and the human self seems to be 'imprisoned' in the process. As a result, and in spite of the numerous benefits of the cultural process for the condition of humankind, a cry for peace and justice is heard from many a hook and corner of the earth whereas, at the same time, it has become clear that the process may also lead to global catastrophe now that the world's ecosystem is under serious threat. Using current terminology, the very 'integrity of creation' is at stake[3]. Consequently, as far as the Conference itself is concerned, the questions to be asked are: What are we - as participants as well as organizers - called upon to do in the present, disastrous state of affairs? And what should be, for this reason, the focus of our concern?

In our opinion, what obviously justifies the enterprise is the help that it provides in sounding and meeting the responsibility that is incumbent upon human beings. Making people conscious of our profound involvement in the cultural process together with contributing to the liberation of the human self is in fact *the* answer that should be given to the questions asked before. In our area of interest the human self clearly occupies a key position. 'Peace' and 'justice' are terms that will remain without significance unless the human self is born again[4] to recognize the untouchable otherness[5], the authenticity of whatever is there, living beings and inanimate matter alike. And the 'integrity of creation' is only discerned in response to a growing integrity of the self which, in its turn, is factually constituted because of the wholeness that makes its impression upon the observing subject. Hence, *the study of human existence in a world dominated by the sciences and their applications* should be the focus of our concern.

What is needed is a greatly increased consciousness of an ethical value of paramount importance - integrity - which, in turn, may generate aesthetic values: wonder, a sense of beauty, and perhaps even harmony. What counts is *not* so much the establishment of a sophisticated view that encompasses both the realm of the sciences and that of religion, as the awareness of a lasting coherence of things, living and inanimate, spiritual and material impartially. For a sophisticated view, that, from its particular perspective, takes in 'everything', presupposes a grand objectivation - and leaves the human being in the margin, if anywhere. Thus, all of the universe becomes one giant object! But the awareness of a lasting coherence of things rests upon experience of what escapes objectivation and remains as subject. It rests upon the observation of what is other, untouchable and sacred, and commands respect. The experience of such unending conviviality is given expression in the explicit recognition of the authenticity of otherness as manifested[6]. In the case of a collective of individuals, e.g. a group of human beings, nations or peoples, this implies the end of imperialism and the recognition of each other's right to self-reliance. Hence, a plurality of vision is accepted along with dialogue in lieu of monologue, a plurality and a dialogue that, in recent years of cultural struggle, have been anticipated as people longed for 'the human face of society'.

Consistent with the preceding considerations the first announcement of the present Conference contained a statement of intention, its central part being[7]: *...Scientific points of view and expectations need to be in dialogue with religious forms of understanding - and religious traditions need to take account of the new scientific perspectives on the world and the ethical problems generated by science, medicine and technology....* For the sake of the humanisation of humanity!

2. The Conference and its patron

Those who attended the Conference in Enschede will have noticed that we had chosen the portrait of Erasmus, painted by Hans Holbein Jun., as the emblem of our gathering. His picture was reproduced on the one thousand and fifty posters that we distributed 'all over Europe'; it appeared also on the front page of the Conference programme, as it does once more on the cover of this book. Desiderius Erasmus Roterodamus, the great Renaissance humanist, who lived before the question of the relation between science and religion had become a controversial issue, held as his considered opinion that the most profound truth is experienced as people live in harmony and mutual respect. It was his conviction that basic truths, that have been put into words as such and are confessed to be 'truths', need not be singular and universal, that is, valid for and accepted by everybody. Hence, in his vision, humankind should be striving after concordance - 'concordia'. As a direct result, closed systems of thinking would open, thereby preparing man for being ultimately transformed[8]. Thus what really counts are the ways that truths come into play. In modern terminology, it is plays of truth that count, *not* the truths themselves. Clearly, Erasmus was of the opinion that humanity is characterized by the possibility of a plurality of positions and, we add tentatively, by a process of growth. Man is always new again! These lines already contain sufficient information to explain why Erasmus has been chosen as the patron of the Conference. There is still another, more specific reason to be considered. This reason seems to suggest a long term task for future conferences on science and religion. Our line of thought is developed here and in the final section.

As the reader will probably know, the later years of Erasmus coincided with the beginnings of the Reformation and of the ensuing Counter-Reformation, a period that led to a major splitting of the Christian world of that time. It is a well-known fact that Erasmus did not want to take sides neither with the one nor the other party in the Church. In particular, his standpoint was that eternal truth, as supposedly transmitted by the reading of the Scriptures, did not lie *in* the interpretation of the texts that were studied but *beyond* them[9]. In point of fact, Erasmus held that knowledge obtained by the reading of the Scriptures is important, not because of the intellectual value of particular pieces of knowledge as such, but because these pieces of knowledge ultimately become vehicles that enable man to experience what remains a mystery, a mystery that conveys truth that is transverbal[10]. Thus, a truth that is eternal can be *received* only by a 'pure heart', that is, by the impressionable nature of a human being who is in a state of innocence - 'innocentia'. The views of Erasmus, which were potentially conciliatory, have not prevented history from taking its bloody course. Moreover, when religious warfare had ended in armistice and the mind of European man was illuminated by the Enlightenment, it became clear that the opposition between the Reformation and the Counter-Reformation was no longer the only split in European culture. For, in addition to the difference in religious matters, a new contrast had appeared, namely, that of science - 'natural philosophy' - over and against religion. It was a contrast that developed into a cleavage in the course of time. And in its wake, the unmistakable possibility of successful knowledge that did not depend on religious convictions stimulated a vision of humankind that is known to this very day as 'humanism', a vision that is mostly considered to be irreconcilable with Christianity.

With respect to the contrast in religious matters, Erasmus had sought means for mediation and reconciliation. Hence, the principal question must now be asked, whether the name of this humanist scholar can be connected in an analogous way with the later cleavage between religion, on the one hand, and the developing sciences, on the other, including in particular the humanist view of humankind. In our opinion such a connection can be rightly asserted. Obviously, the ironical writings of Erasmus appeal implicitly to man to develop and to exercise a critical spirit that will not desist from condemning existing constraints whatever their nature. And a spirit that is truly critical must be a 'free' spirit. It must be in the state of innocence, the mental state to which Erasmus consistently pointed in his writings, and which is the condition necessary to the spirit for finding the proper words to speak. Thus it is certainly legitimate to look upon Erasmus as an early 'free-thinker', although, of course, the comparison must necessarily be restrained within bounds because of his attitude towards religion[11]. In this connection his contacts with the utopian thinker Thomas More should be mentioned too. As a matter of fact, the writings of Erasmus on society and on education testify that his criticism cannot be legitimately denied a utopian point[12].

3. A contemporary anthropology?

Clearly, humanism as referred to in the preceding paragraphs is considered to be in a dialectical relationship to what may be called 'traditional Christian theology.' It is atheistic in so far as theism is in need of being criticized. And Christian theism is in need of criticism wherever, on forgetting the lesson taught by Judaism concerning the Name, it speaks when it should be struck dumb[13]. Consequently, in Western history, humanism is at the root of modernity and in the spirit of secularization, but, in its core, it is also post-modern and beyond secularization. A humanism that retains its critical spirit and does not become an ideology itself is possibly *the* way to overcome the self-destructive forces of secular society.

What is man and what is humanity in the vision of this humanism? They are questions of profound relevance when it comes to organizing a conference like ours. For man evidently finds himself at a definitive meeting point; he finds himself in a crucial position because he alone participates in the two realms at once, the material and the spiritual, the world of science and technology and the world of the spirit. In this regard it is essential to notice that the development of the sciences in our generation has led to a widening of their scope but, at the same time, it has also led to a far better understanding of their intrinsic limitations. It is expedient to enlarge upon one specific aspect: the role of chance, which proves to be objective and non-eliminable, in addition to being subjective; besides as an expression of incomplete knowledge, chance proves to be a fundamental element of the structures used to describe the physical world. In other words, while dissecting an object under investigation, 'chaos' may appear resulting in a certain 'randomness' in the description of the object[14]. Thus, today, science itself teaches us that the reduction of a particular - 'higher' - level of understanding to another - 'lower' - one does not always lead to unambiguous correlations. Expressed the other way round, theorizing on the basis of fundamental presuppositions that are considered evident may easily be open-ended. Consequently, Cartesian world-views, like the famous one given by Pierre Simon de Laplace or modernized versions of it, are no longer compelling. The upshot of it is that, as a matter of principle, in science different levels of description must be discerned that cannot be reduced the one to the other. And it follows that the customary distinction between the world of science and technology and the world of the spirit has become obsolete. Indeed, we are witnessing the birth of a new age in the history of mankind, an age in which traditional antagonisms seem to have lost their virulence, whereas at the same time this new epoch confronts us with never-dreamt-of challenges that require immediate response.

The time has come to venture an answer to the question about man and humanism. We start with the observation that the contingence of the universe has received unexpected emphasis now that it appears that theorizing may be open-ended. It implies that the future is essentially open - as already seen from the standpoint of the sciences; this openness, in its turn, paves the way for a corresponding interpretation of the notion of transcendence. The 'old' notion of transcendence, which refers to the realm of the divine as related to that of the sublunar in a static reciprocity, may be compared to the 'new' concept, which refers to the openness of the future and, more particularly, to the dynamic openness of the human being in his or her process of growth. For reality is in process. In this connection old texts may be read afresh and become transparent to a new significance - which, by the way, may be the old significance rediscovered[15]. In a recent publication by the Ian Ramsey Centre, the ongoing self-transcendence of a growing human being is considered as the encounter with a new being, as a gift which, being a grace, is received no matter how (un)successful man's endeavours are in 'making' his future[16]. We read: '... [it is our vocation] to find within us the place of encounter between the human and the divine, the centre of the self...'[17]. And having found this centre, this 'little point of nothingness' or 'point vierge' - which of course is no *point*[18] - the author, Kallistos Ware, concludes that 'we then become mediators in the truest and fullest sense, through the power and after the example of Christ, the unique Mediator'[17]. Without doubt, the latter are traditional terms, but they are valid Christology of the Chalcedonian era[19], and they may be used to generate an inviting contemporary anthropology! Ware himself explains that, according to the Greek Fathers, anthropology must be considered as an aspect of Christology. More explicitly, he states that there is no anthropology unless that of the man who is his own prolepsis, who is his being-in-becoming and who anticipates existentially, just as there is no Christology but that of Christ who lives in the face of death: 'at evening time there shall be light'[20]. Thus, the heart of this anthropology turns out to be already given in the well-known adage: 'media in vita in morte sumus, media in morte in vita' - words of Pesach, that is a transit or Passover, which hardly need translation[21]. Ware quotes St. Basil of Caesarea to illustrate his statement: 'Christ is in this way *the* man, the model of what it means to be human, the mirror in which I see reflected my own true face, and the incarnation - his human birth - is at the same time the 'birthday' of the human race'[22]. Far from being 'the subjective belief of a private coterie'[23], Christian faith is universal in intention. Without usurping any claim of inclusiveness, however. For everybody's identity is to be respected, and the tradition of any community is a tradition in its own right[24]. Clearly, a universality that triumphantly takes possession of the identity of others, be they individuals or communities, is imperialistic and corrupts itself.

In brief: it is held that the openness of the human being in his or her process of growth, experienced and articulated by making use of scientific terminology, can be compared to the receptiveness implied by Ware's key phrase 'little point of nothingness' or, for that matter, 'point vierge'. *True, proleptic humanity implies the merging into - problematic- harmony of the human and the divine as conceived traditionally, both of which are to be emancipated from their antithetic positions in common discourse.* And it may be concluded that the achievements of the (natural) sciences of today together with those of the Greek Fathers in their disputes on the nature of Christ may contribute essentially to the creation of a contemporary anthropology. This anthropology expresses in words that the cleavage between 'science' and 'religion' - or 'theology' - is bridged, and better still has been bridged forever, in human existence. With this understanding, the opening strophe of an Orthodox Christmas hymn appears as a motto at the beginning of these 'preliminary observations'[25].

4. Erasmus, an inspirer of humanism today

On reflecting upon the contours of an anthropology, as presented in the preceding section, we recall Erasmus, and note, in retrospect, his emphasis on 'innocentia', the state of innocence where man is aware of the limitations inherent in his knowledge and transcends them in his experience. The same recollection, moreover, reminds us that Erasmus called his humanism 'philosophia Christi'. Erasmus has something to say to those of us who, in our day, live to see the culmination of secularity and, beyond it, the drawing near of its demise. We need an awareness of the vista that is offered when humanism and Christian doctrine can be reconciled. A barrier is pulled down, when the traditionally conceived autonomous human being and his heteronomous counterpart are shown to be partners in a process of personal growth. In fact, the words that have been chosen as a motto, which are part of the liturgy of the Eastern Church, describe autonomy *and* heteronomy and their balance[25] in humankind's pilgrim's progress. They describe action, concerted future-directed action in which the awareness of a new vista is consummated. The term 'consummated' has an existential connotation, as has action, one which demands that the person who acts be personally involved. In this connection we should remember that, from ancient times, the term 'liturgy' - ' λειτουργία ' - has carried the usual, well-known meaning of the word and its much less familiar meaning of the accomplishment of duties and tasks for the benefit of society as a whole[26]. Contributing to the liberation of the human self is clearly a case in point!

But the reader should not miss the intrinsic meaning carried by 'existential'. If a human being is 'liberated', it is not solely because of novel insights, which may have remained an intellectual, verbal exercise. For novel insights must be taken to heart, and, if they are 'liberating', they will result in a new creative living. While, if not, they may lead to additional forms of slavery by the subjection of humankind to new objectifying forces[27]. The emancipation that results from the 'dialectics' of man's enlightenment[28] is certainly not straightforward. And instead of positive roads to be followed, there may be first of all only negative paths to be avoided...

There is clearly a need for a careful *de*construction of whatever constraints can be observed in human life[4]. In any process of growth, a critical recollection and reconsideration of the experience of humankind cannot be missed: the past deserves what Gianni Vattimo remarkably calls 'pietas'[29], that is a critical respect. It is the lesson that we are taught today by a remembrance of 'Auschwitz' and 'Hiroshima' that urges us to practise true anamnestic solidarity with the victims of the past. Their suffering should not have been in vain. Humankind may cherish hopes for the future, and certainly Erasmus may be taken as an inspirer of our humanism, but only on the condition that the new age we eagerly expect to enter appropriates a past that saw the fury of sophisticated dehumanizing forces, a past that is a present still.

Saturday before Easter, 1989.

Acknowledgements

These 'preliminary observations' reflect the many inspiring contacts made during the organization of the Second European Conference on Science and Religion. To single out anyone for particular thanks would be invidious. There is clearly a great indebtedness to the members of the Organizing Committee as there is to all those on whose cooperation we could rely, to the various speakers and contributors, and to several (prospective) participants. They are all anonymously acknowledged. Cordially acknowledged are debts to Ir. G. G. Oosterwegel (University of Twente) for his steady encouragement during the process of writing, to Prof. Dr. A. H. Smits (Faculty of Theology Tilburg) for critical discussions as this text neared completion, and to Prof. Dr. Boon (Free University Amsterdam) for his spontaneous commentary on the epoch of the Enlightenment.

References and notes

1. The preceding conference was held on 13-16th. March, 1986, in the Evangelische Akademie Loccum, Federal Republic of Germany. For the papers presented at that conference see:
    Svend Andersen and Arthur Peacocke (eds.), *Evolution and Creation,* Aarhus University Press, Aarhus, 1987; this book also briefly reviews the origins of that conference.

2. See e.g.: Ian G. Barbour, *Issues in Science and Religion,* SCM Press, London 1966, and
    R. Hooykaas, *Religion and the Rise of Modern Science*, Scottish Academic Press, Edinburgh 1972, p. 105 e.s..

3. The terminology reminds us of the present World Council of Churches' programme on Justice, Peace, and the Integrity of Creation, which is in preparation of the World Convocation with the same name, scheduled to take place in 1990.

4. Compare: 'Die eigentliche Aufgabe, mit der die Möglichkeit eines wahren Weltfriedens steht und fällt, ist die Verwirklichung des menschlichen Selbst'; see: Carl Friedrich von Weizsäcker, *Der Garten des Menschlichen,* Carl Hanser Verlag, Munich 1977 (3rd. impression), p. 252.

5. The adjective 'untouchable' has been added to emphasize that true otherness implies a breakdown of the usual methods of categorization with regard to what is 'other'. Compare e.g. Emmanuel Levinas, *Totalité et Infini*, Martinus Nijhoff, The Hague 1974, pp. 52-53. ('Le face-à-face, relation irréductible': 'Le Même et l'Autre ne sauraient entrer dans une connaissance qui les embrasserait.')

6. A classic text which describes the experience of conviviality *together* with all relevant modes of scientific cognition is provided by Martin Buber's description of his encounter with a tree. See: Martin Buber, *Ich und Du*; reprinted in Martin Buber, *Dialogisches Leben*, Gregor Müller Verlag, Zurich 1947, pp. 18-20; English translation: *I and Thou*, T. & T. Clark, Edinburgh 1971 (3rd. edition), pp. 57-59.

7. For the integral text of the Statement of intention see p. 8

8. J. Sperna Weiland et al, *Erasmus, de actualiteit van zijn denken*, Walburgpers, Zutphen 1986; see p. 55. As the author, G. Th. Jensma, explains, Erasmus' irony burst the closed world of the Middle Ages into the open space of the Renaissance.

9. J. Sperna Weiland et al, op. cit.; see p. 47. Truths that lie *in* the texts are necessarily 'contextual'. Truths that do not depend on their contexts, that is, which lie *beyond* any context, are called 'eternal'. In fact, we have here a hermeneutical spiral running the opposite-to-normal way round and leading to mystical knowledge.

10. J. Sperna Weiland et al, op. cit.; see p. 35. The author, G. Th. Jensma, explicitly identifies a mystic element in the theology of Erasmus. Compare reference 9.

11. The term 'free-thinker' may lead to misunderstanding. It is used here more or less in the sense explained in the *Oxford English Dictionary*:
'One who refuses to submit his reason to the control of authority in matters of religious belief'. The Dictionary adds that the term was claimed as a designation by 'the deistic and other rejectors of Christianity at the beginning of the 18th century'.
But, in addition to similar uses of this term, it also gives a quotation of an entirely different nature: 'The modern free-thinker does not attack Christianity; he explains it'.
We hold that it is legitimate to look upon Erasmus as an early free-thinker in the sense of the last quotation. Clearly, Erasmus was not an atheist in disguise. This misconception, which still can be found in the literature today, should be strongly criticized;
see e.g. S. Dresden in J. Sperna Weiland et al, op. cit., p. 102.

12. J. Sperna Weiland et al, op. cit.; see p. 90. According to the author, J. Sperna Weiland, the utopia of Erasmus was a utopia of erudition, humanity and everlasting peace.
His utopia was 'critical' none-the-less; for a utopia which is critical, compare Georg Picht, *Hier und Jetzt, Philosophieren nach Auschwitz und Hiroshima, (II)*, Klett-Cotta, Stuttgart 1981, pp. 335-349.

13. Compare Isaiah, chapter 6 verses 6-7. Some languages called 'theological', for instance, creationist and cosmological languages, imply in their theoretical constructions a conceptual effort concerning the Name - where iconoclasm would be in place.

14. A basic, though by no means 'easy', book to be consulted in this connection is:
    Ilya Prigogine, *From Being to Becoming, Time and Complexity in the Physical Sciences*,
    W.H. Freemann, San Francisco 1980.
    After summarizing the consequences implied by the (non-)existence of relations between
    different levels of description, the author arrives at the following conclusion (see p. 215):
    'The increased limitation of deterministic laws means that we go from a universe that is closed, in
    which all is given, to a new one that is open to fluctuations, to innovations.'

15. An analogous standpoint is taken by A. R. Peacocke in his *Science and the Christian Experiment*,
    Oxford University Press, London 1971, p. 170: 'Science by eliminating a naive literalism has
    restored the credibility of the early Genesis stories as dramatic accounts, not so much of history,
    but of the way things are.'

16. When struggling at the threshold of the future, man encounters the other. Compare Genesis,
    chapter 32 verses 24-31.

17. A. Peacocke and G. Gillet, *Persons and Personality, A Contemporary Inquiry*, Ian Ramsay
    Centre Publication, nr. 1, Basil Blackwell, Oxford 1987; see p. 204.
    The full quotation from Ware's contribution reads: '... [It is our vocation] to find within us the
    place of encounter between the human and the divine, the centre of the self where our created
    personhood opens out upon the uncreated personhood of God - what Thomas Merton styles *le
    point vierge,* the 'little point of nothingness and of absolute poverty' that is 'the pure glory of
    God in us'. Having found this centre, or 'little point', we then become mediators in the truest and
    fullest sense, through the power and after the example of Christ, the unique Mediator.'

18. Any conceiving of Ware's 'little point' as an indication of a place would imply a serious
    misconception, not only of what Ware is aiming at, but also of all Christological disputation.
    Compare the misplaced conception of the pineal gland as a 'point' of contact in Cartesian
    philosophy.

19. Clearly, we cannot discuss here in any detail the significance of the disputes in and around the
    Church Council of Chalcedon, held in 451.

20. Zechariah, chapter 14 verse 7c.

21. Nevertheless, we give the translation: 'in the midst of living we are dead, in the midst of death we
    are alive'.

22. A. Peacocke and G. Gillet, op. cit.; see p. 202.

23. A phrase taken from: A. R. Peacocke, *Science and the Christian Experiment,*
    Oxford University Press, London 1971, p. 176.

24. In this connection the reader is reminded of the opinion of Erasmus that humanity may be characterized by a plurality of positions. In the context of the present Conference this may be explained, for instance, by adding: 'Jewish', 'Christian', 'Islamic', 'Bahá'í' etc..

25. The translation of the Greek text is as follows:
    'Today the Virgin gives birth to the One that surpasses being,
    and the earth turns the cavern towards the Unapproachable...
    (Proper of the Season. December 25)'.
    The words of this strophe may be reasonably taken as introducing a critical conception of man's scientific and technological endeavour.

26. Also in modern Greek!

27. Compare Martin Buber, op. cit.. On p. 29 of the German edition we find: 'Das aber ist die erhabne Schwermut unsres Loses, dass jedes Du in unsrer Welt zum Es werden muss.';
    and on p. 68 of the English translation we read: 'This, however, is the sublime melancholy of our lot that every You must become an It in our world.'

28. After the title of *Die Dialektik der Aufklärung - The dialectics of the Enlightenment -*
    by Max Horkheimer and Theodor Adorno, first published in 1947. This book holds a key position in the ongoing discussion on the transition from modern to post-modern times in our era.

29. See Gianni Vattimo's *Das Ende der Geschichte* in H. Kunneman and H. de Vries (eds.),
    Die Aktualität der "Dialektik der Aufklärung", zwischen Moderne und Postmoderne,
    Campus Verlag, Frankfurt 1989, pp. 168-182.

Part I
Lectures in full sessions

Epitome of Part I

Introduction to the conference theme
A.G.M. van Melsen, *Science and religion*
T.F. Torrance, *Fundamental issues in theology and science*
M. Bloemendal, *Science and religion - the Jewish position*

Reconciling developments in the natural sciences - the question of scientism
A. Gierer, *Physics, life and mind*
W. Weidlich, *Reconciling concepts between natural science and theology*
J.C. Polkinghorne F.R.S., *A revived natural theology*

Reconciling developments in theology - the question of dogmatism
W.B. Drees, *Theology and cosmology beyond the Big Bang theory*
J. Van der Veken, *God's world and man becoming:*
how can science possibly help us transcend dogmatism?

The divorce of science and religion - a process in retrospect
O. Pedersen, *Historical interaction between science and religion*
J.R. Durant, *Is there a role for theology in an age of secular science?*

Science and religion studies today and tomorrow
J. Hübner, *Science and religion coming across*
G. Vahanian, *Creation and Big Bang: the word as space of creation*

Each text is preceded by the particulars of the author.

A.G.M. van Melsen, chemist and philosopher,
Professor emeritus of philosophy, Katholieke Universiteit Nijmegen,
Nijmegen, The Netherlands

Science and religion

A.G.M. van Melsen

The relationship between science and religion has a long history of tensions. When we confine ourselves to Western culture, the first tension arose when in Greece philosophical and scientific explanations began to compete with mythological ones. Usually the latter are called 'irrational', whereas the former are considered to be 'rational', but that distinction is incorrect. In its own way the mythological explanation is also rational. The real difference between the two kinds of explanation is that myth explained the phenomena by referring to divine activity, whereas science refers to internal and external natural causes. The latter causes, however, could not explain everything. As a result the realm of mythological explanations did not completely disappear, but it became more limited. Perhaps it did not entirely disappear because, at that time, the scientific explanations were *de facto* deficient, or was this an indication of more fundamental problems?

The later history of the relationship between science and religion is to a high degree dominated by that problem. The fact that, during a long period, the practical possibilities of science remained limited has particularly caused much misunderstanding about the real relationship between science and religion. For this reason we must examine first why, in the beginning, the practical possibilities of scientific explanations remained so limited. The answer is not difficult. In the beginning, only those sciences could be developed in a satisfactory way in which an intellectual insight was able to distinguish between what was relevant and what was not. In geometry, for example, it is evident that only the form is relevant, and the material way in which this form is present (made of wood or iron, as a drawing in the sand etc.), does not matter. The same thing applies to formal logic; the content of the argument is not relevant, only its structure. It is important to realise how different things are in natural science. Any aspect of the phenomenon involved could be important. Only by a long and careful, empirical and experimental process are we able to decide which aspects are relevant and which are not. In a sense it could even be said that the birth of an empirical science confronts us with a kind of logical circle. On the one hand, in order to find out what aspects of a phenomenon are relevant, we first need some theoretical ideas to guide the empirical and experimental researches. On the other hand, fruitful theoretical ideas can be developed only on the basis of empirical data. No wonder it took such a long time for the empirical and experimental sciences to come into existence. No wonder also that, in the Greek unity of philosophy and science, the philosophical partner was much more developed than the scientific one. Aristotle, for example, raises a lot of scientific questions, but notwithstanding his genuine empirical interest, he always ends up with philosophical problems. Only there could he satisfy his quest for rational insight. Scientific questions lead him via the philosophy of nature to metaphysical problems.

The Church Fathers had no special interest in scientific questions, but it was clear to them that they could make use of Greek philosophy for their apologetical and theological concerns. They were convinced that Divine Revelation could answer the questions raised but unanswered by Greek metaphysics.

In the Middle Ages a new situation arose. Through the close contact with Arabian culture, the full richness of Greek philosophy and science became known. This was a real challenge to Christian intellectual culture. It was a confrontation with pagan philosophy and science, mediated by Islam, at that time the greatest enemy of the Christian world. Yet great philosophers and theologians, such as Albertus Magnus and Thomas Aquinas, evaluated correctly the fundamental importance of that new form of knowledge, that was based upon reason and experience, not upon Divine Revelation. They saw that this new knowledge and Christian thought could be integrated easily. I do not hesitate to consider this integration as one of the great accomplishments of medieval Christian culture. Instead of a conflict between science and religion, that could so easily have arisen, the autonomy of the new philosophy and science was recognized, and the respective realms of theology and science were clearly distinguished, at least in principle.

In view of what happened in the Middle Ages, we could be puzzled by the question why, in the 17th. century, such sharp conflict could arise between science and religion. Then, the conditions seemed so much more favourable. The new science of the 17th. century was not a product from outside, but a development within Christian culture itself. Yet it is not difficult to see that what happened in the 17th. century was a much greater challenge to Christian culture than what had happened in the Middle Ages. The new science, with which the Middle Ages had to cope, was still an undeveloped science. That is to say, its questions led to philosophical problems and answers, rather than to scientific answers. And if scientific answers were given, they were mostly wrong, and they could not lead to further investigations. What we saw with Aristotle, therefore, happened also in the Middle Ages. Scientific questions led to the philosophy of nature and to metaphysics. There was, however, one new element. In the Middle Ages, metaphysical questions invited theological answers. In this important respect nothing had changed since the time of the Church Fathers. As a result, the situation in intellectual life, that is, the situation in the realms of science, philosophy and theology, corresponded fully with that in daily life. As life on earth did not offer many possibilities, daily life was totally oriented towards eternal life. The intellectual possibilities seemed to confirm that orientation. Philosophy and science were both regarded as *ancillae theologiae*, as the servants of theology.

This orientation of science changed radically in the 17th. century. First of all, empirical science discovered the method of solving its own problems in an intellectually satisfactory way. It was no longer necessary to move on to philosophical problems. Secondly, in contrast with traditional science, the new science was progressive. New results made new theories possible, and these in their turn made new experiments possible, and so on. Thirdly, the new science proved to be extremely useful for material culture and for daily life.

Consequently, the whole orientation of both science and life changed from the past to the future (belief in progress) and from eternal life to life on earth. This explains why what happened in the 17th. century was a much greater challenge to Christian faith than what had happened in the Middle Ages.

In order to understand better the conflicts between science and religion, it is necessary to distinguish the different levels on which these conflicts arose:
- The first level is that of actual conflicts (Galileo and Darwin).
- The second level concerns the radical change in intellectual climate, namely, from a dogmatic to an anti-dogmatic attitude.
- The third level is that of the different views of life that we have already mentioned.

In the beginning, the actual conflicts drew the greatest attention. What was the cause of these conflicts? In general terms the answer is not difficult. Neither faith nor science was sufficiently aware of its own subject matter. That is to say, not all that was pronounced in the name of Christian faith really belonged to that faith. Not all that was pronounced in the name of science really belonged to the realm of science. Much more interesting, however, is another question. Why were the respective realms of faith and science so poorly delineated?

The main reason was that, in the Middle Ages, so many problems were passed on to theology, problems that were not theological ones at all, but that were of scientific origin. That they were not recognized as such was not only due to the state of affairs in science, but also to the fact that not everything that is written in the Holy Scriptures is Divine Revelation. The famous conflict between evolutionary theory and the dogma of creation could never have arisen if the story about creation in Genesis had not also been believed to be a more or less accurate description of the origin of the earth. For the sake of fairness, however, let us not forget that, before the existence of natural science in its modern form, there was no 'theory' available other than the description in Genesis. It took some time to realise that, although both creation and evolution are interested in the origin of life, they ask entirely different questions. Evolution tells us something about how and why the different forms of life have been developed. Creation says something about the *existence* of the world, itself, together with its potencies. How did the world come to exist? Does it explain itself? Although there are still some rear-guard actions[1], I do not think that the real tension between science and religion, to-day, actually lies in this kind of conflict. Both science and religion have learned their lesson.

Much more important, however, is the tension on the second level of which I have spoken. It concerns the difference in intellectual climate. Theology as a science was developed in a period, in which each science was believed to take its starting point in fundamental principles based on rational insight. These principles were of necessity true. From these principles all the other theses of a science could be logically derived. In fact, theology was organised in the same way. There was, however, one important difference. The fundamental principles of theology, its *dogmata* were not based upon rational insight. They were revealed and, therefore, true. Because they were true, they could be used as fundamental principles in the same way as the fundamental principles of the other sciences. For this reason the dogmatic character of theology and of the Christian faith did not offend the scientific mind at all. Science and religion were both dogmatic.

The new science, however, was no longer dogmatic. That is to say, its fundamental principles did not form the starting point of science, but its end-point. And even when this end-point was reached, when the fundamental principles were found, they were never then considered as absolutely true, but only as provisionally true. They could always be revised. An important consequence of the new scientific method was that principles had to be *verified* in an empirical way. No verification could ever be absolute. Nevertheless some verification was needed (or at least no falsification). If, in principle, no verification at all was possible, then a scientific principle did not make sense. I am convinced that the change in intellectual climate that I have just described caused the actual conflicts to be much more harmful to religion than they would have originally been. I am not saying that, in the intellectual climate of modern times, there can be no place for any *dogmata* because they cannot be verified in an empirical way; I will discuss that point later. What I am saying is that dogmata should not be used in the same way as scientific theses. And that is precisely what happened in the conflict between 'creation' and 'evolution'.

Let us now turn our attention to the third level of the conflict between science and religion, namely, the different views of life. Whereas the conflicts on the first and second levels interested only relatively small groups of people, mostly the intellectuals, the conflicts on the third level concerned everybody. The societal consequences of the development of science and technology were such that for everybody the whole orientation of life had changed from eternal life to life on earth. The new orientation found its creeds and its apostles in the Enlightenment and in secularized political philosophies, such as liberalism and socialism. On this third level the same thing happened as on the first one. As a rule the churches and their adherents opposed the new creeds because they were thought to deny at least some aspects of Christian faith. The apostles of the new creeds fought against the old one because faith was believed to be essentially associated with a view of the world that was obsolete. Both parties were right in the same sense in which evolutionists and creationists* were. For evolutionists opposed rightly some aspects of the traditional belief in creation, and believers in creation opposed rightly the thesis of the evolutionists that the doctrine of evolution showed that the belief in creation was obsolete.

Nowadays, the smoke of the battles has cleared. We can see better what mistakes have been made, but this does not mean that there is no longer a certain tension between religion and science. Let me try to describe as accurately as possible some of the aspects of the present situation, especially with respect to the tension between the scientific and religious attitudes - for on that level there is still something left of the original conflict, although some interesting developments can be observed. The first aspect concerns the position of science. On the one hand, this position is stronger than ever, thanks to the enormous success of science and technology. On the other hand, however, this position is weakened both in a theoretical sense and in a practical way. In a practical way because science and technology have not fulfilled all the expectations of the belief in progress. There are too many

---

*   The term does *not,* of course, refer to what, in this century, is called 'Creationism' in the U.S.A. and some other countries.

side-effects, some of them of such a nature that they seem to outweigh the benefits of progress. As to the theoretical aspects of the weakened position of science, the most interesting point is that, although science is still proud of its rationality, it is also clear that science cannot work without a certain amount of belief. Science must believe in the reliability of sense experience, in the immutability of nature, in the competence of reason etc.. This is not to say that this belief is unreasonable, but it shows that the scientific method is not completely self-sufficient. Not everything can be verified in an empirical way. In terms of our earlier discussion of the undogmatic character of modern science, it could be said that in a sense science too has to accept certain dogmata. These dogmata are not concerned with scientific theses, but *they delineate the rational sphere in which science lives*, so to speak. In passing I remark that the Christian dogmata are also meant to delineate a sphere, namely, the Christian view of life. This is not to say that these dogmata have no truth-content, but it is not truth in the scientific sense. No particular conclusion about the structure of the world follows from the religious truth that God has created the world.

I am not very happy with a development that is connected with the different contexts in which we can speak of truth, and that is meant to diminish the tension between science and religion. From the side of religion it is sometimes said that religion has nothing to do with truth. The intention of this thesis is clear. If religion has nothing to do with truth, there can be no collisions with science. But that price is too high to pay. Religion should never abandon its claim on truth. Although it is clear that, when we pray the *Credo,* we are not first of all pronouncing a truth, if it was not true that the world was created by God, our prayer would not make any sense. For this reason I said that, by abandoning the claim on truth, we pay too high a price for preventing any conflict between religion and science. More important, however, is the fact that we do not have to pay that price if we distinguish carefully the different realms of truth in the way that we have indicated previously.

There is yet another development that seems to be an important factor in easing the tension between science and religion. In the 19th. century, science itself was a kind of religion with reason as its god. Universities were the temples of this religion, and professors its high priests. Nowadays, there is not much left of that pride. Science has been split into a manifold of specialisms, each studying only certain aspects of reality. This means that science is not aiming at an overall picture of reality. There is, therefore, less chance of colliding with religion. Moreover, the sciences of today are much more pragmatic, less interested in truth than in validity. When something works, that is to say, when it can be applied in a useful way, science is satisfied. The result of these developments in science seems to suggest that there is hardly any connection between science and religion. Many scientists who are also believers have the feeling that they live in two different worlds that are completely apart. (This feeling is perhaps also the source of the idea that religion has nothing to do with truth.)

The developments that we have described offer an overall picture that differs considerably from that of the last century. In that century, Abraham Kuyper, the founding father of the Free (Calvinist) University in Amsterdam could write that the real conflict is not between science and religion. 'Not faith and science, but *two scientific systems*, or if you choose two scientific elaborations, are opposed to each other, *each having its own faith.*'[2] Even if we do not agree with the basic way in which Kuyper - intrinsically - connects faith and science, we must ask if it is really desirable to have the complete separation that nowadays characterizes the realms of faith and science. I do not think so, because this separation does no justice to faith or to science, as the following considerations will show.

On the one hand, we have seen that the pragmatic character of science is one of the reasons for the separation of the respective worlds of science and religion. On the other hand, however, it is precisely this pragmatic or useful character of science that enables science to be an important factor in improving the human situation on earth. All the side-effects of scientific and technological progress do not alter the fact that, without science and technology, we would not be able to fight against all kinds of misery. That fight means caring for people in need. This very caring is one of the fundamental religious obligations in Jewish, Christian and other religious traditions. This perspective justifies the question: Are the side effects of science and technology not partly due to the exclusively pragmatic view of science and technology? Their severance from religion could be one of the reasons why their benefits are less than they could be. Let me give just one example. The care of the sick is one of the great merits of the Middle Ages. At that time, this care was a work of charity. Nowadays, caring for the sick is a professional job that involves, and rightly so, much science and technology. But if we should ever forget that caring for the sick remains an act of charity, then there would be something fundamentally wrong. The modern hospital is no longer a charity. Everybody has a right to medical treatment, but in that same hospital the human face and the human hand must remain visible through all the scientific and technological skills. And we know the deep significance of that fact from Christ. It shows the intrinsic relationship between faith and science.

What happens in the hospital, or better what should happen in the hospital, could be considered as a paradigm of all scientific and technological work. Consequently, there is truth in the claim that, in pursuing and applying science to the benefit of humanity, we are engaged by the Creator in his creative activity and by Christ in his work of liberation. Did I claim too much when I said that the separation of faith and science does no justice to both of them? This example may also help to explain to some extent what I meant when I said that dogmata delineate the realm of faith and the domain of science analogously. From the *dogmata* of science - presuppositions I like to call them - no scientific conclusions can be drawn. In the same way, the *dogmata* of faith do not tell us how to cure the sick, but they do tell us something of the spirit in which we ought to help them.

We have just spoken of the manner in which science through its applications helps to fulfill fundamental religious precepts. Science, however, has a theoretical side too. Is there also a connection between this side of science and religion? It is true, of course, that in the way in which modern science explains phenomena there is never an appeal to religious considerations. In this sense modern science is fully secularized. This is in sharp contrast with the past, when many phenomena were explained as acts of God. Even in the first phase of modern science religious explanations were still given. Newton, for example, explained the actual cosmological order as the result of God's creation because the laws of nature could explain not this order itself, but only that it persisted. Some time later, when asked by

Napoleon if he did not need the Creator, Laplace, however, answered proudly, 'Sire, je n'ai pas besoin de cette hypothèse'. ('Sir, I do not need this hypothesis.') And he did so because he believed that the cosmic order could also be explained by itself.

The same thing happened with the theory of evolution. Some 'jumps' in evolution, such as the transition from non-living matter to life or the transition from animal life to human beings, were difficult to understand. For those transitions were not special creative acts of God necessary? Although the theory of evolution still lacks its 'Laplace', most scientists nowadays do not doubt that the explanation of these transitions will be found eventually. And if they are not found, very few of them will still accept an appeal to acts of God as a satisfactory solution. Even the great majority of religious scientists are not inclined to fill the gaps in their explanations by acts of God.

So it seems that modern scientific theory does not offer any point of contact with religious ideas and feelings. Whereas formerly everything in nature and in history, both in personal history and in history in general, spoke of God, this voice is silenced nowadays. What does this mean? Is the voice simply not there or do we not hear it because we are deaf?

Like all really fundamental questions, the one that we have just asked cannot be answered by a simple yes or no. Yes *and* no would be a better answer, but without further explanation such an answer does not help very much. So we must provide it. In a certain sense, it is fully correct to say that scientific explanations have rightly taken the place of an appeal to supernatural powers. This process, started by Greek philosophy and completed by modern science, has been one of the great accomplishments of human culture. Within the realm of scientific explanations as such, there is certainly no 'deafness' involved when nothing is said about divine acts. Or to put it differently, after a satisfactory scientific explanation has been given, there is no mystery left, so to speak. What at first was a mystery to me, for instance, the development of an embryo to a mature animal, is now made clear. The question, however, is whether or not all mystery is really explained away. The answer to this question is also an answer to the question with which we started our analysis of the special realm of religious considerations. Does this realm really exist or did it only seem to exist because of the actual state of affairs in science?

In order to answer the question, 'Does science explain all mystery away?', the following example may be helpful. If I am confronted with a new technical development, such as a remote control T.V. set, at first the whole thing may be a complete mystery to me. After receiving an explanation of how it works, the mystery has gone (provided I have enough scientific and technical knowledge to understand the explanation). What may remain and should remain, however, is my admiration for the possibilities that nature offers us and for the ingenuity of the human mind that constructed the new gadget out of these possibilities. In this sense I may and should be still wondering at the mystery of reality. The same thing applies to the function of D.N.A. in the development of an embryo. Once we have understood this function, we do not wonder any longer at the development of an embryo, at least not in the same way as before. Yet I do not hesitate in saying that, since I understand that development better, my admiration for the workings of nature is even greater than before. Thus the sense of mystery that nature offers us can even increase after a scientific explanation has been provided!

What conclusions should we draw from these considerations? We should not go as far as to suggest that it is still true that, in experiencing the mystery of nature, nature speaks to every scientist of God. But we are not going too far when we assert that every scientist ought to experience the mystery of nature (and of reality in general), if he or she reflects on what he or she is doing. The lack of this kind of reflection is one of the weakest points in our scientific culture. And I add, in our philosophical culture too. For this reason I feel justified in saying that, for religious scientists and philosophers, it is not enough that the mystery of nature speaks of God to them. They should also reflect in a more systematic way on the philosophical problems involved. This reflection is needed the more so because, in this respect, the religious traditions have committed serious errors (usually with the best intentions). I remind you of the ones that I mentioned before. It is quite understandable that questions about the original state of the cosmos, about the origin of life on earth, and about the origin of human life have especially evoked religious answers. In so far as they were meant as substitutes for scientific answers, those answers were misplaced. In so far as at critical stages in evolution the mystery that is *always* there is condensed, so to speak, there is nothing wrong in experiencing this mystery in association with those stages. It is just like the unfolding of our own life. The birth of our children and the death of someone we love are moments in our life when we experience in an intense way what life means. This is probably also the reason why people who do not frequent the church appreciate church services at those moments. But in the same way as religious life ought to be more than going to church only for marriage, for the baptism of children and for funerals, religious wondering at the miracles of reality should not be confined to the great transitions in evolution. The miracle is always there.

In conclusion, for the religious scientist every phenomenon of nature and every explanation of any particular phenomenon can speak of God, although no religious element will enter into his scientific explanations.

References and note

1. They are rear-guard actions, not only from the side of fundamentalists, but also from the scientific side. See for example J. Monod, *Le hasard et la nécessité, essai sur la philosophie naturelle de la biologie moderne*, Éditions du Seuil, Paris 1970; English translation: *Chance and Necessity*, Collins, London 1972. Compare also E. Schoffeniels, *L'anti-hasard*, Gauthiers-Villars, Paris 1973; English translation: *Anti-chance*, Pergamon Press, Oxford 1976.
2. A. Kuyper, *Calvinism. Six Stone-lectures*, Amsterdam-Pretoria 1898, p. 176.

T.F. Torrance, theologian,
Professor emeritus of Christian dogmatics, University of Edinburgh,
Edinburgh, Scotland

Fundamental issues in theology and science

T. F. Torrance

In recent years significant progress has been made toward Einstein's great objective of a unified field theory combining all primary forces in the universe, through a coordination of relativity, quantum, gravity and thermodynamic theory. One thinks here, for example, of the brilliant work of Stephen Hawking in linking together thermodynamics and the geometrical properties of black holes[1]. I myself do not consider that in principle a complete unified field theory can be achieved, owing to the contingent, unbounded nature of the finite universe, for contingent structures defy precise conceptual analysis and formalisation. Nevertheless, the more deeply scientific inquiry penetrates into the multilevelled intelligibility of nature, the more it needs a unified view of the universe.

The most inveterate problem we have to face remains the deep rift torn in human knowledge during the Enlightenment between the *how* and the *why*, or between the *is* and the *ought*. It is to that rift that all the unhappy splits in our culture ultimately go back, and not least the damaging separation between the physical and the human sciences, or the natural and the moral sciences. Can we ever reach a unified field theory unless we can heal that rift? In order to deal with it, however, we need to operate within a dimensional perspective which transcends that separation, that is theologically speaking, from within the relation of God to the universe. As Max Planck once claimed, the unified view of the world demanded by science requires in some way coordination between the power of God and the power that gives force to the laws of nature, which would have the effect of giving those laws a definitely *teleological character*[2]. In other words, it will be through thinking out the epistemological interrelations of theological science and natural science, where the cultural rift is deepest, that we may be able to find coordinates for the reunification of human knowledge.

Important developments in fundamental inquiry are already taking place in which rigorous questioning refuses to be halted at artificial barriers laid down in the past and reaches out across the *how* to the *why* and beyond the *is* to the *ought*. It is the purpose of this paper to draw attention to several of these areas of investigation where the old rationalist dichotomies are being set aside and where interdisciplinary thinking may open the way for the kind of deep-level integration that we need.

1. The concept of order

All scientific inquiry presupposes that the universe is inherently orderly, for otherwise it would not be understandable or open anywhere to rational investigation and description. This belief in order is not something that we can prove, for it has to be assumed in all proof, and arises irresistibly as a decisive operator in our consciousness under the impact of reality from beyond ourselves. As such it is built into the inner walls of our minds, and exercises a regulative function in all scientific inquiry and explanation. Thus we think scientifically as we must think under the compelling claims of reality and its intrinsic intelligibility. We find ourselves up against an immanent imperative in nature in response to which we frame our understanding of its objective, dynamic arrangements in terms of physical law, and we are deeply aware of an obligation thrust upon us from the ultimate ground of order which gives rise to what we call the *scientific conscience*. This sense of an ultimate obligation, echoed by the lawful claims of reality upon him, was very evident in Einstein's frequent appeals to 'God'. Under the compulsion of a scientific instinct, sympathetically tuned in to the profound intelligibility of the universe reaching out indefinitely beyond him, he dared to think about nature as he felt he ought to think even, as sometimes happened, in the teeth of what was adduced as evidence to the contrary[3].

It was undoubtedly his single-minded commitment to the ultimate unifying ground of order that lay behind Einstein's drive to develop a grand unified field theory. Particularly illuminating in this regard were the opening remarks offered by Einstein in his contribution to the *Stodola Festschrift* in 1929, 'Über den gegenwärtigen Stand der Feld-Theorie'. The ultimate aim of field theory, he claimed, is 'not only to know *how* nature is and how its processes run.... but *why* nature is *what it is and not something else*'[4]. That is to say, Einstein held that physics has reached the point where science can no longer be satisfied with discovering the laws of how nature actually behaves, but must find a way of penetrating into the ultimate unity of those laws and of finding the inner reason for them. That is doubtless 'the Promethean element in scientific experience', but Einstein claimed that so far as he himself was concerned it was, so to speak, 'the religious basis of the scientific enterprise'[5].

Einstein was surely right. When rigorous science refuses to be satisfied with asking the question *how?* but finds that it must press on to ask the question *why?*, if it is to reach the unified view of the world it needs, then it stands on the *religious basis* on which science finally rests. In that case, however, no satisfactory answer to the question *why?* can ever be reached merely through pursuing the quest for an ultimate 'logical unity' *(logische Einheit-lichkeit)*. For that goal to be reached scientific questioning and theological questioning must be allowed to interlock, empower and fructify each other.

Einstein's demand that science must be concerned with the inner justification of natural law also has powerful implications for the moral and social sciences. This was already evident from the massive recovery of *ontology* in the foundations of knowledge brought about through the integration of theoretical and empirical factors in general relativity theory. Recognition of the coinherence of truth and being in nature and in our knowledge of it, to which this gives rise, radically changes the attitude to 'reality' and deepens the sense of obligation generated in the scientific mind under its compelling claims. The effect of this is to call in question the positivist notion of *Wertfreiheit* or 'value-free science' that has become entrenched in social science, together with the separation of the *ought* from the *is* in moral and legal science, and to call for the recovery of ontology in their fields also. This integration of the *ought* with the *is*, however, is not to be confused with the 'naturalistic fallacy', i.e. the identification of what may be regarded as 'natural' or 'conventional' with what is positively obligatory[6]. Instead, it opens the way for an ethic grounded upon an imperative latent in reality itself in which we not only think and speak of things in accordance with their nature, that is, truly, but act toward them in accordance with their nature, that is, truly. Our actions, as St. Anselm reminds us, are capable of signifying truth or falsity just as much as our words[7]. At the same time, the way becomes open for realist social science in which questions of truth and falsity are no longer artificially bracketed off from serious investigation. It would thus seem to be incumbent upon all science for the moral imperative to function as an *internal operator*, and not just in some external utilitarian way.

2. The concept of time

In classical Newtonian mechanics absolute mathematical time, along with absolute space, is no more than an empty static container, an abstract standard for the measurement of velocity. Its differential account of time fails to represent the on-going of real time, much as an action movie fails to represent real movement for which it substitutes countless still pictures run together to give the illusion of movement. Everything began to change, however, with the concept of the continuous dynamic field as an independent reality, when relativity theory dethroned the scientific concept of time from its absolute status and revealed time to be an intrinsic feature of the on-going empirical universe. Moreover, the finiteness of the universe implied by the limited speed of light and Planck's constant h, carried with it the finiteness of time and the contingent nature of empirical reality. Even with relativity theory and quantum theory, however, at least in their traditional forms, time remains in the last analysis an external geometrical parameter, for the dualism between particle and field inherited from Newton has not been entirely resolved away as Einstein had hoped.

That picture has now been radically changed with the recent advances in non-equilibrium thermodynamics made by Katsir, Prigogine and others[8]. Here the notion of the irreversibility of time is not restricted to the macroworld and derived, as with Boltzmann, from time-reversible laws of motion operating in the microworld, but is found to be a primal, fundamental feature of nature. As such, real on-going time requires to be brought into scientific equations as an internal operator. This fits in very consistently with the now generally accepted understanding of the universe as continuously expanding from its original incredibly dense state, which forces us to regard the universe, and all the dynamic states of matter/energy constituting it, as inherently temporal, that is, with history embedded in it. In this event we are forced to ask questions about beginnings and ends, and questions as to why the universe exists rather than not and why it is what it is and not something else.

This reinforces considerably the insistence of Einstein that scientific inquiry must not stop short of trying to discover the ultimate justification of the laws of nature, if we are to reach a unified account of the world and all that happens within it.

The fact that the universe has a history within which the history of humanity is to be understood, implies that the sharp differentiation between nature and mankind that has held sway over the sciences since the Enlightenment is not valid. The history of nature and the history of human beings cannot be finally held apart. There are, of course, important differences that have to be taken into account: the time of an inert inanimate thing is different from the time of a living moving being, and the time of a self-organising biochemical system is different from the time of a self-organising human being. Nevertheless they all belong to the stream of on-going finite time in the expanding universe. Theologically expressed, they all belong to the same contingent order of the created universe. The implications of this are very far-reaching for historical science and for natural science[9].

So far as historical science is concerned, the old distinction with which it has operated since the Enlightenment, between necessary (timeless) truths of reason and accidental (contingent) truths of history is shattered. Since all events in the universe are contingent, scientific truths in which we express their orderly structures are themselves contingent and are neither necessary nor timeless. By the same token, historical truths, far from being merely accidental in character, in contrast to necessary truths of reason, and which as such have to be invested with extraneous meaning, are characterised by a contingent intelligibility of their own and must be interpreted as such. Historical science has not yet begun to adjust to this different concept of real time, for it still appears to operate under the tyranny of a Newtonian conception of absolute mathematical time clamped down upon relative apparent time![10] However, when the implications of this profound change in our scientific understanding of time are taken seriously, they cannot but lead to a radical revolution in historical science and in every human science with which historical science overlaps.

So far as natural science is concerned, the embedding of humanity and its history within the history of the universe has implications of no less significance. The fact that human culture, science, religion and art all arise out of and are part of the expansion of the universe, calls for a radical reconsideration of the nature of nature. It is not only the human brain that gathers up in itself the whole history of nature, but the intellectual, religious, moral, aesthetic, not to mention the scientific, development of mankind. Thus, for example, the embedding of the human being in nature means that the *moral* imperative is not extraneous but intrinsic to the essential nature of nature and its rational order. In other words, it tells us that *the moral ought is ontologically integrated with the intelligibility inherent in the being and becoming of the contingent universe.* Here once again we are forced to abandon the concept of *Wertfreiheit* in every field of scientific inquiry and explanation, for we are concerned not only to describe how things actually are but to determine what they ought to be in accordance with an obligation to an external objective governed by the ultimate ground of order[11].

3. The problem of meaning

At the end of his remarkable book, *The First Three Minutes. A Modern View of the Origin of the Universe,* Stephen Weinberg wrote: 'The more the universe seems incomprehensible, the more it also seems pointless'. There in a sentence we have starkly set out the baffling impasse now reached by quantum physics: the juxtaposition of brilliantly successful mathematical analyses and utter meaninglessness. What seems to lie ultimately behind that is the positivist divorce between *Verstehen* and *Erklären*, or understanding and explaining - for the more abstract formalistic descriptions and explanations of nature take over, the further they are removed from the real world of understanding and meaning. The problem of meaning, as John Archibald Wheeler has pointed out repeatedly, is bound to be uppermost in the new era of physics, which he has named 'meaning physics' or 'recognition physics'[12]. The fundamental question is: *How are we to recover meaning?* Do we correlate mathematically deduced entities complementarily with the human observer, thereby seeking to tie them in with the real everyday world? Or do we seek through a reconciliation of understanding and explaining to penetrate to a deeper level of *embodied* intelligibility and truth, where the foundations of physics and even of existence itself are revealed? Or do we combine both these attempts?

The problem of meaning is particularly acute when investigations touch the zero points at which physical laws become critical. That is the baffling problem now faced in quantum physics: penetrating to the untouchable interior of the elementary quantum phenomenon or 'the act of creation'[13]. There, at the frontiers of knowledge, everything appears to be lawless or without rational form, but we are nevertheless compelled at those very points to press inquiry beyond the limits of what can be conceptualised and explained in explicit terms in order to sustain the inner consistency and meaning of science itself.

In his *Oersted Lecture* of 1983 John Wheeler insisted that the way forward must surely be through discovering a 'regulating principle' under the guidance of which order is found to arise out of disorder. 'I believe that everything is built higgledy-piggledy on the unpredictable outcome of billions upon billions of elementary quantum phenomena, and that the laws and initial conditions of physics arise out of this chaos by the action of a regulating principle, the discovery and proper formulation of which is the number one task of the coming third era of physics.'[14] In his search for a regulating principle that must be 'deep' and 'simple' Wheeler looks to the pattern of thermodynamics and statistical mechanics for his operative cue. At the same time, he insists that such a regulating principle must be one that can account for all the structure that makes physics what it is, and as such must have universal relevance in order to make sense out of our experience - without it 'reality' would not be recognisable. That is to say, it must 'make meaning', but in that case Wheeler asks, 'Will it not be existence itself that comes under the purview of physics?'[15]

We must surely agree with John Wheeler here, not least with his point that for physics to be meaningful it must involve the fundamental metaphysical, and indeed theological, issue of the ultimate ground of all that is. However, when he raises the questions: 'What is the order we seek to understand?' and 'What makes meaning?', two questions may be put to him, that have the same import. Is not the kind of order he is looking for essentially *contingent order,* the kind of order that is what it is precisely through being grounded beyond itself, an open-structured order that is consistent and meaningful only as it is completed beyond itself in meta-reference to a transcendent ground of order? Moreover since, as Michael Polanyi has shown so clearly, meaning is found only in a 'displacement away from ourselves'[16], does physics not require at the frontiers of knowledge a *semantic focus* within which it can be invested with meaning? Does it not need an Archimedean point beyond it from which intelligible coordination could be given to what might otherwise appear disorderly and thereby yield the regulating and unifying principle that it seeks?

John Wheeler has evidently moved further in this direction in his paper of 1984, entitled 'Bits, Quanta and Meaning', contributed to the Caianiello Celebration volume[17]. In it he carries his understanding of quantum theory beyond Bohr's answer to the question of meaning - which implies the coupling of quantum phenomena with the human observer - to an objective registration of elementary quantum phenomena lodged in nature itself, independently of any human 'observer'. What I find most significant, however, is his claim that in *meaning physics* 'we have to seek nothing less than the foundation of physical law itself', while giving basic importance to the problem of *time* in the 'meaning circuit'[18]. Here we make contact again with Einstein's insistence in the *Stodola Festschrift* that we must penetrate into the inner reason or justification for nature's laws if we really are to grasp and to understand reality itself in any way, but also with the far-reaching questions posed by time embedded in nature and functioning as an internal operator in the basic equations of natural science.

Now if we relate Wheeler's search for a 'regulating principle' or for 'law apart from law' to the concept of contingent order and the need of meaning physics for a semantic focus, may we not gain illumination at this decisive point through an intersection of symmetries, as it were, between a theological understanding of creation and a quantum-mechanical (preferably quantum-contingent) penetration down to the mysterious emergence of order as it arises out of nothing? To switch to a musical analogy, it is when a *Logos* from a transcendent level of reality is allowed to call the multivariable events and disparate processes of the contingent universe into contrapuntal relation to itself, that consistency, lawfulness and meaning result, together with a harmonious understanding of the universe and all the structure that makes physics what it is. Wheeler is certainly right when he says that 'no law springs unguided out of absolute chaos'[19]. It may be submitted on the part of theological science, however, that the ultimate regulating principle which he seeks is none other than the *Word of God*, from which and by which the beautiful intelligibility of the universe has been conferred upon it, but which, like the music of the creation, is to be apprehended through hearing[20]. Moreover, the fact that the intelligibility and beauty of the creation derive freely from the unlimited Rationality and Beauty of God helps us to understand why it always takes our scientific investigations by surprise and constantly incites us with the promise of quite unanticipated and unpredictable disclosures in the future[21].

If scientists looking for meaning at the frontiers of knowledge are to reckon seriously with an open-minded semantic focus of this kind in the universe, should they not cultivate the habit of listening for the Voice of the Creator and recognising it? In that event, they might well allow the Word of God to function as a sort of meta-level to the levels at which their fundamental inquiries are made, and to bear meaningfully on them at their boundary conditions. This would not be altogether unlike what takes place in their efforts to decipher the light signals that come to us from all over the universe, laden with information about it, whether in its microphysical or astrophysical aspects. They are able to read those signals and to understand their message only as they correlate the mathematical patterns they carry with language. No science, not even pure mathematics, can be pursued with symbols alone, but only as *number* and *word* are coordinated meaningfully together. While in natural science *number* is primary, it requires the service of *word* to be meaningful. However, if science is to have meaning at the frontiers of knowledge where *number* becomes critical, it is *word* that must surely be allowed to play a more positive role. All this implies that natural science, in being true to itself, might do well to give more attention to the auditive mode of learning and knowing than it has been accustomed to since the self-limitation of classical science to aspects of reality that are only quantifiable or measurable. If that artificial restriction has induced deafness to the Word from beyond, it may well be that cultivation of the auditive mode of knowledge will help science recover the meaning it now seeks.

4. The problem of entropy

Entropy is still one of the most difficult problems in modern science. According to the second law of thermodynamics, which applies to closed systems, all physical and chemical processes tend toward an increase of disorder or entropy. In its classical statistical form this law is relevant only to macroscopic processes, and does not apply either to microsystems or to the universe as a whole, which seriously limits its usefulness in our understanding of the expansion of the universe or of the evolution of living organisms. Today, however, there are startling developments in the thermodynamics of open systems such as living organisms, or non-equilibrium thermodynamics, in which, while the classical formulation of the second law for closed, isolated systems is not challenged, a restatement of that law on a different level has had to be made to cope with the way in which order is found to emerge in the universe. According to classical thermodynamics, increase in order is always at the expense of increase in disorder, which implies that fundamental change takes place only in that one direction, even though there are areas in nature that deviate from this rule. How is it, then, that the whole expansion of the universe shows a steady upward gradient in the emergence of ever richer patterns of order from the 'primeval soup' of its earliest minutes to the wonderful complex order of the human brain and, indeed, of scientific knowledge of the universe? However, Prigogine and others, who have been responsible for the development of non-equilibrium thermodynamics, have shown and accounted for the fact that order is found to arise spontaneously upon the random or disorderly fluctuations that occur far from a state of equilibrium, that is, in the behaviour of open systems in which an exchange of matter and energy takes place between them and their environment. Thus in some respects what Prigogine has been after is something like the regulating principle sought by Wheeler which guides the rise of order out of disorder.

There are evidently deep unresolved tensions in entropy theory that we cannot enter into here, but important issues have been thrown up with which theology and science have to reckon.

Thus face to face with the fact that suffering in the universe affronts us, we can hardly avoid asking *questions* about the relation between natural and moral disorder, and thus even between entropy and evil - although, of course, there could not be any question of a simplistic or direct relation between entropy and evil. We noted earlier that the embedding of the human being in the nature of the expanding universe implies among other things that the moral *ought* has a deep ontological relation with the intelligible structures of created reality, but now the question must be posed whether moral disorder or evil is also somehow rooted in the expansion of the universe. In other words, we have to reckon with the reality of natural as well as moral evil and with some kind of interconnection between them. Natural science, however, especially in its classical way of reaching universal laws through processes of mathematical generalisation, inevitably resolves away any conception of natural evil just as it discounts singularities and discontinuities. Although the situation is now radically changed with relativity and quantum theory, in which we have to reckon with singularities and discontinuities, science still recoils from any linking of disorder with evil, even in face of the fact that under the commanding intelligibility of the natural order we find ourselves grappling not just with what is actually the case but with what ought to be or ought not to be the case.

Theology and ethics, on the other hand, have complementary inhibitions in refusing to consider any relevance, even in an indirect way to their fields, of the law of entropy that good order is achieved and maintained only at the expense of increasing disorder and noise. Yet if human society is recognised to be a self-organising open system, exchanging matter and energy with its environment and thus having a regular input and output of energy in different forms in order to keep going, then *must it not be the case that the more we set out to organise the good society, the more we induce forms of serious disorder in the world around us?* Is not our modern technological society a clear case in point, when through the application of science as an 'entropy-consuming' enterprise in furthering its ends, it seems to generate inevitably ecological disorder around it?[22] Perhaps the lesson to be learned here is that theology and science should think out together the significance and implications of *original sin* or radical evil, not least in regard to the fact that sin, as St. Paul taught us, can gain a strange strength from law and that evil can magnify its force through latching on to order.

This bears upon another difficult question to which much more attention should be given, the implication of the *direction of time* for both disorder and order. In a closed determinist world governed by logico-mathematical connections and the statistically formalised laws of thermodynamics, on the one hand, the arrow of time moves with the ineluctable increase in entropy or disorder. In the open-structured world of relativistic quantum theory and non-equilibrium thermodynamics, on the other hand, the arrow of time moves in the opposite direction with the spontaneous increase in order and the emergence of structure. In the former, time is an external parameter governing nature in a geometrically absolute way without being affected by what happens in the empirical world, and as such it closes the door to the future. In the latter, however, time inheres in the empirical world as an essential dynamic property of nature and operates as an internal parameter in its on-going processes, and as such it opens the door to the future[23]. In the former the irreversibility of time means that time is *unredeemable*, but in the latter the irreversibility of time means that time, as Prigogine points out, is *redeemable*[24]. Thus strangely, the law of entropy operates in a closed deterministic way near a state of equilibrium in terms of the disintegration of structure, but allows for an open creative functioning far from a state of equilibrium in terms of the transformation of structure. The paradox is that order should emerge spontaneously out of disorder, that is, not in spite of entropy but because of entropy. This does not imply, of course, that we may get order through causing disorder, any more than we may sin that grace may abound! Here, it would seem, we arrive at an extremely important point where theological and scientific movements of thought may once more interact to the benefit of both, just where we might not have expected it, at the issue of *redemption*.

A survey of the discussion

In gathering up the discussion let me bring together :
1. Wheeler's ideas about the need for a regulating principle and for law-without-law in the transition from the disorder of initial conditions to order;
2. Prigogine's ideas of the way in which richer patterns of order spontaneously emerge out of unstable, disorderly states far from equilibrium, together with the way in which the ir- reversibility of time leads to a world open to change and innovation in the future; and
3. the points I have made about the undeniable obligation in all scientific inquiry thrust upon us from an ultimate ground of order, and the contingent nature of all order in the universe under the creative and harmonising activity of the Word of God.

However, if in some inexplicable way there is evil at work in the universe, giving disorder a crooked twist so that it is not just a natural feature of nature on the way toward order, but is fraught with destructive tendencies, then the redemption of the universe from disorder requires more than a rearrangement of form like the resolving of dissonance in music, namely, the radical undoing and defeat of evil. In Christian theology that is precisely the bearing of the Cross upon the way things actually are in our universe of space and time. It represents the refusal of God to remain aloof from the disintegration of order in what he has made, or merely to act upon it 'at a distance'. It is his decisive personal intervention in the world through the incarnation of his Word and Love in Jesus Christ. In his life and passion he who is the ultimate source and power of all order has penetrated into the untouchable core of our contingent existence in such a way as to deal with the twisted force of evil entrenched in it, and to bring about an atoning reordering of the creation.

This is not the place to offer an account of the doctrine of atonement, but I cannot help but recall that in St. Paul's theology of the Cross, redemption takes place through a divine act of justification that is both 'under the law' (ὑπὸ τὸν νόμον) and 'apart from law' (χωρὶς νόμου)[25]. On the one hand, it takes place without any violation of the Law of God's own Being, the universal 'Constant', as it were, upon which all order depends and by which all disorder is judged. On the other hand, it takes place in such a way that the deep-rooted tension between what we actually are and what we ought to be is transcended and our life is set on a new basis, where we may live not under the imperative of law but in the indicative of grace. The act of justification in bringing order out of disorder is not just some kind of external forensic transaction but a real ontological event, for it deals decisively with the source of disorder and triumphs over it. The situation is complicated by the fact that guilt has deeply affected the irreversibility of time in such a way that the arrow of time runs from disorder to disorder and thus closes the door to change and renewal in the future. Redemption must involve what St. Paul spoke of as 'recapitulation', the astonishing act of God in the Incarnation and the Cross in which he penetrated back through time to its initial conditions, unravelling the twisted skein of evil, in order to liberate us from the tyranny of guilt-conditioned irreversibility in which our existence had become trapped. In the life and passion of Jesus Christ the order of redemption has intersected the order of creation, judging, forgiving and healing it of malevolent disorder, and making it share in the wholly benign order of divine love. Since in Jesus Christ there became incarnate the very Word of God by whom all things are made and in whom they cohere, the redemption of time applies not just to the human race but to the whole created universe of things visible and invisible.

Let me end by referring to a little book of beautiful and sensitive theological verse, *The Wounds of Love*, recently published by the very distinguished Emeritus Professor of Geography in the University of Edinburgh, J. Wreford Watson[26]. In his preface he tells us that he had taken up the study of natural science, finding in the theory of 'the terrestrial unity of all things' an assurance of the intelligibility of the world, but that the problem of disorder and pain threw the world in doubt - not least the holocausts of the twentieth century. 'Here was a profoundly disturbing thing that crooked the intelligibility of the world.' There seemed no way to resolve this mind-boggling and soul-distressing anomaly until he was confronted with that strangest of phenomena in the universe - the wounds of love. The efficacy of Christ's august anguish is a profound mystery, 'but one that somehow reconciles the particularity of suffering with the universality of order'. That is the most fundamental issue which science and theology must surely consider together.

References and notes

1. For Hawking's own assessment of a complete unified theory, see his inaugural lecture at Cambridge, entitled 'Is the end in sight for theoretical physics?', 1980.

2. Max Planck, *Religion und Naturwissenschaft*, 1937; Cf. Karl Heim's comments, *Christian Faith and Natural Science*, English translation, 1953, pp. 169f. & p. 233.

3. Cf. Einstein's preface to Max Planck, *Where is Science Going?*, English translation, 1933, pp. 9-14.

4. 'Wir wollen nicht nur wissen *wie* die Natur ist (und *wie* ihre Vorgänge ablaufen), sondern wir wollen auch nach Möglichkeit das vielleicht utopisch und anmassend erscheinende Ziel erreichen, zu wissen, warum die Natur *so und nicht anders ist*'; p. 126.

5. '... es ist sozusagen die religiöse Basis des wissenschaftlichen Bemühens', p. 127. Cf. Cornelius Lanczos on this Einsteinian rejection of positivism, 'Rationalism and the Physical World', in *Boston Studies in the Philosophy of Science*, vol. III, 1974, p. 1985.

6. For an instance of this see W. H. Waddington, *The Ethical Animal.*

7. Cf. here my essays: 'The Ethical Implications of Anselm's *De Veritate*', *Theologische Zeitschrift*, vol. 24, 1968, pp. 309-319, and Juridical Law and Physical Law, 1982.

8. See especially Ilya Prigogine, *From Being to Becoming*, W. H. Freeman, San Francisco 1980, and *Order Out of Chaos*, Bantam, New York 1984.

9. See my essay 'Time in Scientific and Historical Research', *Epistemologia X* (1987), pp. 73-80.

10. This is nowhere more evident than in Wilhelm Herrmann's distinction between *Historie* and *Geschichte* with which Bultmann and many other biblical scholars have been operating.

11. Cf. 'The Concept of Order in Theology and Science', chapter 2 of *The Christian Frame of Mind*, The Handsel Press, Edinburgh 1985, p. 17: '... in theology and science alike, we are concerned with *the kind of order that ought to be*, through relating actual order to the ultimate controlling ground of order from which all order proceeds'. An enlarged edition is now published by Helmers and Howard, Colorado Springs.

12. See his *Oersted Lecture*, 'On Recognizing 'Law Without Law'', The American Physical Society, Jan. 25, 1983.

13. J. A. Wheeler, 'Delayed-Choice Experiments and the Bohr-Einstein Dialogue', *Papers Read at a Meeting of the American Philosophical Society and the Royal Society, June 5, 1980*, The American Philosophical Society, 1981, p. 29.

14. Op. cit., p. 4. And see 'Law Without Law', chapter 1.13 of *Quantum Theory And Measurement*, edited by J. A. Wheeler and W. H. Zurek, pp. 182- 221.

15. Op. cit., p. 36.

16. E.g. *The Tacit Dimension*, 1967, p. 11f. Cf. *Scientific Thought and Social Reality*, 1974, p. 137f: 'All meaning lies in higher levels of reality that are not reducible to the laws by which the ultimate particulars of the universe are controlled.'

17. Edited by A. Giovanni, M. Marinaro and A. Rimini.

18. My references are to Wheeler's own typescript, pp. 5ff, 13ff, 20ff.

19. *Oersted Lecture*, p. 15f.

20. See Karl Barth's appreciation of 'the incomparable Mozart', and the pure way in which the music of creation, as expressed by Mozart, is related to the Word of God, *Church Dogmatics, III.3*, English translation, 1960, pp. 297ff; and cf. *III.1*, p. 404f.

21. For Michael Polanyi the capacity of nature to reveal itself in unsuspecting ways in the future is an essential aspect of its *reality, The Tacit Dimension*, 1967, pp. 23, 32f, 77f, 87; *Knowing and Being*, 1969, p. 119f, etc.

22. See the essay by R. B. Lindsay, 'Entropy Consumption and Values in Physical Science', *American Scientist*, 1982, pp. 375-385.

23. This is forcefully argued by Ilya Prigogine in showing that recognition of the inherence of time in nature induces a transition in our thought from being to becoming; see:
From Being to Becoming, 1980, passim, but cf. p. 214f.
(The subtitle of this book is: *Time and complexity in the physical sciences*!)

24. Cf. Prigogine's contribution to *Zygon* in 1984, Vol. 19.4, 'The Rediscovery of Time', p. 444. Prigogine derives the term '(un)redeemable time' from a poem by T. S. Eliot published in 1968: 'Time present and time past/ Are both perhaps present in our future/ And time future contained in time past/ ... / If all time is eternally present/ All time is unredeemable'
('Murder in the Cathedral').

25. See St. Paul's Epistle to the Romans, chapter 2 verse 12 to chapter 10 verse 15.

26. Although privately printed in a limited edition, the book is available from the author at Broomhill, Kippford, Kirkcudbrightshire, Scotland.

M. Bloemendal, physical chemist,
Research associate NWO
(The Netherlands organization for scientific research) / Vrije Universiteit Amsterdam
and lecturer Nederlands Israëlitisch Seminarium,
Amsterdam, The Netherlands

Science and religion, the Jewish position

M. Bloemendal

Contents

1   Introduction
2   Some basic concepts about Judaism
   2.1   The Torah
   2.2   Written law and oral law
   2.3   The Talmud
   2.4   Codices
3   A warning against science
   3.1   Only the truth of the Torah is eternal and absolute
   3.2   The Torah contains everything
   3.3   Science may lead one away from the Torah
4   How is the law?
   4.1   Books of 'other religions' and biblical criticism
   4.2   Philosophy, mystics and metaphysics
   4.3   Natural and human sciences, and history
   4.4   Science and its applications
5   Science within the rules of religion
6   Summary and conclusions

1. Introduction

Almost every year, at least one of the Nobel Prize winners is a Jew. Considering that only about 0.3% of the world's population is Jewish, this suggests a close relationship between Judaism and science. The Jewish Talmudic specialist, Maimonides, was one of the most famous physicians of his time, and he was asked to serve as court physician by Richard I, the Lion Heart. More than 1000 years before Galileo Galilei, Rabban Gamaliel already had an extensive knowledge of astronomy (e.g. he seems to have known that comets have a period of appearance[1], an observation that was first made in Europe as late as the 17th. century). Thus, it is clear that science has always held an important place in the life of the Jews.

In fact, many of the famous rabbis were also excellent scientists. Rabbi Jochanan ben Zakkai*, who lived shortly after Jesus, was a known specialist in linguistics, grammar, astronomy, mathematics and biology[2]. Scientific developments were incorporated in Judaism at a time when the Catholic church was burning scientists for anti-Christian ideas. Many modern scientific concepts can be found in the Talmud, which was completed in its current form at the beginning of the 7th. century. Examples can be found for almost any field of scientific endeavour. It is known, for instance, that Rabban Gamaliel had some kind of instrument for studying the stars (an early type of telescope?)[3]. Everyone knows about the hygienic rules that were practised by the Jews during the Middle Ages, and that saved their lives during epidemics of pestilence. The 'Shemittah year', the obligation to let the land lie fallow in the seventh year, is a biblical commandment[4]. Nowadays, agricultural schools teach that the land should not be eroded by continuous cultivation. Lastly, in the Talmud, Horayot[1], Rabbi Joshua refers to a star that appears every 70 years and might have been Halley's comet[5] (Halley discovered its period in 1682[6]).

I could spend the rest of this lecture giving examples of Jewish traditions that have been confirmed as useful by contemporary science. However, let me finish this introduction with an example of an arithmetical joke that can be found in the Talmud. The section concerning the Passover[7] relates that Rav Papa ate four times as much as Rav Huna, whereas Ravina consumed eight times as much as Rav Huna. About his two friends, Rav Huna says: 'I prefer to eat with a hundred Papas rather than have dinner with one Ravina'. At first, this may be regarded as a gross exaggeration since, assuming that Rav Huna himself eats a standard meal, a hundred Papas would eat four hundred meals, but one Ravina only eight. However, the statement by Rav Huna is accurate if the bill is shared equally by all who attend the meal. In that case one hundred Papas and one Huna have to pay for four hundred and one meals for one hundred and one persons, which means that 3.97 meals are paid for by each person. On the other hand one Ravina together with Rav Huna have to pay for nine meals, which means that 4.5 meals are paid per person, an obviously larger number.

2. Some basic concepts of Judaism

Apparently, there is a reasonable harmony between the Jewish religion and science. A closer look, however, reveals that things are far less simple. In order to present the Jewish attitude towards science and religion, first of all, I will explain a few of the fundamental principles of Judaism and Jewish learning.

---

*   As the reader may not be familiar with the transcription of Hebrew letters as proposed by the *Encyclopedia Judaica* we have transcribed consistently ח ('chet') by ch and כ ('khaf') by kh, *both* pronounced like the 'ch' in the Scottish word 'loch'; similarly, ש ('shin') has been transcribed by sh.

2.1 The Torah

It is assumed that the Pentateuch (the five books of Moses, the Torah in Hebrew) was given from beginning to end by G-d on mount Sinai. Let me stress that, although only the ten commandments (or according to some traditions only the first two of them) were communicated directly to the whole nation, it is believed that the complete five books of the Pentateuch were dictated by G-d to Moses. This means that each and every single word and letter is Divine and is assumed to have a purpose. Recalling that Jesus was a Jewish boy with a good Jewish education, the origin of his warning not to change one iota or one tittle is clear. It reflects the old Jewish tradition that every letter in the Torah has its meaning and, indeed, in some cases conclusions are drawn from the use of single letters, e.g. in the case of the old philosophical and theological discussion about whether a baby is born good or bad. The English poet, Wordsworth, who said[8], 'And much it grieved my heart to think what man has made of man', supported the idea that a child is born pure and is corrupted by its surroundings. Yet, at least according to some Christian sources, a baby is baptised in order to remove the original sin from him. This means that the baby is born wicked. In the Hebrew version of Genesis, when Adam is created, it is written 'vayyatzar' with a double jod. As the commentaries point out, this is to indicate that man was created ambivalently, which means with both a good and a bad inclination. In other words, according to Jewish tradition, a baby is born neither good nor bad, but neutral with both a good and a bad disposition. This example illustrates clearly that Jesus' words about the tittle and the iota are taken seriously by the Jews until this very day. It emphasizes that, in fact, every letter in the Torah has to be explained. Moreover, it is not difficult to appreciate that, if this holds true for letters, it must hold even more so for all those words that may appear to be superfluous.

2.2 Written law and oral law

The preceding ideas may not be particularly surprising, but less well-known is the fact that Jews believe that in addition to this written law, there was also an oral explanation given by G-d to Moses on mount Sinai. In fact, the Jewish tradition speaks about written Torah (Torah she-bi-khetav) and oral Torah (Torah she-be-al peh) in order to stress that both are of the same Divine origin. This oral tradition is utterly essential because it is completely impossible to understand the written Torah without it. For example, the Torah simply reads[9]: 'And thou shalt bind them (the words of G-d) for a sign upon thy hand, and they shall be for frontlets between thine eyes'. From the oral tradition, we learn that these frontlets are the black leather prayer-straps that orthodox Jewish men wear during their daily morning prayers on weekdays.

Another example of the importance of the oral law is the death penalty. Upon reading certain parts of Leviticus and Deuteronomy, one may get the impression that ancient Israel was a country with weekly executions. The oral law teaches us that, although in principle quite a few transgressions have capital punishment as the maximum sentence, such a verdict requires conditions to be satisfied which are so strict that the death penalty was hardly ever given, so much so that a court, that once in seven years put a man to death, was termed a tyrannical one[10]. According to other sources, this term was even applied to a court that gave one such verdict in seventy years[10]. Obviously in some cases the existence of the oral law is a matter of life and death!

The Torah she-be-al peh was passed orally from generation to generation, until finally, after the destruction of the second temple in 70, it was written down in a book, called the Mishnah in later times, because the rabbis of that period were afraid that it would get lost in the exile to come. The Mishnah was completed around the year 200. But, in contrast to the written law, which was *and is* always copied literally from an older version, one cannot be sure about the exact content of the original version of the Mishnah, especially after an oral tradition spanning more than 1500 years. Indeed, the rabbis of the Mishnah disagree with each other on several points. It is certain that some parts of the original Divine oral law have been lost, that other parts have been changed, and that some new concepts have been added. However, since no one knows which parts are Divine, and which are not, the orthodox Jew chooses to obey the human commands rather than risk disobeying the Divine ones. So he keeps the whole Mishnah as true.

2.3 The Talmud

The discussions of the early rabbis on the subjects laid down in the Mishnah have also been recorded. This work, completed about the year 600 and called the Talmud, may be considered as the jurisprudence of Judaism. Since Judaism is extremely conservative (in this respect the current Pope could be a Jew) everything that we do nowadays is based on the Talmud. For with every new problem or innovation that we encounter, we look to the Talmud, and we try by analogy to make statements and judgements about modern problems. It is surprising just how much can be learned about modern problems in these books. This guidance actually ranges from abortion to euthanasia and from living together instead of marriage to women's rights. It may be clear that every lecture on Judaism, and therefore also one on the stance of Judaism on science and religion, should be based (soundly) on Talmudic sources.

2.4 Codices

Later sages realised how important it was to have a short summary of the conclusions of the Talmudic discussions, and they also came to ultimate conclusions when this was not already done in the Talmud itself. Thus, Maimonides, around 1200, and Joseph Caro, around 1550, wrote their respective codices, the Mishneh Torah and the Shulchan Arukh.

3. A warning against science

Since the origin of the Torah is Divine, a first conclusion to be drawn is that it has absolute dominion over science, which is only human. Compared to the 'wisdom of the Torah', science is classed in Talmudic sources as 'external wisdom' or 'wisdom of the world'. This means that all scientific developments should be discussed and placed within the framework of the Talmud. Consequently, discussions by the rabbis on every scientific topic that you could imagine can be found, and a lecture on the Jewish stance on any one of them could be delivered. In this presentation, I would like to confine myself to a fundamental discussion of the concepts of science and religion in the Jewish tradition.

3.1 Only the truth of the Torah is eternal and absolute

Let us see first what we can learn about our topic from the Torah. In Leviticus it is written [11]: MINE ORDINANCES SHALL YE DO AND MY STATUTES SHALL YE KEEP, TO WALK THEREIN. A typical example of Jewish learning will now be given. In the previous section it was pointed out that there is a reason for the presence of every word in the Torah. We must ask, therefore, three questions:

- Why is there a double commandment? ('Mine ordinances shall ye do' and 'My statutes shall ye keep')
- What is the difference between these two commandments, or more specifically between ordinances and statutes?
- What is the meaning of 'to walk therein'? If I keep the statutes and the ordinances, don't I automatically walk therein?

The difference between ordinances and statutes (in Hebrew, between mishpat and chok) is explained elsewhere. A mishpat (ordinance) is a Torah law that we can understand (often related to justice), whereas a chok (statute) is a law that we don't understand, e.g. the law that allows us to eat cow but not rabbit. This shows us immediately something about the Jewish attitude towards science. Human understanding is of no consequence for the truth and the absoluteness of G-d's commandments. Both the laws that we do understand (mishpat, ordinance) and those that we do not understand (chok, statute) are equally true and should be kept. We could argue that, in fact, it would not be a matter of faith to believe in G-d if we could understand everything. We may say that G-d gave us some laws and commandments that we don't understand in order to test the strength of our religious conviction. In other words, believing in matters that we know for certain is not belief but knowledge.

As a scientist I should like to emphasize at this particular stage that science changes continuously. Certain facts that science can explain today could not be explained some years ago. The example of circumcision makes the point clearly and persuasively. For someone living a century ago, this practice must have seemed unscientific and very cruel to the baby. Why operate on a baby and risk an infection? Therefore, at that time, science opposed this commandment. Later, when the findings of physicians supported the view of circumcision as a healthy procedure, science advocated its practice. And so ten years ago, the majority of the baby boys who were born in the U.S.A. were circumcised, although not on religious grounds. Now, in recent reports some physicians have suggested that circumcision is not healthy after all, and so science may be opposed once more to the practice of circumcision.

Another example is the celebration of the Jewish festivals with all their symbolism. Before the fifties, people thought that this was an archaic form of religion. The early reform Jews relied on human understanding to decide whether to keep the old Jewish traditions, and they cancelled the celebration of those festivals. But as psychology and sociology developed, it was suggested that man needs symbolism as a support, as something to go on. For example, the weekly celebration of the Friday evening (the Shabbat night) possibly strengthens the emotional ties within the family. In response, therefore, they decided to reintroduce the celebration of the festivals with their symbolism. This example shows that the Torah may be ahead of modern scientific developments, and it cautions us that no one knows what science will find in the future.

The example of circumcision demonstrates clearly that scientific viewpoints change. Of course, we all know this. Indeed, it is vividly illustrated by the history of the effort to understand the nature of light. First, light was thought to consist of little particles. Then everyone believed that this had been proved false, and that light was a wave phenomenon. Nowadays, we recognize that only a combination of those two models can describe the behaviour of light, although the newest theories show that light is really neither of them. Despite the fact that every scientist knows that scientific theories regularly change or are proved untrue, the contemporary man, including the scientist himself, often forgets this very important point. A commercial on T.V. that cribs scientific credibility sells well because, if the man in the laboratory says that washing powder X is better than washing powder Y, then it must be so! We all know that, in the past, great scientists have erred. There are more than four elements, the globe is not flat, there is no generatio spontanea, and even some of Einstein's theories appear to be fundamentally wrong. We all know those things, but in my opinion (and this opinion was strongly reinforced during this second European Conference on Science and Religion!) we still tend to forget that contemporary science may be wrong too. If anyone argues that our modern scientific ideas are based on direct observations, he should consider that many observations are made, for example, by spectroscopic techniques, that are certainly indirect methods. No one has ever seen an atom directly. Nevertheless, almost everyone is certain that they do exist. So I conclude this part of the lecture with the statement that the reliability of science is grossly overestimated: science is at best a working model of reality. The orthodox Jew believes that the only eternal truth is the Divine truth of the Torah.

3.2 The Torah contains everything

Let us go back to the sentence of Leviticus quoted earlier. What does 'to walk therein' mean? The Sifrei explains[12]: 'One could say, 'I have learned the wisdom of the Torah; I know the Divine rules; now I shall learn the wisdom of the world'. Says the Torah, 'to walk therein'; you have no permission to leave its contents; you should be continuously involved'. This seems to be a warning against science. The prophet, Isaiah, is possibly subscribing to this caution, when he says[13]: 'Wherefore do you spend money for that which is not bread?' On this question from Isaiah, rabbi David Kimchi, a 12th. century commentator on the Holy Scriptures, notes[14]: 'Your efforts to acquire foreign sciences instead of the knowledge of the Torah is a waste of energy for they satisfy neither your material nor your spiritual needs'.

As I said already, if we really want to understand the Torah, we must seek the guidance of the oral tradition, the Mishnah. So let us look at what is written about this subject there. The Mishnah in Avot (Chapters of the Fathers) tells us that Ben Bag Bag says[15]: 'Turn it [the Torah] over and over for everything is in it, see with it, grow old and worn with it and do not depart from it, for you do not have a better pursuit'. This is perfectly straightforward. Ben Bag Bag is saying that you have to study Torah wisdom over and over and never think, 'Now, I have done enough'. You must learn it again and again. You must never tell yourself: 'I have learned enough', for there is actually no better way, nothing more useful, than the Torah. Here we find a reason for rejecting the study of science; that is, it is a waste of time, for everything that you may find through science, you could also find, in principle, in the Torah.

3.3 Science may lead one away from the Torah

A very strict statement against science is made in the mystical book of the Zohar. The Torah says in Exodus[16]: 'And make no mention of the name of other gods, neither let it be heard out of thy mouth'. The Zohar explains[17]: 'From here, we learn that one shall not occupy himself with books other than the Torah, and that it is even forbidden to mention them; certainly you shall not try to explain the Torah from them'. This seems to be a total rejection of science. This rejection, however, may be limited to those aspects of science that are in conflict with the Torah, or to a scientific explanation of the Torah (including biblical criticism).

Why are we warned against such things? The Torah is known to forbid a Jewish king to have a multitude of wives, money and/or horses[18]. The Torah also provides, as an exception, an explanation for this prohibition, viz. 'that his heart turns not away'[19]. We know that king Solomon neglected this commandment. He did acquire a multitude of wives, horses and money. The reason seems clear. He thought: 'I, in my great wisdom, will not turn away from G-d's path'. He knew the reason for the prohibition, and he convinced himself by logical reasoning that this commandment did not apply to him. As history tells us, in the end he failed and served idols. We can compare this with someone who, having drunk some alcohol, thinks: 'O.K. Someone who drinks should not drive a car. However, I have not drunk too much and, in any case, I can hold much more alcohol than most men without loosing control of my senses'.

Another example is the ritual immersion of women after their monthly period of menstruation. This requirement is readily explained as sound scientific practice for hygienic reasons. Hence, many people say: 'This commandment was rather important in ancient times, when attitudes to hygiene were generally poor, but nowadays when everybody has at least a shower, if not a bathtub, there is certainly no reason to go to the ritual bath'. However, when we investigate the rules for this immersion, we find that, before going to the ritual bath, a woman should thoroughly wash and clean herself. This includes brushing her teeth, removing her nail-varnish, and so on. If she does not clean herself thoroughly, the immersion is rendered ineffective! This shows us that the reason for this commandment is not just a hygienic one because, if the matter was that simple, then the cleaning beforehand would be enough and the ritual immersion would be superfluous. These examples allow us to conclude that a scientific explanation may lead to an erroneous abandonment of old rules, a conclusion that answers partly the question why we are warned against science. As Rabbenu Bachya puts it[20]: 'Other sciences sometimes lead a man away from the path of the Torah', which, as shown by the examples that I have given, might be by giving a false reason or by thinking: 'It (this warning) does not apply to me'.

In this connection one further point should be discussed. How should we deal with the problem that sometimes science seems to be true, yet it contradicts the Torah? In fact, the answer to this question is given in Deuteronomy where it says[21]: 'If there arises in the midst of thee a prophet or a dreamer - and he gives thee a sign or a wonder. And the sign or wonder comes to pass, whereof he spoke unto thee - saying, 'Let us go after other gods ... and let us serve them'. Thou shalt not hearken unto the words of that prophet ... for G-d putteth you to proof, to know whether ye do love G-d with all your heart and soul'.

4. How is the law?

The question now is whether the actual law is really as strict as has been suggested thus far. As I explained in subsection 2.4, we have to search the codices of Maimonides and Joseph Caro in order to learn the ultimate rules.

The Shulchan Arukh, Yoreh De'ah 246.4, deals with the obligation of a Jew to learn the Torah, the Mishnah and the Talmud. There Rabbi Mosheh ben Isserles - Rema - says: AND ONE SHOULD LEARN JUST THESE THREE, HOWEVER, NOT OTHER WISDOM. IN ANY CASE ONE MAY LEARN THEM ACCIDENTALLY. BUT DEFINITELY NOT THE BOOKS OF THE MINIM (see below). AND THIS (OTHER WISDOM) IS WHAT THE SAGES CALL 'STROLLING IN THE GARDEN': AND ONE SHALL NOT MAKE SUCH A STROLL UNLESS ONE HAS ENOUGH MEAT AND WINE (KNOWS WHAT IS ALLOWED AND WHAT IS NOT).
What then do we conclude from Rema's saying?
–   The main accent is always on the Torah, the Mishnah and the Talmud.
–   We are allowed to learn science ('accidentally').
–   Not all aspects of science are allowed (not 'the books of the Minim').
–   Not everyone is allowed (or able) to study science; only those who have 'bread and wine', who know enough about the science of the Torah.

4.1 Books of 'other religions' and biblical criticism
Who are the 'Minim', whose books are so strictly forbidden? On this subject we find different opinions. The Talmud gives a general definition[22]: 'Who is a 'Min'? One who actually worships idols'. Rambam explains in more detail[23]: 'Five are called Minim. The one who says there is no G-d and no Ruler in the world. The one who acknowledges that there is a Ruler, but believes in two or more. The one who acknowledges that there is one Ruler, but says that He has a body or an image. The one who says that this Ruler is not the only origin of everything. The one who serves a star or something else as an intermediate between G-d and man'. The second and last categories might also include Christian books, and, indeed, at several places in the Talmud Rashi translates Minim as Christians[24]. As we noted previously, biblical criticism is also a prohibited science.

Actually the Shulchan Arukh, mentioned in the preceding subsection, is based on Maimonides' Mishneh Torah, which in turn refers to the Talmud, Chagigah[25]. 'Four men entered 'the Garden', namely Ben Azzai, Ben Zoma, Acher and Rabbi Akiva. Ben Azzai died, Ben Zoma became stricken, Acher made mistakes (apostatized) and only Rabbi Akiva departed unhurt.' Maimonides says[26]: 'Although they were great men of Israel and outstanding sages, they had not enough power to understand and to reach completely their Creator'. Thus, one may study science, but only if one takes great care not to lose the right path! The same idea was expressed in subsection 3.3.

4.2 Philosophy, mystics and metaphysics

Let us study in more detail what the Talmud, Chagigah tells us about science. The Torah says[27]: FOR ASK THOU NOW OF THE DAYS PAST WHICH WERE BEFORE THEE, SINCE THE DAY THAT G-D CREATED MAN UPON THE EARTH AND FROM THE ONE END OF HEAVEN UNTO THE OTHER, WHETHER THERE HATH BEEN ANY SUCH THING AS THIS GREAT THING, OR HATH BEEN HEARD LIKE IT. The Talmud says[28]: 'One might have thought that one may inquire concerning the period before the creation; therefore, the Torah teaches: 'Since the day that G-d created man upon earth'. But then one might have thought that one may not inquire concerning the creation; therefore, the Torah teaches: 'The days past, which were before thee'. One might have thought one may inquire concerning what is above and what is below, what is before and what after (the world); therefore, the Torah teaches: 'And from one end of heaven unto the other'.' This means that we may occupy ourselves with an explanation of the physical world but not with what is above or outside it. Several rabbis[29], therefore, explain that the Shulchan Arukh, quoted before, speaks about sciences like metaphysics, mystics and philosophy, which deal with 'matters' outside and before our physical world.

4.3 Natural and human sciences, and history

From the Talmud, Chagigah it is evident that the pursuit of natural science (including the human sciences) and the study of history are allowed. Furthermore, the Jewish tradition even teaches that it is advisable to study them. The statement in Ecclesiastes[30], 'It is good that thou shouldest take hold of the one; yea, also from the other withdraw not thy hand; for he that feareth G-d will discharge himself of them all', has been explained[31] as speaking about science. It has also been mentioned that the sciences are essential in learning the Torah. They have been likened to a ladder upon which to climb towards the wisdom of the Torah[32], and they also have been described as being doors leading to it[33]. Maimonides[34] stated that the sciences are like perfumers, cooks and bakers for the Torah. The Vilna Gaon - the 'genius from Vilnius', a famous opponent of the Chasidim - has said[35] that 'a man who is lacking knowledge about secular sciences will lack one hundredfold in the wisdom of the Torah', and that 'those who despise these sciences do so because of their lack of wisdom, and are considered as a child fleeing from school'.

The high esteem enjoyed by science, and therefore shared by scientists, within Judaism is perhaps best appreciated from the fact that a Jew is expected to say a special benediction whenever he sees a great scholar[36]; that is, 'Blessed is He who gave from His wisdom to flesh and blood'. (This benediction, of course, is only said on the condition that the scholar does not use his knowledge against the Torah![37])

One may wonder why Judaism values these sciences to such an extent. A primary reason is 'in order to know and to appreciate our Creator'[37,38]. In fact, this idea is also expressed in the quote cited from Deuteronomy in subsection 4.2, which continues with the words[39]: 'Unto thee it was shown, that thou mightest know the Lord; He is G-d; there is none else beside Him'. From Deuteronomy several rabbis[37,38,40] not only allow, but even require, the study of the sciences, that 'make one better acquainted with G-d; everyone according to his ability to understand'[40]. Yet here we have encountered an interesting point. Often it is felt that science and religion are contradictory, and that knowledge about nature may lead man away from religion, whereas the Jewish tradition suggests the opposite. A true knowledge of nature may strengthen religious belief through the increased admiration of the believer for the greatness of the creation. In the next section we will find another reason for studying the sciences.

4.4 Science and its applications

The importance of science for the Jew and Judaism is probably best illustrated by a quotation from the Talmud, where the qualities required of a candidate for election to the Sanhedrin are summed up by Rabbi Jochanan[41]: 'None are to be appointed members of the Sanhedrin but men of ... and of science'. The sciences in question are given by Maimonides in the Mishneh Torah[42]: 'We don't appoint in a Sanhedrin whether it is a big one (which means the Sanhedrin of 71 men, comparable with the Supreme Court) or a small one (a court of three judges, comparable with a district court) but sages excellent in the wisdom of the Torah, and owners of great intellect, people who at least know something about other sciences like medicine, mathematics and astronomy; moreover, something about astrology and idolatry in order to judge them'. (Astronomy is important for the Sanhedrin because of the calculation of the calendar.) This quote from the Mishneh Torah tells us that the judges should even know something about the usually strictly forbidden books on idolatry in order to judge them. In a comparable way some rabbis explain the Mishnahic statement[43], 'know what to answer a non-believer', as a reason for allowing, or for requiring, the study of philosophy and of 'other religions'[44]. However, it is made clear that one should do so with extreme care not to become confused and not to lose the right path (recall the picture of the four strolling in 'the Garden', mentioned above). Apparently, science has also a role to play in decision making.

Another very important reason for studying the natural and human sciences, medicine and so on is their applications. How do we know that medical science is allowed? The Torah says in Exodus[45]: 'And if men contend and one smite the other with a stone or with a fist and he die not, but keep bed; if he rise again and walk around upon his staff.... you shall pay for the loss of time and shall cause him to be thoroughly healed'. From this extract we learn that we are allowed to practise medicine[46]. Of course, one could always argue that the passage deals primarily with the harm caused by men. However, we also find in the Torah[47]: 'Thou shalt not see thy brother's ox or his sheep driven away and hide thyself from them, thou shalt surely bring them back unto thy brother and so shalt thou do with his ass and with his garment and *with every lost thing* of thy brother's which he hath lost and thou hast found; *thou mayest not hide thyself*. This quotation is generally understood as stating the obligation to return to someone everything that he has lost, including his health[48]. On the basis of this verse, moreover, Judaism rejects the argument that, as diseases are sent by G-d, interference is forbidden.

No doubt the analogy between an ox and the health of a man seems rather strange. Yet, in the case of the ox or of the garment we could also reason: 'If G-d makes this fellow lose his coat, who am I to give it back? G-d has his reasons for it'. One may also compare it with the obligation to help the poor, which is a feature of almost every religion. Why should we give something to a poor man, if G-d made him that way? G-d knows why he is poor and why I am rich! The answer is that G-d presents us with the opportunities to help others. And the same thing applies to scientists. G-d provides for us the opportunities to enrich and to improve life. 'You shall not hide yourself from it', says the Torah. If G-d gives us the opportunity to be scientists, 'to make us rich', then we are obliged to acquire this spiritual money and also to give charity, to help other 'poor' people with our knowledge. Here we meet another reason for allowing and requiring the study of the sciences; that is, in order to help our fellow human beings and to improve life. Included in the range of allowable sciences are the life-sciences and life-improving sciences in the broadest sense of these terms. Some rabbis even classify music in this group[35b].

The tasks of helping mankind and of improving life lay a heavy ethical and moral burden on the scientist. The Talmud, Shabbat[49] goes so far as to say: 'He who is able to calculate the cycles and the planetary courses and does not, one may hold no conversation with him'. Rabbi Shim'on ben Pazzi in the name of Rabbi Joshua ben Levi on the authority of Bar Kappara said: 'He who knows how to calculate but does not, of him it is said in Isaiah[50] but they regard not the work of G-d, neither have they considered the operation of His hands'. In the Sefer Chasidim it is said[51]: 'One who is in a position to learn medicine but does not, it is as if he had killed the sick person'. Evidently, then, it is a great sin not to apply science when its use is possible.

5. Science within the rules of religion

Although science is considered to be of paramount importance, it is always subordinate to the rules of the Jewish religion. One can find several examples of this subordination. We discussed the strict obligation to heal, which, in cases of neglect, was even compared to murder. However, a priest, a descendant from the high priest Aaron, a kohen, is forbidden to defile himself by contact with a dead body[52]. What does this mean? We all know the New Testament story of the good Samaritan[53] who helped the sick man on the road, whereas the priest passed by, apparently in order not to defile himself. According to the Jewish religion, the New Testament condemns correctly the priest. For in an emergency Judaism says, 'and ye shall live by them'[54], and therefore the priest should have helped. There is, however, no good reason a priori for a priest to put himself in a position where he has to defile himself. Consequently, a kohen should not study medicine[55], because the training involves necessarily the dissection of cadavers, and because the practice of medicine in a hospital exposes inevitably the physician to dead bodies. Another example is organ transplantation. If it is urgent and someone's life can be saved as a direct result of taking an organ from a dead body, it may be permissible[56]. However, if there is no immediate need, the removal of such organs is not permitted. Hence, organ banks are forbidden[56]. Another problem that is encountered with transplantation is the method used to determine when someone is dead - for if the person is alive during the removal of such organs, the practice is vivisection, which is strictly forbidden in Jewish law, and may even be regarded as murder[57]. This moment of death is determined not on scientific grounds, but on religious ones. Thus, it is made abundantly clear that even the life-sciences must be practised within the context of the Torah and the Talmud.

6. Summary and conclusions

In Jewish tradition there is no doubt about the absolute dominance of religion ('the wisdom of the Torah') over that of the secular sciences ('external wisdom' or 'wisdom of the world'). Consequently, the tension between religion and science, so apparent in some other religions, is absent from orthodox Judaism, although it is certainly felt by Jewish individuals. The basic principle of the Jewish religion is the absolute and eternal truth and value of every word, even of every letter, of the Torah (Pentateuch). In this respect human understanding has no role to play. Thus, if science claims to have proved something against the Torah, then science is wrong by religious fiat! Nevertheless, as early as Talmudic times, it was realised that many people trust scientists far more readily than they do clergymen. Many warnings against science, therefore, are found in the Talmud, and some of the former sages even go so far as to forbid the study of the sciences. Two basic reasons *against* the study of the sciences can be found:
- *Everything is in the Torah, so the study of other sciences might well be a waste of time and effort.*
- *Science can take one away from G-d and from the Torah by mistaken rationalization.*

Notwithstanding this apparently fundamentalistic point of view, the importance of science was acknowledged from the very beginning of Judaism and, in fact, one can also find two main reasons in favour of the study of the sciences:
- *In order to know and to appreciate the Creator of the world, and to strengthen our religious convictions.*
- *For practical purposes, including judgement, decision-making, the answering of non-believers, and applications that save, enrich and improve life.*

The latter is so important that the study of the life-sciences is not only allowed but mandatory, it being judged a great sin not to apply science when its use is possible.

The practical Jewish law concerning secular science may be summarized as follows:
a. We are allowed to learn science (accidentally), but the primary interest always should be in the Torah, the Mishnah and the Talmud. Thus, not everybody is allowed to study the sciences. Only those who know enough about the latter three. Even then, one should study with great care in order not to lose the right path.
b. The preceding warning applies particularly to those sciences specifically concerned with matters 'outside and before our world', like metaphysics, mystics and philosophy.
c. In general, science that conflicts with the Torah, such as biblical criticism, and books about other religions are strictly forbidden. According to some sources, this prohibition covers every effort to explain the Torah in a scientific way.
d. The natural sciences, including the human sciences, history and possibly even music, are not only allowed but mandatory. Everyone should pursue them according to his ability.
e. IN ANY EVENT, ALTHOUGH SCIENCE IS OF PARAMOUNT IMPORTANCE, IT IS ALWAYS SUB-ORDINATE TO RELIGION. In this respect, even medical science is answerable to the Torah. Thus, on ethical questions about the practice of euthanasia, organ transplan-

tation, vivisection, in vitro fertilization and so on, it is the rabbi who decides (usually after he has consulted the physician).

The author acknowledges gratefully the support received from The Netherlands organization for scientific research (NWO).

References

1. Talmud, Horayot 10a.
2. Talmud, Sukkah 28a and Me-iri on that place.
3. Talmud, Eruvim 43b.
4. Leviticus 25:1-7.
5. Epistle to Slonimsky in Toledot Ha-shamayim, Warsaw 1938.
6. P. Moore and J. Mason, *The return of Halley's comet* (2nd. ed.), Patrick Stephens Ltd., Wellingborough 1985; Ch.4.
7. Talmud, Pesachim 89b.
8. W. Wordsworth, *Lines written in the spring*, 8.
9. Deuteronomy 6:8.
10. Mishnah, Makkot 1:10.
11. Leviticus 18:4.
12. Sifrei on Ecclesiastes 5:17.
13. Isaiah 55:2.
14. Radak on Isaiah 55:2.
15. Mishnah, Avot 5:23.
16. Exodus 23:13.
17. Zohar II:124.
18. Deuteronomy 17:14-20.
19. ibid. v.17.
20. Rabbenu Bachya on Avot 5:23.
21. Deuteronomy 13:2-4.
22. Talmud, Avodah Zarah 26b.
23. Mishneh Torah, Teshuvah 3:7.
24. Talmud, Berakhot 12b, Steinsalz edition, Jerusalem 1970.
25. Talmud, Chagigah 14b.
26. Mishneh Torah, Yesodei Torah 4:13.
27. Deuteronomy 4:32.
28. Talmud, Chagigah 11b.
29. Siftei Kohen on Shulchan Arukh, Yoreh De'ah 264:4; Be-er Heitev on the same place; Response of Hai Gaon to Shmu-el Hanaggid on the study of philosophy; Letter of Rambam to the sages of France; see also *Encyclopedia Talmudit on philosophy*, Talmudic Encyclopedia Publ., Jerusalem 1979; Vol. 15, pp. 79-80.

30. Ecclesiastes 7:18.
31. Iggerot Kena-ot, response of the Radak, p. 3; Zohar on Tazry'a 47:2-48:1.
32. Rabbenu Bachya on Avot 3:23; Maharal, Netivot Olam on the same place.
33. Sermons of the Chatam Sofer 112b (on Beshalach).
34. Letters of Rambam to R. Jonathan Hakohen, Responsa of Rambam, J. Blau edition, Vol. III, p. 57 (compare Samuel I 8:13).
35. (a) R. Barukh of Shklov, Introduction on the book Euclid;
    (b) R. Israel of Shklov, Introduction on the Pe-at Ha-shulchan.
36. Talmud, Berakhot 58a.
37. Maharal, Netivot Ha-olam, Netiv Ha-torah, Ch. 14.
38. Responses of Rema, no. VII.
39. Deuteronomy 4:35.
40. Mishneh Torah, Teshuvah 10:6.
41. Talmud, Sanhedrin 17a.
42. Mishneh Torah, Sanhedrin 2:1.
43. Mishnah, Avot 2:14.
44. Me-iri on Mishnah, Avot 2:14; Talmud, Bava Kamma 83a.
45. Exodus 21:18,19.
46. Talmud, Berakhot 60a.
47. Deuteronomy 22:1-3.
48. Sifrei on Deutoronomy 22:1-3; Talmud, Bava Kamma 81b; Rambam, Torat Ha-adam, subject Sakkanah; Rambam, Perush Ha-mishnah on Nedarim 4:4.
49. Talmud, Shabbat 75a.
50. Isaiah 5:12.
51. Sefer Chasidim, Machberet 150, 1469.
52. Leviticus 21:1.
53. Lucas 10:33.
54. Leviticus 18:5.
55. Iggerot Mosheh, Yoreh De'ah, Vol. III, 155.
56. ibid. Yoreh De'ah, Vol. III, 150; E. Landau, Responsa Noda Biyhudah, Mahadura Tinyana, Yoreh De'ah, no. 210.
57. See e.g., Iggerot Mosheh, Yoreh De'ah, Vol. II, 286.

A. Gierer, biophysicist,
Director Max-Planck-Institut für Entwicklungsbiologie
(Max Planck Institute for Developmental Biology),
Tübingen, The Federal Republic of Germany

Physics, life and mind:
The scope and limitations of science

Alfred Gierer

Abstract

What, precisely, are the 'changing perspectives on reality' in contemporary scientific thought? The topics of the lecture are the scope and the limits of science with emphasis on the physical foundations of biology. The laws of physics in general and the physics of molecules in particular form the basis for explaining the mechanism of reproduction, the generation of structure and form in the course of the development of the individual organism, the evolution of the diversity and complexity of organisms by mutation and selection, and the control of behaviour by information processing in the nervous system. However, the application of scientific thought to its own foundations reveals some basic limitations in science: indeterminacy in quantum physics, the limits of decidability in mathematics, and, most likely, the limitations of an algorithmic theory of the brain-mind relationship. In all these cases, the application of scientific methods to their own presuppositions leads us to recognize their intrinsic limitations. These limits, in turn, are closely related to fundamental philosophical questions on the relationship between human knowledge and reality. Modern science is consistent with different, though of course not all, interpretations of man and the universe, including the religious interpretations of the universe as God's creation and man as God's (mentally creative) image.

Science is often said to support a materialistic and mechanistic view of nature and man, and to contradict traditional religions, explaining belief in God as superfluous, though historically understandable. In recent times, however, an opposing approach has gained attention. It claims that so-called scientific truth depends on historical conditions and cultural contexts, and that metaphysical ideas are more fundamental than scientific formalisms and need not surrender to allegedly scientific facts. Further, it is argued that the misuse of scientific skills for the arms race and the consequences of science-based technology in generating environmental hazards cast doubt on the value of science as such.

I will try to explain in my lecture that both extreme notions of science are unconvincing. The scope and the limits of science are themselves meta-scientific problems, that can be assessed by applying scientific methodology to its own presuppositions. In this way, it is possible to detect some intrinsic, unsurmountable limitations of science, limitations that are themselves open to philosophical interpretations. The latter, in turn, are relevant to the relation between science and religion. The scientific assessment of these limits of science is an advantage rather than a drawback, and the scope of science *within* these limits is still very impressive. In particular, phenomena in all domains of nature - including chemistry and biology - appear to be formally interrelated, following ultimately the basic laws of physics.

The scope and the limits of modern science thus assessed are still far from being common knowledge. In fact, many of the naive notions of 19th. century materialism still survive. My talk aims at summarizing arguments in favour of the unity of nature given by the basic laws of physics, the intrinsic limits of science as assessed by science itself, the interpretation of these limits, and possible consequences for the relation between scientific truth and cultural, as well as religious, pluralism.

If we ask for explanations of natural phenomena, e.g. Why is the sun shining? How do plants grow? How does a muscle contract? Why is the sky blue? How does a cloud form? How does a fly chase another fly? ...., then we get involved in various branches of science - physics, chemistry, biology - but, ultimately, the explanation of such strikingly different phenomena rests on one and the same set of laws, the basic laws of physics. Admittedly, physics as a science is still incomplete, but quantum theory as developed in the nineteentwenties appears as the complete and adequate explanatory basis for processes in the energy ranges of chemistry and biology. None of our questions can be answered directly by studying the equations of quantum mechanics; but for all of them the chain of explanations eventually leads back to the basic laws of physics. This establishes a unity of all nature or, at least, of all of natural science.

Such an understanding of 'unity' does not imply reductionism; the basic laws of physics themselves do not tell us all about chemistry or biology. Chemical compounds and living organisms are systems of components. Physics applies, but a system of components has properties that the components themselves do not have. 'The whole is more than the sum of its parts' is the essence of contemporary mathematical systems theory. Explanations require adequate conceptualization and mathematical methods, in addition to a knowledge of the basic laws for the interaction and movement of the constituent components. A given formalism - such as the set of basic physical laws - does not allow us, in principle, to draw all possible conclusions solely from a case by case theoretical analysis. There are too many potential cases. Therefore, we can understand living organisms only by analyzing *existing* biological phenomena that have to be known and conceptualized in the first place. Thus, by referring to the unity of nature, we do not imply that physics explains everything. The meaning of unity, in this context, is rather that all natural phenomena are interconnected and that the *central role in the network of explanations* is played by the laws of physics, abstract laws that are fairly simple, formally beautiful and accessible to the human mind.

Let me explain the physical foundations of science with respect to the most recent and most impressive development, the understanding of the basic phenomena of life. To begin with, we may ask what are the characteristics of all living systems, from bacteria to man, that distinguish them from the inorganic domain. There are three characteristic features:

reproduction of organisms in each generation, metabolism (by which energy and material from the environment are recruited for the growth and the proliferation of the organism), and mutation (that is, changes of hereditary properties as a basis for selection and evolution). In 1944, Avery discovered that the genetic material is DNA, and, in the decade from 1952 till 1962, the basic discoveries were made that led to a molecular understanding of the fundamental biological processes mentioned. The hereditary substance DNA consists of long sequences made up of four types of units, the four nucleotides. These sequences contain the genetic information for the organism, in analogy to a written text that contains information in its sequence of letters. DNA has two functions: it can be replicated identically by a molecular copying mechanism, and it can determine the synthesis of specific proteins with specific catalytic and other functions. Mutations are random changes, deletions or additions of nucleotide sequences; some of them have positive consequences for selective value, thus allowing for evolution. These basic insights of molecular biology, nowadays rather common knowledge and part of high school curricula, explain the essential properties of living systems - reproduction, metabolism and mutagenesis - as the properties of molecules. Molecular properties, in turn, can be understood in terms of the basic laws of physics, because quantum mechanics has proved to be the adequate basis for them all, including organic chemistry. While physical laws hold fully in the living domain, an adequate explanation of that domain requires concepts specific to biology, such as those of genetic information. These concepts are not inherent in the laws of physics themselves.

In the nineteensixties, after the main facts of molecular biology had been established, some scientists thought that the essential biological problems had been solved in principle, the remainder being concerned 'only' with the details. However, this view overrates the explanatory power of molecular biology as such. The most impressive features of higher organisms are not the metabolic reactions but the specific form and the complex behaviour of plants and animals. It is true that these features are also based on molecular genetics, but clearly the relation, say, between the form of a mouse and the structure of its DNA is a very indirect one. To begin with, the question is how genetically determined biochemical reactions can lead, in each generation, to the characteristic structure and form of the organism. Particularly impressive are the striking regulatory properties of biological development. For instance, half of an early sea-urchin embryo can still generate a complete animal with the sizes of its parts adapting in proportion to the reduced size of the whole. Such holistic features have been considered as a challenge for physical explanations.

In the last decades, we have learned that chemical reactions are in principle capable of generating patterns with the holistic properties encountered in developmental regulation. What is required is some local activating reaction with autocatalytic, self-enhancing features coupled to a more widely diffusing, inhibitory effect. Then even a slight initial advantage is self-enhancing, but because of the wider range inhibition, a local activation in a tissue can proceed only at the expense of de-activation elsewhere, thus producing a strikingly unequal distribution of molecules. In this way, a specific, spatial concentration pattern can be formed that can serve then as a 'morphogenetic field' directing the spatial organization of cells and tissues. Though the biochemical basis of morphogenetic fields is not yet known, the dynamics of self-organization accounts for the self-regulatory features on the basis of fairly conventional reactions and movements of molecules.

The development of biological structures is the result of many processes, such as induction by interaction between tissues, as well as the differentiation, proliferation, movement and death of cells, in conjunction with, and in response to, the establishment and function of such morphogenetic fields. Much has still to be learned about the details, but there is little doubt that the basic phenomena are within the reach of present-day physics.

Another main feature of living organisms is the complex behaviour of higher animals and man, controlled by the nervous system. Some of its properties are genetically specified. Others are the result of learning. The individual nerve cell is the element of information processing; each cell receives electric signals from certain cells and transfers these signals to other cells. In addition to electric signals transferred between nerve cells by close contacts called synapses, there are also less localized, biochemical signals that appear to be part of information processing. Learning and memory are probably based on changes of the efficiency of transmission of the synapses between nerve cells, changes that occur in response to certain types of activities within the neural network.

Most of the nervous system in higher animals consists of sheeted structures made up of different cell layers and subdivided into different functional areas. The cerebral cortex of man is the best- known example. It covers an area of 0.2 square meters. It contains some ten billion* cells, connected by some hundred thousand miles of nerve fibres, forming about one hundred thousand billion* synaptic connections. There is considerable knowledge about the biophysical and chemical bases of information processing by the individual nerve cell, and increasing insight into the function of the systems of such cells, for instance, in the processing of visual information by subareas of the cerebral cortex. However, we are still far from a satisfactory understanding of most brain functions. Nevertheless, there are good reasons to believe that physics is fully applicable to all brain processes, and that all brain properties and functions that are detectable by objective analysis will be accounted for eventually by information processing mediated by physical signalling in the neural network.

This view is supported by a general mathematical insight, namely, that in principle *any* task of information processing that can be fully specified can also be implemented by suitable networks of elements of information processing. We are used to these notions, on which the ever-increasing capabilities of electronic computers are based. Though the construction principle of the brain is different from that of existing computers, the same mathematical principle - 'what can be formalized can also be mechanized' - applies to the neural network as well. 'Higher' tasks like abstract analysis, forecasting, decisions can be formally implemented in such systems. Therefore, we have good reasons for assuming that higher brain functions can be understood, in principle, as information processing based on the physical transmission of signals in the neural network. Understanding such brain functions, of course, requires extensive mathematical analysis. Whether or not there may be

---

* American usage is followed here: 1 billion = 1 thousand millions.

limits of formalization, in particular with respect to the mind-body problem, will be discussed later. At this stage we summarize that physics is the explanatory basis not only of chemistry, but also of biology, including genetics, evolution, the development of pattern and form, and the processing of information in the nervous system.

However, the development of science in our century has also revealed that there are intrinsic limits to scientific knowledge. Not all questions that can be asked in scientific terms can be given scientific answers, leaving aside questions that are not scientific from the outset. It turns out that the main limitations of science are not uncovered by external criticism (such as the dubious claims of some historians that scientific methodology is a culture-specific vogue without objective validity), but by applying scientific methods to its own presuppositions. Such internal analysis has profoundly changed the notions of science, and it has profound philosophical implications. We will discuss briefly a few particularly instructive cases.

a. *The theory of relativity.* An early example is Einstein's theory of relativity. It shows that a consistent understanding of certain aspects of electrodynamics and optics is obtained only if we give up our intuitive notion of space and time in favour of a more abstract and counter-intuitive concept. The maximum velocity of signals under any circumstances and in any reference system is the velocity of light. This theory reveals a formal symmetry of physical laws with respect to space *and* time coordinates; it includes the famous formula $E = mc^2$, i.e. energy (E) equals mass (m) times the square of the velocity of light (c), the basis of all nuclear physics. The theory of relativity demonstrates that, while epistemological reasoning contradicts common intuition, it may nevertheless lead to universally applicable, experimentally confirmed, physical laws, laws that are conceptually abstract but formally beautiful.

b. *Quantum physics and indeterminacy.* Even more fundamental was the revolution of physics resulting from the development of quantum mechanics. The physics of the previous century was based on mechanics in a sense that we would describe today as naively materialistic and deterministic. Modern atomic physics has shown, however, that prediction at atomic dimensions depends on the precision of measurements, a precision that is limited because the process of measuring interferes with the states of the atoms to be measured. Therefore, the future cannot be fully deduced, in principle, from parameters measurable at present. In the case of processes involving strong enhancement - for example, the nucleation of turbulences or the expression of genetic mutations - atomic processes are re-inforced giving rise to macroscopic effects. In such aspects the future is open. For example, long-term weather trends, and also genetic recombination, are not strictly determinable. Many characteristics of any living being arising from sexual reproduction are unpredictable in principle. Furthermore, the notion that at atomic dimensions small but real particles assume well-defined positions and velocities in the course of their movement is no longer acceptable in modern physics. Modern physics is not a theory of a concrete reality, but a theory of possible knowledge. This knowledge is limited - and the limitations are just as deeply anchored in the laws of nature as is, for instance, the principle of the conservation of energy.

c. *The logic and limits of decidability.* Another example refers to the limits of formal thinking. Natural phenomena are explained on the basis of laws of nature by means of mathematics. Mathematical thinking is logical thinking; logic in turn is an object of mathematics. How logical is logic? In the nineteentwenties, it was still a major aim of mathematics to substantiate fully the system of formal, logical thinking by the formalism of logic itself. This failed. It has been proven that the 'rich' logical systems required to encompass the essential capabilities of human thought, in principle, cannot provide their own foundation. No computer can be programmed to find every true theorem valid for a given formal system, or to decide for every given theorem whether it is true. Here only luck and intuition can help. It is impossible to prove the consistency of a 'rich' formal system by methods limited to its own formalism, and thus the possibility of future contradictions can never be excluded. All formal thinking depends on unformalized assumptions.

d. *The finiteness of the world*. According to modern cosmology the universe is finite in size and age and consists of a limited number of material components (at least within the range of possible human knowledge). Therefore the number of physically possible processes and operations in the universe is also finite. This number, though very large - estimates based on cosmological data are of the order 10^{120} -, is nevertheless much smaller than the number of possibilities resulting from combinatorial considerations even for everyday problems - like the possible arrangements of people fitting into a lecture hall. The constraints imposed by the physical universe support a 'finitistic' epistemology. But verification of general statements cannot always be based on a case-by-case analysis; even mathematically finite problems can be physically insoluble. Although often intuition and luck may lead to a general proof (just as in cases of mathematical theorems valid for an infinite number of cases), there is no logical guarantee for decidability.

e. *Chaos*. The theory of chaos, a modern branch of mathematics, shows that there are limits to the predictability of processes in which extremely small fluctuations in the present would lead to large-scale differences in the future. This means that the formalism of the natural sciences can predict some aspects of the behaviour of systems very well but others not at all, conditions that cannot be altered by further investigation.

And also:

f. *The philosophy of science*. It was a major aim of the philosophy of science - particularly in the nineteentwenties - to define and to substantiate comprehensively the procedures and prerequisites of science: for example, measurements, conceptualization, logical deduction. In particular, it was claimed that scientific concepts are to be anchored exclusively in experience by indicating the methods of measurement. Further analysis has shown, however, that this is impossible. Although the theoretical concepts of natural science are only reasonable if they have some experimental implications, a *complete* reduction of these concepts to processes of observation cannot be achieved, and it is not even attempted by the scientists who do the real work. In general the development of the philosophy of science led to an attenuation of exaggerated expectations. The theory of science is a metatheory that is *less* precise compared to the sciences that are its objects. It is interesting, but it is never free of open or tacit assumptions. The philosophy of science is quite naturally more controversial than science itself. Presumably this is not due to a transitory lack of insight, but rather to the scientific ambiguity of any interpretation of the world as a whole.

A final case to be discussed is:

g. *The mind-body problem.* The classical, mechanistic notions of the world, and biological theories based on them (particularly classical behaviourism), regarded soul and sentiment as superfluous concepts, and maintained that scientific reality should only consist of the behaviour of organisms and the control of that behaviour. Today, few scientists would subscribe fully to this opinion. Feeling pain is not identical with observing one's expressions of pain. It is known that we have access to our own consciousness in a way that is direct and often independent of the senses. This conscious experience need not be unequivocably and completely reducible to physics. As mentioned, we expect any formalizable function of the brain to be eventually explainable on a physical basis. The question is left open, however, whether or not all mental aspects of brain function actually can be described in objective terms.

One may argue that anything that can be described can also be formalized, but this is not true for the relation of the mental to the physical. Mental aspects, such as feelings, emotions, our own moods, preferences and intentions, are given to ourselves immediately in consciousness without reference to any knowledge of our brain. These mental aspects are not just a few raw feelings that can be inferred from psychophysical reactions, like blushing or a trembling voice. Roget's *Pocket Thesaurus,* a dictionary for synonyms and antonyms, contains about fifteen thousand entries of English words. About half of them belong to the mental domain, and even a rigorous classification would leave us with several thousand. The so-called mind-body problem has many aspects that are difficult to define unambiguously, and so scientific discussion of it is somewhat inhibited because our deep interest in this problem is in conflict with its conceptual evasiveness. One aspect that has a defined meaning is the following: can we expect an algorithmic theory of the correlation between the mental states of a person (moods, dispositions, intentions, aversions, judgements, as well as integrated properties such as 'Selbstverständnis' - the understanding of oneself - and 'Lebensgefühl' - the awareness of the quality of one's life), expressible by combinations chosen from the thousands of words belonging to the mental domain, and the measurable physical state of his or her brain? In other words, can we expect a satisfactory theory of the correlation of mental and neurophysiological states?

Our present knowledge is still far from a solution. Many correlations between perception, as well as emotion, and neurophysiological structures and activities in the brain are known; effects of ablations and of drugs also show psychophysical relations. It is very likely that any mental state corresponds to just one physical state. But will there ever be a complete algorithm for this correlation?

The validity of the laws of physics in the brain does not imply of necessity that such an algorithm is possible. We may explain this by discussing the dispositions of a given person for future behaviour. Such dispositions, resulting, for instance, from past experience and strategic thinking, are *present* in the memory of the brain but refer to an open *future* with many different possible sequences of events. Their number, as well as the number of conceivable behavioural dispositions, exceed by far the finite number of possible physical operations in our finite universe; an upper limit of this number can be estimated, on the basis of cosmological data as 10^{120}. Therefore, in principle, not all possibilities could be checked individually, even with the help of the largest conceivable assembly of computers.

Hence, there is no guarantee that all dispositions corresponding to a given brain state actually can be decoded by systematic analysis.

Moreover, there are specific reasons supporting our assumption that brain states are not fully decodable with respect to mental states. Mathematical decision theory, such as Goedel's theorem, teaches us that a full intrinsic formalization of a logical system is impossible. Certain questions that can be formalized within the system, especially if they are self-referential and involve metatheoretical levels, have no finite answers within the formal system in which they are asked. In point of fact, these theorems have no immediate bearing on the limits of understanding the brain. The mathematics refers to infinite entities, whereas the brain is a complex but finite unit with a finite number of states. However, by analogy, one may guess that there are self-referential aspects of the mind-body problem that would require - in principle, not just in practice - algorithms of a size surpassing any order of magnitude consistent with the finite world - . In that case certain, especially self-referential, aspects of the mind-body problem may not be decodable in principle by finite procedures, although relatively simple, crude and partial aspects are expected to be resolvable.

These thoughts on the scope and limits of the physical foundation of biology indicate that physics is, indeed, the universal basis of all events in time and space, including those in living organisms. Nevertheless there exist limits to our possible knowledge as revealed by science itself. These limits are related to ambiguities involved in self-referential operations. Quantum indeterminacy has its root in the unavoidable interference of measurements with the measured object, an interference that cannot be avoided by the measurement of the instruments of measurement because this would lead to an infinite regress. The logical analysis of systems of logic gives rise to limits of decidability. Similarly, a complete algorithmic theory of the mind-body relation appears to be impossible because mental states cannot be fully analyzed by mental procedures, neither directly nor by an analysis of the physical basis of mental processes in the brain.

The interesting aspect of all these limitations of science is not just their existence, but the fact that they can be subjected to quite different philosophical interpretations. Such interpretations are not ambiguous - usually each of us has quite a strong inclination to one of several possible lines of thought - but supporting reasoning is far less stringent than, say, an experimental demonstration or a mathematical deduction. For instance, the theory of relativity can, but need not, be interpreted as suggesting that 'time' is a human mode of cognition, whereas truth, not only mathematical truth, is 'beyond time'. Obviously, not everybody will subscribe to this interpretation. Quantum mechanics is held to be a - probabilistic - theory of possible knowledge of reality, not a theory of reality itself. This interpretation has been considered by Bohr and Heisenberg (I think adequately) as the conclusive, epistemologically satisfactory, formally beautiful answer of nature to our sense of curiosity, whereas Einstein and others claim that there must be real, underlying events subject to deterministic laws. Finally, theorems of undecidability in mathematics, such as Goedel's theorem, are interpreted by most professional mathematicians with great caution; they consider them as formal theorems valid only for certain formalisms. Yet these theorems may also be taken as an indication that human thought cannot comprehend itself completely.

Similarly, our analysis of the mind-body relation - as well as other approaches to this problem in the literature - may be subject to different interpretations. I suggest that the mind-body relation is not fully resolvable in principle. My reasoning is partially based on the finite number of analytical steps consistent with the finite size and time-scale of the universe. Of course, one may question whether the proposed 'finitistic' epistemology is philosophically acceptable, that is, whether the term 'in principle' has been applied correctly. One may still consider the limits of our potential knowledge as consistent with determinism in the naive sense of the word, and even with the notions that conscious experience is an epiphenomenon and free will is an illusion. But alternatively, one may accept, as I do, a 'finitistic' epistemology based as it is on physical cosmological parameters. The underlying notion is that, *what is determined only for an imaginary super-cosmic computer, is undetermined.* Thus, presumably, the mind-body relation is not decodable for fundamental scientific reasons. This inference has far-reaching consequences. In fact, one expects that there cannot be a complete definition of mental concepts in terms of objective criteria. Now, with respect to the 'man-versus-machine' - or the 'brain-versus-computer' - issue, it appears that the brain follows the laws of physics completely. At the same time, however, there is no evidence of the interference of mental states with physical states of the brain in voluntary actions. So we arrive at the conclusion that a machine that we fully understand does not have the full range of human capacities, whereas we would not understand fully a machine with the capacity of man. The full range of mental experience, and its expression by human communication, proves to be beyond the information derivable from an objective analysis of brain states alone.

Generally we arrive at the conclusion that physics is the basis of all science, but that science has limitations that allow for and require a metatheoretical interpretation. These limitations refer to the relation between human insight and reality in general. This relation, in turn, is connected with the deepest questions elaborated in the history of philosophy from the presocratic 'physicists' onward.

The metatheoretical ambiguities that cannot be resolved in principle constitute a positive aspect of human freedom: it is possible to interpret the world in agreement with scientific facts and logic in an agnostic or a theistic way; it is possible to claim or to disclaim sense in evolution, in history and in personal life, to regard consciousness as the inexplicable basis of all objective knowledge or as a marginal feature of neural networks, to consider the future as open or as essentially determined by hidden parameters, etc.. But these metatheoretical ambiguities, though unresolvable by science, do not permit us to refrain from choosing for ourselves an interpretation of the world and the self, and from choosing a style of life. Science helps us in this interpretation and orientation and in solving practical problems, but the enigmatic and ambiguous character of man's self-understanding cannot be scientifically resolved. Rather it is consistent with cultural and philosophical pluralism, and fortunately so, because the development toward cultural uniformity and sterility would be hardly desirable. Compared to today, many more people would have claimed only a few decades ago that science is the one dominant basis of our culture, that it is superior to the unscientific interpretations that preceded a fully rational approach and that, because of its progressiveness, it will eventually transform divergent cultures into a more or less uniform, rational, consistent and efficient civilization. Clearly, even with the limits of science in mind, scientific knowledge is still a challenge to any traditional interpretation. It has changed religions and ideologies, and it will continue to do so. Yet religions and ideologies have always changed, even without the aid of science, and so it is only to be expected that they will neither vanish nor merge under the influence of science.

What then are the implications for the topic of this meeting, for the relation between science and religion? This question is not new. It can be traced back to medieval philosophy and beyond, but the question has to be posed afresh by each generation because the notion of science itself is changing with the progress of science. Let me emphasize that doubts about religious beliefs are much older than science. We find scepticism as early as 5000 years ago in the Sumerean story of Gilgamesh; we find it in the weariness of life expressed by the ancient Egyptian 'letter to the soul', in the Koheleth of the Old Testament - the book Ecclesiastes or The Preacher - and in philosophical treatises from Protagoras onwards: 'I have nothing to say about the Gods; neither that they exist nor that they don't exist. There are many reasons for our ignorance. The subject is too difficult, and life is too short.' Nevertheless, many of the pioneers of modern science had deeply religious motives for pursuing science. But clearly, the progress of science undoubtedly encouraged religious scepticism, which perhaps reached its peak in late 19th. and early 20th. century materialism. In our time, there is less hostility between science and religion, the prevailing attitudes ranging mostly from indifference to critical sympathy.

In my view, scientific claims on the truth of religious traditions require us to distinguish between factual and metatheoretical statements. For instance, the statement in Genesis that there were plants before there was the sun is definitely wrong. In this regard, modern science has disproved the ancient scriptures. Yet, the statement that man is God's image is not describing an established fact. Rather it provides a general interpretation of man and the universe (not excluding the capacity of man to pursue science in order to understand the universe). This interpretation cannot be proven or disproven by scientific arguments. It is fully consistent with scientific facts. Its acceptance or rejection, however, is based on intuition as related to many facets of life, not on deduction based merely on facts and logic.

However, the distinction between factual and metatheoretical statements cannot lead to a complete separation of the domains of science and religion. Though many statements clearly belong either to the one or the other of these domains, such distinctions fail as soon as science analyzes religion, for instance, its psychological and historical bases, and as soon as religious thoughts include the interpretation of science. Evidently, science and religion are then ultimately dealing with their own respective presuppositions. As far as a religious view of science is concerned, one can, but need not, interpret science as the creative participation of the human mind in God's creation. Also, scientific analyses of religion cannot claim objective truth either, based as they are on conscious or unconscious philosophical presuppositions on which their conclusions implicitly depend.

Let me summarize my talk. The basis of all sciences is uniquely given by the laws of physics that are applicable to all events in space and time, including biological phenomena such as evolution, reproduction, pattern formation and information processing. These laws apply fully to man, including the human brain and its functions. Yet the analysis of the conceptualization and methodology of science by science itself leads to scientifically established limits - quantum indeterminacy in physics, undecidability in mathematics and, as I tried to explain, limits on a complete algorithmic theory of consciousness and the human mind.

I do not suggest that the gaps in our scientific understanding of the real world should be filled by philosophical or theological speculation. Instead, I stress that metatheoretical aspects, namely, the scope of science as a whole together with the existence and the logical structure of its limitations, allow for and require philosophical interpretation. The scope and limits of science have implications for the relation between human knowledge and reality, and this relation, in turn, is connected with the deepest questions of philosophy and religion. Science is consistent with quite different - though, of course, not all - religious ideas. Such consistency, however, allows for controversies, but it does not imply ambiguity. For opinions and decisions on 'metaphysical' matters necessarily involve intuition, judgement on values and notions on life styles, none of which can be decided upon by factual and logical argument alone, and, therefore, all of which require wisdom and discourse in a spirit of tolerance.

References

A more extensive discussion of the topics of this lecture, including references to the literature, is given in the author's book:
A. Gierer, *Die Physik, das Leben und die Seele*, Piper, Munich 1985.

Aspects of the mind-body problem are discussed in:
A. Gierer, 'Überlegungen zur Leib-Seele-Beziehung: Gibt es Grenzen der Decodierbarkeit?', published in *Zeitschrift für Theologie und Kirche*, vol. 84 (1987), pp. 254-266.

W. Weidlich, physicist,
Professor of theoretical physics, Universität Stuttgart,
Stuttgart, The Federal Republic of Germany

Reconciling concepts
between natural science and theology

Wolfgang Weidlich

Contents

1   Introduction
2   General remarks about the relation between religion and science
3   The emergence of new structures in natural science
    3.1 The scope of classical physics
    3.2 New views necessitated by quantum theory
    3.3 The framework of synergetics
4   Towards a synthesis between scientific and religious thought
    4.1 The disaster of determinism
    4.2 Chance and necessity from a theological perspective
    4.3 Is there a fundamental role of the subject in quantum theory?
    4.4 The hierarchy of structures of relative self-containedness
    4.5 God as originator and God as projection
    4.6 The openness of science to transcendence
5   The dimensions of truth

1. Introduction

Since the dawn of mankind, man's perception of fate has been accompanied and determined by religion. The deepest thoughts about the existence of man, about the meaning of his life and the origin of the world originated in religious faith. It is only recently, i.e. within the last 400 years, that within the family of basic ideas and conceptions a brother of religion was born, namely, natural science who has been prospering since that time. And what can happen in a human family also occurred in the case of sister religion and brother science. The older sister did not like her brother too much because he partially distracted attention from her. The situation worsened when he grew into adolescence. Both the older sister and the younger brother believed that they had good reasons for maintaining their own right of existence and for refusing the claims of their rival. As one knows from family disputes, it is not easy in such cases to disentangle the justified arguments from the unjustified ones.

Fortunately, however, we are witnesses of another very recent development. Living in a century of catastrophes, like the two world wars, we observe a growing maturity in the relationship between sister religion and brother science, at least in Europe, which may be even partially due to these catastrophes. Religion and science now understand each other better. They seem to have become aware of the fact that they are committed to complementary dimensions of the all-embracing truth!

In the following sections we shall give a brief survey of some more recent insights into natural science, insights that have helped in reaching this new level of mutual understanding. But first let us ask in retrospect some *systemic questions* about religion and science which pass beyond the discussion of historical details.

These systemic questions are: Do or did there exist *plausible if not unavoidable reasons* on the side of religion, and of science as well, making it difficult to avoid conflicts, at least at certain stages of their mutual relations? Do there exist *general basic arguments,* independent of transitory stages of science and of the fleeting interpretations of theologians, that hint at a general structural compatibility of science and religion? We shall consider these questions in the next section.

2. General remarks about the relation between religion and science

Let us begin with a criticism of a view still silently shared by many theologians and scientists and by most contemporaries, although it will turn out to be a prejudice. This view arises as follows. Since religion is essentially concerned with the ultimate meaning of human existence and with interpretations of the hazards and deep secrets of life, a silent widespread opinion has evolved that God has primarily to do with the non-understandable, unforeseeable facts of life and of the world. In this understanding all facts and relations rationally explainable by science no longer belong to the competence of God but fall under the purely manipulatory disposal of man.

Theologians adopting this view are automatically thrust into an apologetic situation where they must protect the realm of religion against the progress of science. And scientists adhering to that view are tempted to celebrate their results as a victory over 'religious obscurantism'. We know that this attitude played an important role in former centuries and does so even now in orthodox Marxist philosophy.

But this division into the realm of God and the realm of rational thought must be rejected as a whole, and for simple reasons. If God is the power bringing the world into existence, it follows directly that the explainable as well as the inexplicable belong to the unity of his Creation. The wonder of this Creation is not diminished but heightened by including individuals who are able to understand parts of it. Einstein once said: 'Raffiniert ist der Herrgott, aber boshaft ist er nicht' - 'Subtle is the Lord, but never malicious'. And when asked to give an interpretation of his remark, he answered, 'The creation impresses by its own sublimity, so that it is not necessary for God to conceal it from the thought of man'.

Let us now consider briefly the main thrust of those arguments in religion on the one hand, and in science on the other, that have led frequently to conflict and confrontation in the past and that still do so today. Both sides can claim the evidence of fundamental experience, that is, the experience of faith in the revelation of divine truth and the experience of the far-reaching validity of rational thought in finding and formulating universal laws of nature, respectively. These two types of experience are not as such incompatible, but they may lead to conflict if they are rigidly extrapolated into absoluteness and dogmatism, thereby becoming inadequate. On the religious side, there is always the lure of *fundamentalism*, i.e. the attraction of a literal interpretation of biblical revelation down to the last cosmographic detail. But in science the sore temptation is to embrace *premature universalism* by extrapolating the role of structures found in one layer of reality to the whole of reality where, however, it may prove insufficient.

Both attitudes are understandable and even partially excusable. On the one hand, fundamentalism arises from religious ardour and from fear of relativism in the interpretation of the word of God. On the other hand, scientific claims of universal validity for the laws of nature may originate in the previously unrefuted application of such laws at a certain stage of research. Nevertheless, the dogmatic attitude of both fundamentalism and scientism must be rejected on general grounds that are essential to the structures of religion and of science themselves.

In contrast to a fundamentalist interpretation of biblical revelation, it must be stressed that God can never be labelled and disposed of in an absolute manner. Even with respect to the Bible, which is also only a book written in finite words and at certain historical places and times, it must be left to God what degree of absolute and invariant inspiration and revelation can emanate from it over the centuries, and what degree of literalness proves possible and adequate in the process of its theological interpretation. On the scientific side, one must argue, against a dogmatic generalization of those laws of nature that have proved empirically successful within a certain layer of reality, that the reach of a theory cannot be postulated *a priori* and remains indefinite and open to further research. The history of science itself provides ample evidence against such premature generalizations, as demonstrated, for example, in the cases of quantum theory and the theories of relativity, in which new concepts replace those of classical physics in extended domains of reality.

These considerations provide a general guideline. Whenever a conflict between religious faith and scientific discussion is immanent, both parties should recognize the need to ask themselves if their standpoint is truly inevitable with respect to the constitutive elements of their faith or thought, or if perhaps a premature and misleading, absolute claim will lead to conflict. Instances of the (avoidable) second alternative seem to have prevailed throughout the history of the disputes between science and religion.

Following these remarks let us consider briefly the *relationship between religion and philosophy*. In this case the relationship is not so much concerned with the compatibility or the reconcilability of a set of concrete statements made on both sides, as with the most fundamental level of basic convictions.

Our basic conviction as 'Christians' is that God has given us *His revelation* in terms of the Bible, and that this revelation can be mediated to us through our faith. In contrast, the basic conviction of the philosopher is that *nothing* is given to us with certainty, and that the only means of attaining cognition and orientation is through probing questions and by arguing on the basis of logic and reason. These mutually exclusive principles lead to the very boundaries of conceptual thought. Does a purely logical decision exist which favours one of these convictions? The answer seems to be 'no' because of the following arguments.

On the most fundamental level every thought has a quasi-circular character, since on the one hand it must assume at least its own validity, but on the other hand, at this basic level, no genuinely independent means of verification can be found outside this thought. In this circular sense, then, the religious man has faith because revelation exists, but only within the context of this faith can he justify his confidence that the Bible bears the mark of revelation. In an analogous way the philosopher trusts in the efficacy of his probing questions, but only within the framework of this analysis can he justify the confidence that his method of radical questioning is applicable and makes sense[1,2].

That, in both cases, the modes of substantiation have no absolute character and are only self-consistent can be seen from the doubts of the opposing positions. Thus the philosophical position doubts by its radical questioning the very existence of anything having the nature of revelation. And the religious position, arguing from within the framework of faith, doubts the range and validity of the method of radical questioning where God and the existence and meaning of the world as a whole are concerned.

Summarizing, one must conclude from the antithetic character of the arguments alone that there is no logical way of outmanoevring or invalidating the alternative standpoint. Moreover, since no logical decidability exists for choosing between the fundamental positions of religious faith and philosophical thought, the only explanation is that God has left it to man to make his *existential* decision in that fundamental domain. Although the overall scope for such a decision is partially conditioned by the religious and cultural environment, the domain of decision still presents the individual with a basic range of freedom that may be seen to correspond to the width of God himself.

3. The emergence of new structures in natural science

We now return to the question of natural science and its relationship to religion. Since natural science is the attempt to find the objective structures of the world using well-defined though limited methods, it is *not* concerned with the dispute between fundamental convictions. Instead, its relationship to religion refers to a different problem. Is the structure of the world, as represented and understood in terms of the objective laws of nature, *reconcilable, compatible or even open* to the vision and faith of religion with respect to the essence and meaning of the existence of man and his world? We shall discuss this question in line with new structures that have arisen during the progress of modern research. The focus will be on physics. But many concepts have radiated from this fundamental natural science to the other sciences. For instance, quantum theory leads to the understanding of the chemical bond, and synergetics facilitates the understanding of biological pattern formation and pattern recognition. Therefore, at the very least, some highly relevant conceptual developments can be grasped from this perspective.

To anticipate the result, a fortunate situation will emerge from these considerations. The newly emerging structures lend themselves to a deeper, more open and more constructive formulation of the relationship between the natural and religious dimensions, although we are still at the beginning of this new era of understanding. Two remarks should be made at this point. First, it must be stated that the problem of compatibility cannot be evaded by a dualistic approach, that is, by assuming two completely independent dimensions of 'matter' and 'mind' or of the 'material' and 'spiritual' spheres. This assumption would simply contradict the overwhelming evidence of the unity of the Creation, including the extremely complex interrelation between material and spiritual processes, for instance, in the human being. Secondly, one should be aware that God, not the devil, is entangled in the intricate details of nature, since he has created them. And God did not make them as would a bad clockmaker who interferes here and there in his own work in order to keep it going according to his wishes. Instead, God's ingenuity and authority find their expression in the self-organizing emergence of the structures of the cosmos, from the simplest to the most complex subsystems, including mankind, due to the inherent potentiality of His Creation.

The presentation that follows is organized in this way. In the subsections 3.1 - 3.3 a short survey of concepts as they evolved in physics is given starting with classical physics, continuing with quantum theory, and ending with some more recent developments in synergetics. Tentative interpretations of these results, that may be relevant to theology, are then presented in section 4.

3.1 The scope of classical physics

Classical physics comprises mechanics and electrodynamics. In a sense the theory of relativity also belongs to classical physics, because the most important, classical, fundamental structures remain valid in that theory. Two main concepts, that are directly accessible to the imagination, dominate classical physics: the *particle*, a spacially existing, sharply concentrated centre of mass or of electric charge (a 'point mass' or a 'point charge') and the *field*, a state of excitation continuously expanding over its space. If this excitation is periodic and propagates with time through space, the field is called a *wave* which is characterized by a wavelength, a frequency and a velocity of propagation. An example of a static field is the field of gravitation exerting a force upon any point of mass in its domain. An example of a dynamic wave field is the electromagnetic radiation field ranging from radio waves through visible light waves to X-rays.

Evidently, the concepts of 'particle' and of 'field' are *mutually exclusive*, since something concentrated at a point cannot be simultaneously spread out over the whole space. Nevertheless, particles and fields are not independent. On one hand, particles generate fields in their environment (masses generate gravitational fields, electric charges generate electromagnetic fields). On the other hand, fields exert forces upon particles (the gravitational field acts on masses, the electromagnetic field acts on resting or moving charges). The resulting forces give rise to the motion of particles according to Newtonian mechanics, and the resulting moving particles generate dynamic fields etc.. Generally speaking in the picture that emerges each particle moves because of the force exerted on it by the fields generated by all other particles. In principle, therefore, everything interacts with everything else! And so the main problem of classical physics consists in setting up and solving the equations of motion for the system that we have just described. These equations are differential equations for the positions and velocities of all particles and for all fields as continuous functions of space and time.

Such a system of coupled differential equations implies *full determinism*. This means that, if the positions and velocities of all particles and all fields in the world were known at one point in time, it would be possible in principle to calculate the same quantities for any future (or past) point in time. The only elements of *contingency* left open in this classical description are the *initial conditions*, namely, all the positions, velocities and fields at one point of time, for instance, 'at the beginning of the world'.

Causality can also be brought into this picture. The *principle of causality* states: effects are uniquely determined by causes (provided these causes are complete). In the deterministic picture of the evolution of the world we can consider the coordinates of the particles and the fields at one time, t_1, as the *complete system of causes*, and the same variables at a later time, t_2, as the *complete system of effects*. (It is surprising, however, that 'causes' and 'effects' can be interchanged, since all variables at t_2 also determine all variables at time t_1.)

Only very recently has the immense complexity of this classical picture come fully to the awareness of scientists. While formerly it seemed plausible not only that 'equal causes have equal effects', but also that 'similar causes have similar effects', it can now be proved that there exist even very simple dynamic systems exhibiting so-called *deterministic chaos*. In such systems microscopic variations in the initial conditions - the causes - lead to fundamentally different later states - the effects. Therefore, determinism, although still valid in principle, loses its realizability in practice in classical physics! A good example is the impossibility of exact long-term predictions of the weather. Apart from these subtleties, however, the framework of classical physics was impressively confirmed in the whole macroscopic world, ranging from the dynamics of galaxies to that of gases and fluids, and from electromagnetism to optics and radio-engineering. It found the limits of its applicability only in the microscopic domain of atoms and of elementary particles.

3.2 New views necessitated by quantum theory

The results of quantum physics in the microscopic domain carry us to the boundaries of imagination as well as highlighting the necessity of a revision of concepts as fundamental as the principle of deterministic description. We begin with the discussion of the famous *wave-particle-dualism*. An experimentum crucis exists which shows that this dualism is *unavoidable*. Take a beam of monochromatic light, or a beam of electrons moving at constant velocity, and let it traverse a lattice (a regular array of slits). Let it fall onto a screen lying beyond the lattice and consisting of a photographic film. One then observes an intensity pattern which is typical of interference-phenomena. The partial beams from the slits have mutually cancelled each other out at certain places on the film (producing zero intensity) and mutually enhanced each other at different places on the film (producing high intensity). This behaviour is typical of wave-phenomena, since only the elevations and troughs of waves are capable of amplifying or extinguishing each other. Thus we are forced to conclude that the beam consists of *waves* whose wavelength can be determined. The surprise comes as we scrutinize the film. The intensity patterns on the film consist of microscopic traces of the trajectories of single particles (photons or electrons)! So we are also forced to conclude that the beam consists of *particles*. The mutually exclusive pictures of 'wave' and of 'particle', therefore, are, on one hand, both indispensable to the explanation of different aspects of the phenomenon and, on the other hand, each of these pictures proves insufficient to describe the whole experiment. This strange conceptual structure is denoted as the *complementarity* of the wave-picture and the particle-picture.

Nevertheless *quantum theory* has found a unified description of the paradoxical wave-particle-dualism and even of much more general 'quantum effects'. The fundamental quantity of quantum theory is called the *wave function* ψ ('psi'), which describes the state of the elementary system (e.g. an atom). It obeys an equation of motion, the famous *Schrödinger equation*. The function ψ comprises both wave and particle aspects, but at the cost of a fully deterministic description of these aspects. In general, the function ψ must be given a *statistical interpretation*. This means that for a given ψ one can calculate only the *probability* of obtaining certain values of specific *observables* of the elementary system, like the position or the momentum of an electron. Strangely enough, however, *no* ψ can be found for which all observables could have *simultaneously* definite values *with certainty*. On the contrary, there exist what are termed *complementary variables*, say A and B, whose measurable values are never simultaneously realizable with certainty. If A has a definite value, one is not even allowed to assume in principle that the complementary variable B also has simultaneously a definite value! By the way, the famous uncertainty principle of Heisenberg is a special case of this general statement.

In order to see just how surprising these consequences are, let us formulate them in philosophical terms. Consider the elementary system as 'substratum' and its observables as its 'attributes'. According to classical logic all attributes are expected to be realized simultaneously, each by one of its possible 'measurable values' (as it was in classical physics). But things are quite different in quantum theory! If one attribute, say A, is realized as a definite value, the complementary attribute B cannot be realized simultaneously, but is, in the meantime, 'suspended into potentiality'. (As soon as B is measured, and thus a definite value is obtained for B, the definite value of A is destroyed and A is now 'suspended into potentiality'.)

There have been many attempts to avoid the statistical interpretation of the wave function and to return to a fully deterministic form of quantum theory by introducing so-called 'hidden variables'. But these attempts have all failed! Recently, according to a proposal by Bell, certain experiments designed to investigate a special case (the well-known EPR-paradox: the paradox of Einstein, Podolsky and Rosen) could actually disprove the very existence of these hidden (localized) variables. In the meantime, quantum theory exhibits such an extremely wide-ranging, and as yet unrefuted, quantitative validity that it must be regarded as *the basic theory* on the microscopic level of nature, this theory dealing especially with elementary particles, with atoms and molecules, and with their respective interactions. Its most interesting feature in our context seems to be its inherent *fundamental indeterminism*. This means that chance or the element of contingency plays a much more prominent role in nature than was assumed in classical physics. 'Chance' was only an expression of incomplete knowledge in classical physics, whereas, according to quantum theory, it assumes the new role of an objective non-eliminable structure of nature.

3.3 The framework of synergetics

In the last few decades a new interdisciplinary branch of science has developed which my colleague, H. Haken, has named 'synergetics'[3]. This new field developed from non-equilibrium statistical physics and from quantum optics, in which the laser plays a central role.

Synergetics can be defined as the science of macroscopic collective phenomena in space and time arising in a closed or open multi-component system with 'cooperative' interactions between the units of the system. It originates from the study of one of the general problems of science, namely, how the phenomena on the *macrolevel* of a complex system can be derived from its *microlevel*. Intriguingly, one result of such research is that, on the macrolevel, close analogies exist between the structures of very different systems, although these systems are composed of completely different units with different elementary interactions at the microlevel. This means that the macrolevel exhibits a relative - though not absolute - structural independence from the lower level. Therefore, a *relatively self-contained* unifying description of the macrolevel with more or less universal analogies between very different systems becomes possible. This is the objective of synergetics, and also the origin of the interdisciplinary universality of its concepts.

Let us go into a little more detail! Complex systems have an immense number of variables at the microlevel, whereas they are describable by relatively few variables at the macrolevel. Under favourable conditions the dynamics of these macrovariables are derivable from microscopic laws of nature and are governed in general by a set of *nonlinear differential equations*. These equations exhibit in particular the phenomenon of *self-organization* of *space-time patterns*. This means, for instance, that in such systems order can arise out of chaos without ex- ternal interference, and it can be fully explained in terms of equations of this type. Therefore, the macrovariables characterizing this order are often denoted as *order-parameters*.

Examples are the generation of coherent space-time patterns in chemical reactions out of an originally homogeneous system, the self-formation of the coherent and highly space-time-ordered beam of light in a laser, the spontaneous generation of rolls and hexagons in the Benard-instability, and the generation of the premorphological concentration-variations of activator-inhibitor enzymes in cell systems that give rise to the self-organization of differentiated organisms. (One should remember that, some decades ago, vitalism took the differentiation of an organism out of the blastula as an argument *against* the physico-chemical explanation of biological phenomena, because the promoters of this philosophy could *not* imagine *any* kind of physical explanation at all!)

If the systems described so far are *open*, that is, in contact with an environment by exchange of energy, particles etc., then generally certain *control parameters* of the external environment can be changed. If the control parameters pass certain critical values, the global state of the system will be strongly affected, and the system may undergo a radical change into another mode, so that new order parameters arise and old ones decay. Such a change is denoted as a *phase transition*. Sometimes, it is uncertain which of the several possible new macroscopic phases the system will adopt. It can be shown that in such cases the *micro-fluctuations*, that may even be due to quantum-mechanical uncertainty and chance, make all the difference. In synergetics, therefore, we now understand much better how in certain ambivalent macrostates, for instance, in an unstable equilibrium, chance at the microlevel can be enhanced to produce a macroscopic decision-effect.

The interdisciplinary applicability of synergetics is not restricted to natural science. It extends to the social sciences, for which it can provide a scheme for the construction of quantitative models[4]. Within such a framework the individual is the basic unit, and society is the macrosystem. Indeed, the dynamics of society bear many structural analogies to those of the systems of natural science. For instance, phase-transitions correspond to revolutions. Also, more refined phenomena, like the processes of formation of collective opinions, of economic instabilities and of migration, including the self-organizing formation of metropoles etc., can be successfully treated quantitatively using synergetic models.

4. Towards a synthesis between scientific and religious thought

We are now approaching the core of our considerations, which is the philosophical and theological evaluation of these recent advances in scientific understanding in order to gain a greater appreciation of the relationship between science and religion, and to attempt a synthesis of scientific and religious thought (see also references 5,6,7). We begin with the discussion of some consequences more or less directly connected with the stages of the evolution of science as described in sections 3.1 to 3.3 and then proceed to more general considerations about the nature of science as a whole, including some speculative views that lie 'at the limits of conceptual thought'.

4.1. The disaster of determinism
Classical physics culminated in the endorsement of a deterministic description of the world (see section 3.1). It is obvious that, if this picture were true in all its consequences, then it would lend itself to theological interpretation only with great difficulty. As an example of this difficulty, let us assume that the dynamics of the human brain are also completely deterministic, including the thoughts connected uniquely with the processes in the brain. Then, as no genuine decision-making can occur, there can be no genuine merit, guilt or sin, and no genuine responsibility at all. The only possible interpretation of the impressions of decision-making and of merit, guilt, sin and responsibility, that are undoubtedly present to the human mind, would be then that they are irrelevant 'epiphenomena' or side-effects

accompanying the real processes. This, however, would deprive most theological (and philosophical) concepts of their deeper interpretation.

Therefore, a far-reaching insight that brought considerable relief to this discussion was the recognition that the determinism found by classical physics in the macroscopic domain was only an approximate one, whereas at the microscopic level all phenomena contain necessarily contingent elements, as quantum theory has taught us. Indeed, if quantum theory is correct, then it is not only in the measuring processes that are purposefully devised by man, but also in the natural flow of events, whenever elementary particles leave irreversible traces of their interaction with the macroscopic world, that chance, probability and indeterminism are involved. One could say that, due to quantum theory, the contingent elements of the world are not concentrated only in the initial conditions (as in classical physics), but distributed along the whole time-axis.

Nevertheless, this fact would remain irrelevant so long as chance and statistics were confined to the small fluctuations of an otherwise well-determined flow of processes. From synergetics we know (see section 3.3), however, that sensitive systems exist in which the micro-fluctuations associated with the critical states of the particular system can lead to a phase transition into one of several possible alternatives at the macrolevel. It is most probable - although not yet understood in sufficient detail - that the brain in particular behaves like one of these sensitive multi-mode systems in which transitions between modes, corresponding for example to decision-making and thought, can be produced by micro-fluctuations that can even have quantum characteristics. The basic method of interpreting the very important general roles of chance and necessity can be instructively approached in this way, a way that we shall now discuss briefly from a theological perspective.

4.2 Chance and necessity from a theological perspective

In a very general way the intertwinement of chance and necessity can be seen as a structure of the Creation and as a prerequisite for the possible existence of individuals capable of carrying 'meaning' (in German: 'Sinn'). Of course, the 'meaning of life' cannot be defined in general terms, since this concept hinges on individual fate, but the general properties of this concept and the preconditions of its origination can be characterized.

In the first place, 'meaning' must be distinguished from finite intentions, purposes and achievements. Instead, 'meaning' is the infinite nondelimitable perspective and value of all finite events of life, including them but reaching beyond them as well. Being infinite, 'meaning' cannot aim at any finite elements of the world whatsoever, but only at the origin of all finiteness, namely, God.

Secondly, the two elements, the laws of nature and contingency, are indispensible for the evolution of 'meaning'. On one hand, the laws of nature provide the well-ordered reliable structures of the world on which any meaningful activity must be based. On the other hand, a range of possible alternatives is necessary for the evolution of meaning because evaluations and decisions concerning a set of different possible actions are indispensible for its realization!

The role of man as the carrier of meaning within the intertwined field of chance and necessity may even provide a new perspective of the human being as 'God's image':

whereas God is the power who creates existence as such, man in his existence is able to dispose freely of ranges of alternatives in order to find, or to lose, the meaning of his life.

4.3 Is there a fundamental role of the subject in quantum theory?

Before leaving the quantum theory which has provided us with a deeper understanding of the principal role of chance in nature, a comment is necessary concerning the role of the subject in quantum theory, a role that often has been stressed beyond measure, even by renowned quantum physicists.

The author, however, cannot accept a subjectivistic interpretation of quantum theory that considers the wave function as 'a measure of the knowledge of an observer'. This seems to be a philosophical overinterpretation inspired by neo-idealism. In fact, the role of the subject remains modest even in quantum physics! It is true that the observer can decide *which* of the complementary observables should be measured by his selection of the appropriate measuring device. But thereafter, *no special role of the subject* is played in the measuring process. Since the result of this process is registered automatically and controlled intersubjectively, it is completely independent of the observing subject. (The very concept of 'measurement' would lose its meaning if the result depended on the special way in which it was received by a subject!) Clearly, it is more appropriate to consider the wave function *not* as a *measure of the knowledge of the subject*, but, in view of its probabilistic yet objective meaning, as an *objective measure of the potentialities* of the elementary system with respect to the possible results of the measurement of its observables.

4.4 The hierarchy of structures of relative self-containedness

Let us now consider some philosophical and theological implications of the concepts that are emerging from synergetics, in particular the hierarchy of structures of relative self-containedness. One result of the investigations is the discovery that structural levels of *relative self-containedness* exist in physics, chemistry, biology, and in the social science etc., that exhibit *new qualitative properties*, for example, the level of macroscopic space-time patterns in a multi-component system. As these new qualities only emerge at a higher level of co-operative behaviour, synergetics justifies the statement that 'the whole is more than the sum of its parts'. By generalizing the results of synergetics, one may conclude that there is relative - though not absolute - justification for treating the new qualities of the higher levels in a separate self-consistent way.

The most striking case of the emergence of new qualities at a higher level is widely recognised as the fundamental psycho-physical problem which deals with the relationship between the abstract ideas in the mind and their material basis in brain dynamics. (For a detailed discussion of this intriguing problem see reference 8.) Indeed, the self-containedness of thoughts and emotions is almost perfect. Even penetrating psychological introspection only leads to a dissection of thoughts and feelings but never directly to their neurological basis! Nevertheless, the higher and qualitatively different level of the 'content of the mind' is supported by, and uniquely coupled to, the lower-level neurological functions that obey physico-chemical laws! Abstract ideas, therefore, must have a representation at the lower level of their biological basis, even if that representation is not necessarily decodable (see reference 8).

If it is a general rule that the higher level - although exhibiting a new quality - already has forms of representation at the lower level, then questions of theological relevance appear under new guises. For instance, it can be understood, at least in principle, that a faculty of the sphere of thought may exist that represents entities of a still higher level, the level of 'eternal truth'. In simpler cases, this capacity is certainly given. Mathematical truth, namely, true relations within abstract structures, has an existence of its own beyond space and time, and is perhaps best classified ontologically as virtually 'Platonic ideas'. This truth is independent of the individual who understands it, but it can be represented in his mind. Similarly, the laws of nature exist independently of man's understanding of them, but, as natural science has verified, they can also be represented, at least partially, in the human mind.

From these considerations it seems reasonable to assume the existence of a faculty of the human mind that represents what I propose to call 'ultimate truth', although the range of this representation must remain indefinite, since no independent method of verification is available. It is remarkable that at this deepest level of thought about God a circular structure reappears which seems to be associated with the most fundamental level of the phenomenon of self-organization. Let us venture to speculate on the basis of this idea.

4.5 God as originator and God as projection

We know that no finite thing within the Creation has the cause of its existence in itself. But 'God exists because God exists'. Thus the infinite *regressus* of asking for causes finds its formal end by saying that God is 'the self-organizer with respect to his own existence'. Recalling the fundamental importance within the world of self-organizing structures with a cyclical relationship of causes and effects, we can interpret this phenomenon as an expression of the *analogia entis* (The analogy in being between creature and Creator as held to be the basis of knowledge of God). In God himself the reflexive principle finds its ultimate unsurpassable form as *'self-creation'*, whereas in the world created by him reflexivity is repeated at the fundamentally lower level of the *self-organization of structures under the given existence of the material and of the laws of nature.*

From such a perspective a bridge can be constructed even between the seemingly very different views of 'God as the originator of the world' and 'God as projection of the human mind', views that traditionally demarcate faith from atheism. On the one hand, the originator has endowed His Creation with the principle of self-organization which leads to a hierarchy of structures of relative self-containedness, in particular, in the field of biology up to the human being. On the other hand, at the crown of evolution God appears as an idea in the human mind, because He is the necessary ultimate idea of reference within the self-organizing process of discovering the meaning of individual life.

4.6 The openness of science to transcendence

Finally, we shall discuss the question whether science as a whole has a natural openness towards transcendence or whether it is purely a world-immanent endeavour, as scientism believes. We shall now present two general arguments that substantiate the claim that modern science is fundamentally non-exhaustible and non-finalizable. Moreover, in these two characteristics transcendence becomes apparent!

The fundamental openness of science first becomes obvious through the open logical structure of thought which leads via a *regressus ad infinitum* to never-ending questions about the deeper and deeper foundations of every law of nature: as such each law is contingent and needs to be derived from deeper laws. Transcendence also appears in the openness of the laws of nature through a potentially infinite number of possible ways of fulfilling them. The overwhelming variety of already realized possibilities becomes particularly obvious in the evolution of life, but perhaps the most persuasive multiplicity is represented by all the as-yet-unrealized possibilities.

5. The dimensions of truth

In the preceding sections we tried to show that the constitutive concepts of a mature science, and of science as a whole, are reconcilable with religious thought, including faith based on revelation. In this final section we consider the relationship of scientific truth and religious truth. It will be seen that both dimensions of truth are complementary to each other. This means that each dimension of truth has its own characteristic method of substantiation, but that neither of them is complete, each needing to be complemented by the other.

The *objectifying truth* of natural science consists of the structural isomorphisms of its conceptual models and theories with sectors of reality. These theories are based on the universal laws that are valid in the corresponding domain of reality. Naturally, such theories can only capture the universal, reproducible and general aspects of the lawful behaviour of nature. The specific aspects, always singular individual circumstances, lie outside the scope of natural science. This marks the principal limit of the dimension of objectifying truth and indicates its need for completion.

In contrast, the very existence of each man is an individual singular event without any reproducibility. In the individual life chance and necessity are intertwined, and they give rise to personal fate and to a personal way and meaning of life. Using words like destiny, fortune, tragedy, vicissitudes of life etc., language describes the effects of the co-operation of chance and necessity as they culminate in that unique life. It is obvious that the kind of truth that gives rise to insight, understanding and orientation on this individual path of life must differ from purely objectifying truth. We call this second dimension of truth the *existential truth*. This kind of truth refers to the person and to his individual fate; it explains, enlightens and interprets the meaning of his destiny. Objectifying truth has universal breadth, whereas existential truth has individual depth.

Evidently, the religious form of existential truth, being founded in faith, is the form most directly connected with the 'point of reference of ultimate meaning', namely, with God. And, since God is the originator both of meaning and of the laws of nature, only the two complementary dimensions of truth working together can lead to the full measure of insight available to man.

References

1. W. Weischedel, *Der Gott der Philosophen, Vol. I* and *II,* Wissenschaftliche Buchgesellschaft, Darmstadt 1971 and 1972.

2. For a further analysis of these problems see: W. Weidlich, 'Befragung der philosophischen Theologie der radikalen Fraglichkeit', *Zeitschrift für Theologie und Kirche,* vol. 70 (1973), pp. 226-243.

3. H. Haken, *Synergetics - An Introduction,* Springer, Hamburg 1977.

4. W. Weidlich and G. Haag, *Concepts and Models of a Quantitative Sociology*, Springer, Hamburg 1983.

5. W. Weidlich, 'Fragen der Naturwissenschaft an den christlichen Glauben', *Zeitschrift für Theologie und Kirche,* vol. 64 (1967), pp. 241-257.

6. W. Weidlich, 'Zum Begriff Gottes im Felde zwischen Theologie, Philosophie und Naturwissenschaft', *Zeitschrift für Theologie und Kirche,* vol. 86 (1971), pp. 381-394.

7. W. Weidlich, 'Naturwissenschaft und Gottesbegriff', *Zeitwende,* vol. 53 (1982), pp. 16-27.

8. A. Gierer, 'Überlegungen zur Leib-Seele-Beziehung: Gibt es Grenzen der Decodierbarkeit?', *Zeitschrift für Theologie und Kirche,* vol. 84 (1987), pp. 254-266.

J.C. Polkinghorne F.R.S., S.O.Sc., mathematical physicist,
President of Queens' College, University of Cambridge,
Cambridge, England

A revived natural theology

J. C. Polkinghorne, F.R.S.

A Conference with the title 'One World' (which seems to me to be a very good title!) is bound to reject the idea that science and theology coexist in insulated separation. Yet this is, perhaps, the most widespread of the variety of mistaken views currently held about their mutual relationship. It has a certain specious plausibility. Science is concerned with matter, with asking the mechanistic question 'How?'; theology is concerned with spirit, with asking the teleological question 'Why?'. Each, therefore, has its own domain, its own language (indeed, its own language game, in the Wittgensteinian sense). So the story goes, and it leads to a *modus vivendi,* in which science is allocated its role in a public domain of fact, whilst theology is relegated to a private domain of opinion. ('True for me' is the best that it can aspire to.) Lesslie Newbigin has eloquently warned us of the dangers of such a compromise[1]. The true God is not a private, existentially-meaningful symbol; he is the Lord of all that is - the God of science as well as the God of the soul. Such a compartmentalised view of the relation between science and theology would be false to history. The two disciplines have always interacted with each other. One has only to think of the changes in the tone of theological discourse brought about by Darwinism and by discoveries of physical cosmology, to get the point. Necessarily science and theology impinge upon each other because, inescapably, they meet in us. We are both evolved physical systems, with a continuous history stretching back over thousands of millions of years, and also, if Christianity is true, men and women for whom Christ died. Science and theology just cannot be treated in isolation from each other.

What then is the true nature of their relationship? I think that the answer is to be found in that area of intellectual activity traditionally called natural theology. I see natural theology as the completion of the task, instinctive to the scientist, of seeking the deepest possible explanation of what is going on, the most comprehensive available account of the one world of our experience. In that search for an understanding through and through, the insights of science are to be taken with the utmost seriousness. In its own terms, it is very successful. Scientific questions demand scientific answers, and they seem to get them even if, as Professor Gierer* has pointed out, the answer is sometimes 'no-go'. Yet that success is purchased by the modesty of the inquiry. Science limits itself to a certain general,

---

*   This volume pp. 61-71.

impersonal, testable, sort of knowledge. Within the realm of that kind of experience, I am sure that it needs no augmentation from theology. The one god who is well and truly dead is the God of the Gaps, that Cheshire cat deity* appealed to as the 'explanation' of the currently scientifically inexplicable, and so always liable to vanish with the advance of scientific knowledge. We have learnt *not* to make rash claims, such as 'Scientists will never understand how life arose from inanimate matter - only the direct intervention of God could achieve that'. At present we do not actually have a good account of that remarkable development of terrestrial life, but there is no reason to think that the scientifically posable question of how it came about will not, one day, receive a scientifically stateable answer. In that sense, science *is* complete, but in another it is woefully incomplete.

First, it describes a beautiful, clear world, rather like a lunar landscape. It can speak of metastable replicating systems, but there are no *people* in the world that science portrays. To talk of them we must move from the general, impersonal, testable inquiry of science to the realm of particular, personal, trusting encounter. No account of the way things are, which can only describe a Rembrandt self-portrait as a collection of specks of paint of known chemical composition, is in the least adequate to the richness of reality.

Secondly - and this is one of the points I most want to emphasise in this lecture - there are questions which arise from science and which insistently demand an answer, but which by their very character transcend that of which science itself is competent to speak. There is a widespread feeling among practising scientists, particularly those of us who have worked in fundamental physics, that there is more to the physical world than has met the scientific eye. As a result of that feeling, we are living at a time when there is a revival of natural theology taking place, largely at the hands of the scientists rather than the theologians[2]. Thus, someone like Paul Davies, who is rather hostile to conventional religion, can nevertheless write, 'It may seem bizarre to say so but I believe that science offers a surer path to God than religion'[3]. In fact I think that remark *is* rather bizarre, a fact that Davies himself might be able to recognise if he showed signs of a greater acquaintance with what religion has to say. There is a longstanding tradition of natural theology which would find no surprise at science's offering *a* path to God. However, it is a path of limited investigation and so will only yield limited insight. It is no use complaining that the God and Father of Our Lord Jesus Christ is not to be discerned that way. He is to be encountered in an altogether different, and altogether more personal, realm of human experience. Nevertheless, we should not decline the modest insights that the new natural theology has to offer. In an age whose vision into the scope of reality is often myopic, anything which encourages the lifting of the eyes to wider horizons is to be welcomed. Because I do indeed believe that we live in 'One World', I also believe that the search for truth will always prove a path to God. I have great sympathy with Bernard Lonergan's view of God as the Great and all-sufficient Explanation. He says, 'God is the unrestricted act of understanding, the eternal rapture glimpsed in every Archimedean cry of Eureka'[4].

---

*   A *phantom of a God* invoked in statements like 'Only the intervention of God could bring life out of inanimate matter'.

This new natural theology is not only a revived natural theology but it is also *revised* in two important respects. First, it is more modest in its aim than the old-style natural theology of Anselm, Aquinas and Paley. The latter spoke of the 'proofs' of God's existence. We recognise today that we are operating in an area where a mathematical type of demonstration is not available either to the theist or to the atheist. Instead we must speak of 'insight', of a way of looking at the totality of things which has coherence and intelligibility. It is not the claim of the new natural theology that atheism is stupidity, but that theism offers a more satisfying and more extensive explanation of what is going on. Secondly, and most importantly, the appeal of the new natural theology is not to particular occurrences ('Only God could have made the complex system of the eye') but to the law and circumstance which underlie all physical occurrences. This law and circumstance is science's given, the starting point it assumes as the basis necessary for all its explanations. It is, therefore, something which science itself is powerless to explain, though it has not seemed something without need of explanation. Any further understanding is a task that naturally falls to theology in its role of providing the deepest possible explanation required. In this way theology is not attempting to rival science in the latter's own domain. It leaves the explanation of how occurrences happen for science to deal with, but it seeks to set that explanation within a more profound and comprehensive understanding. The appeal is not to the God of the Gaps, only discerned in the murkier parts of physical process and so apt to prove a vanishing shadow as the light of knowledge increases, but to the true Creator, who is the ground of *all* physical process. We are then looking at the right place in which to find theological understanding. If God is the Creator, he is consistent with all that is and the ground of all that is. And if we are to find scientific straws in what might prove to be a divine wind, it will be by examining the foundations of science itself. Prudence encourages us to look only to such aspects of the pattern and structure of the physical world as are likely to remain part of the scientific world view and to eschew the dazzling but deceptive edges of speculation. Fortunately there are plenty of well-winnowed insights for our consideration.

Twin pillars of this new natural theology are the appeals to *intelligibility* and to the *cosmological anthropic principle*. The physical world is marvellously rationally transparent to our enquiry and mathematics is 'unreasonably effective' (in Wigner's phrase) in providing the key to its structure. Some of its most beautiful patterns, dreamed up by the mathematicians in the isolation of their studies, are found actually to occur in the physical world around us. Whence comes this deep-seated congruence between the experienced rationality of our minds and the observed rationality of the universe? It is surely a significant fact demanding an explanation. Einstein once said that the only incomprehensible thing about the universe is that it is comprehensible. Cosmology and elementary particle physics deal with regimes so remote from everyday experience, and need for their formulation mathematics so abstract in its character, that a mere appeal to the evolutionary need to survive will not serve to explain how this comes about. Survival would be adequately safeguarded at the level of everyday thought and everyday experience. It does not call for the abstract mathematics employed to describe the remote regimes of quantum theory and general relativity. A coherent explanation of the consonance of the reason within and the reason without would be that both have their origin in the Rationality of the Creator.

The appeal to intelligibility is a variation on the cosmological theme of natural theology - that great question, 'Why is there something rather than nothing?'

Besides, as need be emphasized, we have come to realise in recent years that we do not seem to live in 'any old world'. The insights of the cosmological anthropic principle point to a delicate balance in the law and circumstance of the universe - one might almost say a 'fine tuning' - necessary in order that its evolving process might produce such complex and interesting systems as ourselves[5].

If you were loaned the use of a 'universe creating machine' you would find it had a row of knobs labelled with the laws of physics for the world you were to create. For example, if you turned up the knob labelled 'gravity' that force would become stronger in your intended world; if you turned it down, it would become weaker. There would be another row of knobs labelled by circumstance. For example, you could decide how big your world was to be - 10^{11} galaxies, like our own, or something a little cosier, say no more than the Milky Way? After you had pulled the handle and your world had appeared you would have to be a little patient, because billions of years is the appropriate cosmic timescale. The cosmological anthropic principle suggests that unless you had been careful to set these knobs close to their settings for this world, a very boring universe would result, incapable of evolving such complex systems as you and me. I will not go into the details which have often been presented. Of all the features of the physical universe to which I shall appeal this is the most recently recognised and so the one with which we need the greatest caution. I think it possible that some of the life-giving coincidences that we now identify may find underlying explanations, but the delicate balances required are so widespread and so intricately interlaced (think of the nuclear level structure in carbon required for the possibility of the stellar synthesis of the heavier elements necessary for life) that I believe the insight that an anthropically fruitful world is a very special kind of world is a reliable conclusion of physical cosmology. To suppose otherwise is to draw a large blank cheque on an unknown intellectual account.

It is against the instinct of the scientist just to say, 'We are here because we are here'. The remarkable fruitful coincidences of the cosmological anthropic principle seem to call for some explanation. Some have suggested that there is a great portfolio of different universes, each with its own law and circumstance. If that were so, it would not be surprising if one of them were more or less 'right' to evolve life, and that of course is the one that we live in since we could appear in no other. This somewhat prodigal suggestion is not physics (which knows only this universe) but metaphysics. A metaphysical suggestion of equal coherence and greater economy would be that there is only one universe, which is the way it is because it is not 'any old world' but the creation of a Creator who wills it to be capable of fruitful process. This appeal to the cosmological anthropic principle is a wholly new variation on the design theme of natural theology, based on a designed *potentiality* built into the very fabric of cosmic law and circumstance. What sort of universe is it that is thus perceived as God's creation? It is characterised by three features:

1. The interplay of chance and necessity.

This is seen, not only in evolutionary biology (random genetic mutations sifted and preserved in regular environment), but also, for instance, in the coming-to-be of galaxies by gravitational condensation. This role of chance implies that the end is not foreseeable in the beginning. Small triggers induce large consequences. Some have thought that this challenges theology's claim that there is a purpose at work in the world. The great French biochemist, Jacques Monod, wrote with Gallic passion and intensity, 'Pure chance, absolutely free but blind, is at the very root of the stupendous edifice of evolution'[6]. The word where Monod puts the knife in is, of course, 'blind'. Yet one need not see things that way. The theist can interpret the dialectic of chance and necessity as reflecting the gifts of freedom and reliability to the creation by a God who is at once loving and faithful. The random 'shuffling' operations of chance are then seen as the way in which the universe explores its God-given (anthropic) potentiality, incorporated in the lawfulness of necessity. If the resulting picture is of a precarious process, that is because love always accepts the precariousness inherent in the independence of the beloved. W. H. Vanstone wrote,

'If the creation is the work of love then its shape cannot be predetermined by the Creator, nor its triumph foreknown; it is the realisation of vision, but of vision which is discovered by its own realisation'[7].

Vanstone makes no reference to the insights of modern science, but his picture of 'the realisation of vision, but of vision which is discovered by its own realisation' is strictly consonant with our understanding of physical process as the interplay of chance and necessity.

2.1 No mere mechanism: the general openness of physical process[8].

The apparently clockwork universe of Newton has disappeared in modern science, not only because of the cloudy fitfulness of quantum theory at the constituent roots of the world, but also because even classical dynamical systems are now known, in general, to be so exquisitely sensitive to circumstance as to be intrinsically unpredictable. That observation is epistemological in character (it concerns what we can know about such delicate systems) but I believe that it also points to an ontological openness present in physical process. Science is beginning to discern what we, as humans experiencing choice and responsibility, have always known, namely, that the future is not just a spelling out of what was already present in the past, but that it is something really new. We live in a world, not only of being, but also of genuine becoming.

What is the origin of this indefiniteness, or open flexibility, which makes cosmic process open to the genuine novelty of the future? Which, thus, begins to describe a world of which we could conceive ourselves as inhabitants? Which, thereby, begins to permit us even to conceive of God's purposeful and providential action within that world? An obvious candidate might have appeared to be provided by quantum phenomena. It is notorious that quantum events are believed by the majority of physicists to be constrained only by overall statistical regularity in their patterns of occurrence. In accordance with Heisenberg uncertainty, individual events are characterised by a radical randomness and are even spoken of as being 'uncaused'. It might be thought that here is to be found the necessary room for manoeuver, both for God and for ourselves. Such a view has been proposed[9], but it has not commended itself widely. It fails to meet its goal for it is likely to founder on the propensity for randomness to generate regularity, that is, for order to arise out of chaos. The aggregation of individual chance events at one level is liable to compose itself into a highly predictable pattern at a higher level. The practice of Life Insurance Offices is based upon this very tendency. The life expectancy of an individual client is extremely uncertain, but the actuaries can be tolerably secure in their forecasts of how many people in a large sample of given age will die in the next few years. In an exactly similar way, the everyday certainties of the world of Newtonian mechanics arise from out of their fitful quantum substrate. As far as we can tell, most of the processes likely to be of significance for our action on the world (such as those involved in the neurophysiological operations of our brain) proceed at levels above those characterised by quantum indeterminacy[10]. Thus if exploitation of Heisenberg uncertainty is *not* the way in which we are able to be ourselves, it is also unlikely to be the way in which God exercises his purposive will. I am not saying that there are never circumstances in which quantum effects are amplified to have macroscopic consequences, only that they are unlikely by themselves to provide a sufficient basis for human or divine freedom, even supposing God's will and ours to be exercised in the hole-and-corner way of influencing quantum events.

A much more promising line of enquiry would seem to be provided by the modern recognition of the subtlety of behaviour enjoyed by complex dynamical systems. When one speaks of the process of the physical world, the picture which often arises in the layman's mind is that of an intricate piece of machinery, regular and reliable in its operation. A steadily ticking clock would be the paradigm case. From Newton almost to the present day, the study of classical dynamical systems has concentrated on just such predictable cases. From the turn of this century, in the work of Poincaré, and with greatly accelerating progress in recent years, we have come to realise that 'tame' systems of this kind, open to prediction and control, are very untypical of dynamical behaviour. The typical case, on the contrary, involves such an infinitesimally balanced sensitivity to circumstance (one might almost say, such a degree of vulnerability) that it results in an almost infinitely multiplying variety of possible behaviours. How the system threads its way through this maze of possibilities is not open to prior prediction. As an example, consider the continued successive collisions of a collection of many billiard-ball-like objects. One might suppose that to be a pretty well determined system. However, the way the balls emerge from each separate collision depends sensitively upon the precise details of impact. Small uncertainties in the angle of incidence rapidly accumulate to produce exponentially diverging consequences. Molecules in a gas behave, in many ways, like small colliding billiard balls. After only 10^{-10} seconds, fifty or more collisions have taken place for each molecule. After even so few collisions the resulting outcome is so sensitive that it would be strikingly different if the overall gravitational field were changed as the result of 'adding one extra electron on the other side of the universe'!* This example teaches us that, in general, predictability and control may be lost very rapidly. We are necessarily ignorant of how complex systems will behave. If you are a realist and believe, as I believe, that what we know - epistemology - and what is the case - ontology - are clearly linked to each other, it is natural to go on to interpret this state of affairs as reflecting an intrinsic openness in the behaviour of such systems[11]. There is an emergent property of flexible process, even within the world of classical physics, which encourages us to see Newton's rigidly deterministic account as no more than an approximation to a more supple reality. The clockwork regularity of planetary motion, for so long taken to be the very paradigm of what goes on in the physical world, proves then to be just a singularly special sector within the general openness of physical process. Our primary human experience of sharing in that openness can only reinforce that view.

Such delicate systems are never truly isolated or self-contained. Causality cannot be strictly localised within them or within their constituent parts - once again the fragmentary approach of reductionism is seen to be only part of the story. 'Downward causation', such as we experience when we will the movement of our arm, becomes a distinct possibility. Arthur Peacocke is right to say that: 'There is no sense in which subatomic particles are to be graded as 'more real' than, say, a bacterial cell or a human person, or even social facts'[12]. Every level of description is needed in our effort to do justice to the rich and varied process of the world, in its nature both flexible and reliable - including the category of divine providence. And every level of description may impose its own organizing pattern upon the flexibility of what can occur.

2.2 No mere mechanism: the world as fruitful.
This is not the place to describe dynamical instabilities or the theory of chaos. It is sufficient to say that these modern dynamical insights assert the possibility of the generation of a new order within their process (for example, by convergence upon what are called 'attractors'). We see emerging from this study of the dynamics of complex systems just those characteristics of structured openness which seem to offer hope that the super-complex systems, which we ourselves are, might indeed manifest the freedom-within-regularity that is our basic human experience. And might not one go on to suppose that similarly the super-super-system of the cosmos might be capable, in an analogous way, of sustaining the operation of the providential will of its Creator, within the flexibility of its lawful process?

Of course, a considerable extrapolation is needed beyond what we comprehend in order to reach an understanding of the capacity for human or divine action. I do not say that these age-old problems are solved, only that there is a hopeful direction in which to look for their solution. The rigid mechanism of nineteenth century physics first began to dissolve with the discovery of the cloudy fitfulness of quantum theory. We now understand that even at those macroscopic levels where classical physics gives an adequate account, there is an openness

---

*   Indeed, it is beyond doubt that the slightest change of the value of the gravitational constant produces an entirely different world.

to the future which relaxes the unrelenting grip of mechanical determinism. The universe may not look like an organism but it looks even less like a machine.

A consequence of the decay of predictability is a freedom for development, which enables physics to accommodate not only the idea of being (the timeless regularity of physical law) but also that of becoming (the evolving history of complex systems). The future is not already implied by the present. Time is no longer a mere index, parametrising the inexorable disclosure of a determined state of affairs, but it more closely approximates to our psychological experience of its irreversible flow, with the fixity of the past but the openness of the future. Prigogine and Stengers say,

> 'Only when a system behaves in a sufficiently random way may the difference between past and future, and therefore irreversibility, enter into its description ... The arrow of time is the manifestation of the fact that the future is not given, that, as the French poet Paul Valéry emphasised, 'time is a construction''[13].

The degree of randomness of which they speak arises from the labyrinthine possibilities open to an inherently undetermined complex system. They conclude their summary of the capacity for becoming, with which unstable dynamical systems far from equilibrium are endowed, by saying, 'we can see ourselves as part of the universe we describe'[14]. This is no mere reductionist manner of speaking but the recognition that at last physics is beginning to be able to describe a world consonant with being the home of humankind. There is set before us the hope of a synthesis in which the perceived regularity of the physical world and the experienced freedom within ourselves are reconciled in an unfolding act of genuine becoming. Prigogine and Stengers chose for the title of their concluding Chapter: 'From Earth to Heaven - the Re-enchantment of Nature'.

2.3 No mere mechanism: beyond deistic theology.

The picture of God at work within the flexibility of its process seems consonant with theological talk about his purposive immanent presence. John V. Taylor writes of the Creator-Spirit that

> 'if we think of a Creator at all, we are to find him always on the inside of creation. And if God is really on the inside, we must find him in the process, not in the gaps. We know now that there are no gaps .... If the hand of God is to be recognised in His continuous creation, it must be found not in isolated intrusions, not in any gaps, but in the very process itself'[15].

To this I want to add the *counterbalancing* recognition of the transcendent Creator, who is the ground of those laws which make the cosmic process anthropically fruitful, whilst conceding that, without the corrective of the hidden working of the Spirit, that transcendent God would be left in deistic detachment. He is the God of both being and becoming.

The concept of divine immanent action helps us in particular to understand something of the scope of God's activity. Origen wrote that 'It would be utterly absurd for a man who was troubled by the scorching sun at the summer solstice to imagine that by his prayer the sun could be shifted back to its springtime place among the heavenly bodies'. Maurice Wiles, from whom that quotation is culled, goes on to say, 'Once that principle is acknowledged, it is difficult to define its limits'[16], and so he wants to discount the possibility of any specific action whatsoever. I agree that one cannot draw precise lines, but the notion of flexible process helps us to see where there might be room for divine manoeuvre, within the limits of divine faithfulness. The motions of the solar system are mechanical in nature, with a predictability over long periods of time which permits the construction of almanacs. Thus the succession of the seasons will be guaranteed by transcendent divine reliability and it would indeed be foolish to pray for their alteration. The generation of weather is a much more complex process, within which it is conceivable that small triggers could generate large effects. Thus prayer for rain does not seem totally ruled out of court! In this way one can gain some rough comprehension of the range of immanent action. It will always lie hidden in those complexes whose precarious balance makes them unsusceptible to prediction. The recently gained understanding of the distinction between physical systems which exhibit being and those which exhibit becoming may be seen as a pale reflection of the theological dialectic of God's transcendence and God's immanence - consequences, respectively, of divine reliability and of the loving gift of freedom by the Creator.

Finally it is necessary to acknowledge that a subtle and respectful balance is required if the flexibility of physical process is to accommodate both God's action and our own and also the freedom of the universe to explore its own potential. How these intertwine and how each finds space for its own fulfilment without usurping the room necessary for the other, is a profound problem beyond our power to resolve in detail. It is a problem of which theology has long been aware, for it is the expression, in the widest cosmic terms, of the delicate dialectic of divine grace and creaturely free-will.

We perceive here also the possibility of natural theology's contributing to another of theology's classic problems - perhaps the most important and difficult of all for the possibility of theistic belief - the problem of theodicy. The free-will defence, given as the answer to the problem of moral evil, needs augmenting by what we may call the free-process defence in relation to the problem of physical evil. Austin Farrer asked what was God's will in the Lisbon earthquake. He was surely right to say that it was his will for the crust of the Earth, that it should behave in accordance with its created nature[17].

Let me sum up. The clockwork universe is dead. The future is not just the tautologous spelling-out of what was already present in the past. Physics shows an openness to new possibility at all levels, from the microscopic (where quantum theory is important) to the macroscopic (where it is not). In that sense, physics describes a world of which we can conceive ourselves as being inhabitants. The division - quite as sharp as the Aristotelian division between celestial permanence and sub-lunar decay - which seemed to exist between the exterior world of inexorable process and the interior world of willed choice, is beginning to break down. Yet we must not exaggerate the extent to which the two worlds are successfully integrated in our understanding. Many puzzles remain, but there is a hopeful direction in which to look for their eventual reconciliation. Even in its own modest sphere of investigation, natural theology is not after all condemned to speaking solely of the Cosmic Architect or the Great Mathematician. It is not confined to a merely deistic theology. Rather, it can perceive *the possibility of the action of the true and living God within his creation.*

3. Ultimate futility.

Science can not only peer into the cosmic past, it can also seek to discern the eventual cosmic fate. In the end, the universe will either fly apart for ever and decay, or it will fall in upon itself and collapse. We are not sure which, because the balance between expansive and contractive forces is too fine for us to be sure which will prove to be in the ascendancy. Either way the future is bleak, in terms of a final fulfilment solely within the physical process of this world. However, I do not think that this need present a difficulty for the theologian. He has always known that the only possible source of lasting hope is God himself, whether we are thinking of ourselves or of the cosmos. Our physical bodies will decay on a timescale of tens of years, the universe on a timescale of thousands of millions of years. If there is a true hope for either (as I believe there is) it lies in the redeeming faithfulness of the eternal Creator alone.

I have sought to survey the interaction of science and theology. I claim that they do impinge upon each other in ways that are fruitful. The resulting interplay is not without its perplexities but I think that it is mutually enhancing. I have written elsewhere[18]:

> 'Einstein once said that 'Religion without science is blind. Science without religion is lame'. His instinct that they need each other was right, though I would not describe their separate shortcomings in quite the terms he chose. Rather I would say, 'Religion without science is confined; it fails to be completely open to reality. Science without religion is incomplete; it fails to attain the deepest possible understanding'. The remarkable insights that science affords us into the intelligible workings of the world cry out for an explanation more profound than that which it can itself provide. Religion, if it is to take seriously its claim that the world is the creation of God must be humble enough to learn from science what that world is actually like.'

The instinct of the physical scientist is to seek the most all-embracing explanation available to him. Hence the search for GUTS (Grand Unified TheorieS) in elementary particle physics. The thirst for that unified understanding will not be quenched by science alone. Ultimately it will prove to be the search for God, and so natural theology will have an indispensable role in its achievement. In that way I find a fruitful reconciliation of my experience as a theoretical physicist and my experience as a priest.

Notes

1. L. Newbigin, *Foolishness to the Greeks*, S.P.C.K., 1986.

2. P. Davies, *God and the New Physics,* Dent, 1983;
    H. Montefiore, *The Probability of God*, S.C.M. Press, 1985;
    A.R. Peacocke, *Creation and the World of Science*, Oxford University Press, 1979;
    J.C. Polkinghorne, *One world*, S.P.C.K., 1986, and *Science and Creation*, S.P.C.K., 1988.

3. Davies, op. cit, p. ix.

4. B. Lonergan, *Insight,* Longman, 1957, p. 684.

5. J. Barrow and F. Tipler, *The Anthropic Cosmological Principle,* Oxford University Press, 1986;
    see also Montefiore, op. cit..

6. J. Monod, *Chance and Necessity,* Collins, 1972, p. 110.

7. W.H. Vanstone, *Love's Endeavour, Love's Expense*, Darton/Longman and Todd, 1977, p. 63.

8. The material in this section is taken from: J.C. Polkinghorne,
    Science and Providence, S.P.C.K., 1989.

9. W. Pollard, *Chance and Providence*, Faber, 1958.

10. J.C. Eccles would not agree.

11. Similarly, Heisenberg's epistemological argument for the uncertainty principle has led the
    majority of physicists to embrace an ontological uncertainty for quantum entities;
    see J.C. Polkinghorne, *The Quantum World,* Longman, 1984.

12. A.R. Peacocke, *God and the New Biology,* Dent, 1986, p. 28.

13. I. Prigogine and I. Stengers, *Order out of Chaos*, Heineman, 1984, p. 16.

14. ibid., p. 300.

15. J.V. Taylor, *The Go-between God*, S.C.M. Press, 1972, p. 28.

16. M. Wiles, *God's Interaction with the World,* S.C.M. Press, 1986, p. 100.

17. A. Farrer, *A Science of God?,* Geoffrey Bles, 1966, p. 87.

18. J.C. Polkinghorne, *Science and Creation*, S.P.C.K., 1988, pp. 97-98.

W.B. Drees, physicist and theologian,
Staff member of Bezinningscentrum
(Interdisciplinary centre for the study of science, society and religion), Vrije Universiteit,
Amsterdam, The Netherlands

Theology and cosmology beyond the Big Bang theory[1]

Willem B. Drees

'The most miraculous thing is happening. (...) The physicists are getting down to the nitty-gritty, they've really just pared things down to the ultimate details, and the last thing they expected to happen is happening. God is shining through. They hate it, but they can't do anything about it. Facts are facts. And I don't think people in the religious business, so to speak, are really aware of this - aware, that is, that their case, far-out as it always seemed, at last is being proven.'
(...)
'Mr. Kohler. What kind of God is showing through, exactly?'
Dialogue between a computerfreak and a divinity school professor, in
Roger's Version by John Updike (1986, p. 10).

Contents

1. Introduction: why do theology and science
2. What do we do in theology and science?
    2.1   No need for religion and science!
    2.2   The highroad of metaphysics
    2.3   Theology interpreting science and explicating faith
    2.4   Consonance: E. McMullin
    2.5   Constructive consonance
3. Theology in the context of astrophysical cosmology
    3.1   A beginning?
    3.1.1. Limitations of the Big Bang theory
    3.1.2. Diversity at the frontier
    3.2   Complete theories of everything, contingency, and God
    3.2.2. Quantum cosmology without initial conditions
    3.2.3. Three inadequate responses
    3.2.4. Types of contingency and the mystery of existence
    3.2.5. The relevance of transcendence against holism
    3.3   A dynamic or a timeless universe?
4. Down to earth: the integrity of creation

1. Introduction: why do theology and science?

When pressed to explain why one should relate theology and science*, two kinds of answers are often given. On the one hand, ethical issues surround the application of science. The place of values in a world dominated by science must be determined. And in that context science-and-religion* sometimes is even seen as necessary for the continued existence of life on Earth. On the other hand, relating theology to science might be necessary for the intelligibility and credibility of faith and, therefore, for the continued existence of Christianity in our time.

However, integrating science and theology at an intellectual level will not solve the moral issues of our time. Emphasizing the 'Integrity of Creation' might contribute to responsible behaviour, but the relevance of the churches should not be overestimated. Besides, as much confusion exists inside the churches as outside them. Nor will relating science and religion lead to increasing church membership. Instead, growing churches will probably continue to be mostly those that offer a simple package of opinions and guidelines; they provide a safety that relies upon an escape from the complexities of the modern world, science included.

Might we gain then by doing science-and-theology at the other end of the spectrum - among those who take science seriously? A new religiosity, that is apparently based upon science, is now visible in the bookstores as a quest for 'holism'. Although its adherents seem much more promising as allies for those doing science-and-theology, this quest accentuates some important differences, especially with regard to the Christian emphases on a Beyond and on the significance of particular events and persons, all of which are more than a general immanent presence within creation. I am not too optimistic about the effect that science-and-religion will have on morality, church membership or Christianity. Spending time on it cannot be justified on primarily utilitarian grounds. However, I do believe that there are at least two good reasons for engaging in science-and-theology. To relate different kinds of human ideas is to respond to a thirst for understanding, one which appears to be widespread among human beings even when that understanding is not believed to be directly to their benefit. Curiosity seems to be one of the main driving forces behind fundamental scientific research as well as philosophy and theology. Honesty is another motive. We need to make sense of our scientific and religious ideas or else to forget them if we continue to fail to do so. But honesty need not be profitable.

Relating religion to science is the twofold task of *changing* the language used to express the religion and, thereby, changing the religion itself, and also of *preserving* those elements of the tradition that are still considered valuable. Such a project is similar to that of the feminist, black or other contextual theologies: that is, we are working on a reconceptualization while struggling to preserve the valuable elements of the classical tradition. It is not sufficient to make God-talk scientific talk, and thus a superfluous duplication[2]. We are also striving to sustain genuine God-talk.

There are many different approaches to science-and-religion. I will briefly consider some of them and also present my own version of *constructive consonance* between theology,

---

*   In relation to science the terms 'religion' and 'theology' are mostly used interchangeably.

science and metaphysics (section 2). In section 3, I will look at 'theology in the context of astrophysical cosmology'. Granted cosmology is not typical of the sciences, but it does touch on many questions of philosophical and theological interest. Three aspects of the Big Bang theory, namely, the 'beginning', contingency, and the dynamic nature of the Universe, have been used in science-and-religion. I will argue that these issues lie outside the domain of validity of the Big Bang theory, and that a wide variety of ideas exist about theories beyond the limits of the Big Bang theory. In addition this discussion will illustrate some methodological aspects of the task of relating science and theology. To relate theology and science at the frontiers of scientific knowledge is quite different from, and sometimes much more interesting than, relating theology to the well-established consensus of scientific knowledge. It is at those frontiers that the monologue from science to theology may occasionally turn into a dialogue (section 3.1).

Some people claim that science is approaching a complete theory of everything. Is God then shining through or has God become a superfluous hypothesis? This issue will be illustrated by a quantum cosmology without boundary conditions. The discussion focuses on the anthropic principles, contingency and holism (section 3.2). Cosmology offers both a perspective from *within time* and a *timeless perspective*. I argue that this double description presents us with the opportunity to express constructively certain theological themes (section 3.3). Finally, section 4 reviews my ideas while contrasting them with the discussions of the World Council of Churches (WCC) on the theme of the Integrity of Creation.

2.   What do we do in theology and science?

The task of relating science-and-theology is generally a rather vague one. The Second European Conference on Science and Religion was like a crowded market place with many individuals exchanging ideas in order to further their own particular programmes. I will look at a few approaches that I will use as stepping stones to my personal view of the nature of this task. Should theology adapt itself to the truths of science? Or does it function quite differently? Is theology leading or is it following science? Which one is supposed to *change*?

A second challenging aspect is *pluralism*. Does this variety of views result from some basic limitations on our part? If we were sufficiently clever and suitably open-minded, could we agree on a unique way of putting everything together? Or is pluralism inherent, with each individual left to make his or her personal synthesis as if *anything goes*? The position I wish to defend lies somewhere between these two extremes. In several respects this task resembles the building of a house: there is more than one way to put the bricks together. A building plan is required. But not every building plan is acceptable. There are rules restricting the number of realizable plans, for instance, those governing the stability and strength of the construction. This model suggests a pluralism of overall plans according to which the bricks from science and religion are put together. However, if some novel aspect of a plan turns out to be exceptionally important, then it is always possible to search for other kinds of brick. Neither science nor theology is beyond change.

2.1 No need for religion *and* science!

We begin with pluralism. According to some people, science and religion are building different houses with different bricks and different plans on different grounds. There is no interaction; they do their own things. This is - broadly speaking - an existentialistic position which locates faith exclusively in the personal realm in such a way that it is supposedly out of touch with science. This approach eliminates many questions.

A strategic objection to this approach is that the 'safe domain' of faith might be more like an iceberg than like a rock; that is, it might be melting away! A philosophical objection is that it is simply impossible: the words of one domain are related to those of the other, and values imply assumptions about the way the world is. A theological objection is that it attempts to restrict God's relevance to an unacceptably small domain. In the Christian tradition with its notions of covenant and conversion, personal aspects are essential - and that is the 'truth' of the existentialistic position. But these aspects get their force and urgency through their embedment in a relation to God who is claimed to be the Only One, the Ground and Ruler of all.

A similar invalid reduction is associated with the great emphasis placed on language games. American theologians, like Ronald F. Thiemann (1985) and George A. Lindbeck (1984), have argued that we should accept religious pluralism and search for our strength by focusing on our own traditions. For truth is in use, that is, in the life of the community. Theology is dogmatics, not apologetics; it is internal discussion within a system, not the justification of a view to those outside. Such a retreat to individual traditions is unsatisfactory for reasons very similar to those given above. The unity of the sciences, despite the multiplicity of disciplines, challenges any easy acceptance of religious diversity even before trying to enter a rational dialogue. And apologetics is a part of science; one argues partly for the benefit of those outside one's research programme that one theory is better than another. Besides, science is always changing. Therefore, coupling a dynamic science to a static theology, that preserves unchanged its tradition, is mismatching them, for it is like putting new wine in old vessels (cf. Matt. 9:17).

For those who take science seriously, a more interesting defense of separation is the one presented by the English philosopher of science, Mary Hesse. She acknowledges science as a constructive activity *underdetermined* by observations. Future science will conceive of the fundamental nature of things very differently from present science. Science is progressive in its knowledge, but 'it is the kind of knowledge precisely appropriate to prediction and control. (...) It does not yield truth about the essential nature of things, the significance of its own place in the universe, or how it should conduct its life' (Hesse 1975, p. 389).

There is indeed a genuine distance between scientific theories and reality 'an sich' ('in itself'). But the conclusion need not be that science is *only* relevant to prediction and control and thus irrelevant to the things in which religion is interested: value and meaning, the essential nature of things. Science is a construction based on 'data' that relate it to reality while constraining the construction considerably. There is some underdetermination but not total indeterminism. Science is our best available way to knowledge, but to a knowledge which is far more than prediction. Among its components is an understanding of how the world works. There is also a strategic reason for taking science seriously; it enjoys great credibility in our world. To be credible, 'myths' need to take science into account. Theology has a stake in a modest realism too, for 'trust in God' assumes something about reality. But theology has traditionally acknowledged that there is also a genuine distance between the images and the stories we use and the reality to which they intend to refer.

2.2   The highroad of metaphysics

In some theologies, for example process theology, metaphysics functions as a mediating partner between science and theology by placing their mutual influence and coherence in a wider perspective. The theology appears as the most fluid contribution as it is reformulated to fit the metaphysical scheme. And it also seems to me that the metaphysics often determines the way the science is understood; the modern understanding of biological evolution, quantum phenomena or time being very much to the point. While I agree about the unavoidability of metaphysical elements, I have doubts about their dominance. Should one start with a metaphysics or at least get there shortly after take off? This approach builds in coherence, but it does so at the risk of forcing either the science or the religion, or perhaps both (for a similar criticism see Plomp 1987). Besides, it raises the problem of choice: which metaphysics should be adopted?

2.3   Theology interpreting science and explicating faith

According to Phil Hefner, an American Lutheran theologian, theology should 'discern how the world scientifically perceived is referable to God and how it can be the *effect* of God' (Hefner 1984a, p. 198). This position embraces an explicit *asymmetry* between science and theology. Theology has to live with the world as perceived through science. While theological arguments do not count in scientific discussions, science can falsify theological views. Interpretation is essential for meaning. As we don't find meaning at hand, we construct it with our interpretation. 'We struggle, as the poets often remind us, to forge meaning, and we try to test our forged meanings to determine their reliability' (Hefner 1984b, p. 484). It is a view that grants science its autonomy. In sharp contrast the theologian accepts humbly the conclusions of science, adapts his concepts, and changes his construction. But Hefner also acknowledges explicitly the traditional theological elements 'in their identity-bestowing role' (Hefner 1984a, p. 199).

I find myself in sympathy to some extent with this description of what usually happens. However, it turns 'science and religion' into too much of a monologue from science to theology. The interaction is certainly asymmetric, but there may be some influence in the other direction, especially if the constructive side of science is taken into account. Within science scope for construction exists by virtue of the distance between science and reality, and this scope makes theological or metaphysical influence on science possible. I will return to this point in my own proposal and illustrate it in the section on contemporary cosmological theories.

A similar position, which places a much greater emphasis on theology as an independent source because 'it begins with an experience with the Beyond', has been taken by another American Lutheran theologian, Ted Peters. He has argued for the use of scientific language and imagery in theology in the service of evangelical explication: 'Theology may begin with an experience of the Beyond, but it does not end there. It seeks to *explicate* the experience *in terms of the scientific knowledge available'* (Peters 1984, p. 388).

The German theologian Wolfhart Pannenberg claims even more for theology. He entitled an article, 'Theological questions to scientists'. As he sees it, there is scope for questioning in the opposite direction. For example, he asks whether science should revise the principle of inertia (mass continuing in rectilinear motion) or its interpretation because in its present form '[it deprives] God of his function in the conservation of nature' (Pannenberg 1981, p. 6).

I think this is a legitimate position: a certain element of one's theological system might be considered so essential that one prefers to question the science rather than the theology. Science is an enterprise in which conceptual shifts are legitimate. A theological perspective might provide sufficient reason to seek a definite modification of the science - a change of concepts or perhaps only a reinterpretation. Such an eventuality fits neither Hefner's nor Peter's description, both of which take science for granted. Clearly, interpretation and evangelical explication need to be supplemented in some way.

2.4 Consonance: E. McMullin

The Catholic philosopher Ernan McMullin (1981, p. 52) introduced the image of *consonance* which he defined as coherence in a world-view: 'The Christian cannot separate his science from his theology as though they were in principle incapable of interrelation. On the one hand, he has learned to distrust the simpler pathways from one to the other. He has to aim at some sort of coherence of world-view (...). He may, indeed he *must*, strive to make his theology and his cosmology consonant in the contributions they make to this world-view.' Admittedly there is a strong but tacit assumption behind McMullin's view. Consonance seems to involve more than the logical requirement of non-contradiction. It assumes that there is a relevant and largely independent theological contribution, and that the two contributions have to be made to fit 'in harmony'. These assumptions can be defended theologically (everything has to be related to God), or by an appeal to reality (maps of the same reality must show some correspondence), or psychologically (internal tensions within the faithful scientist must be avoided).

This approach allows both science and theology their freedom. However, as McMullin's writings (1981, 1985) make clear, it is *not* strictly true that the one is independent of other. Theological views incorporate some 'science', often the science of a distant past or some popular ideas about 'the way the world is' and about 'true knowledge'. The influence of theology on science is less visible. More often, the world-view is already there, influencing the theology and the science, for instance, through criteria that determine the preferences among theories and among possible interpretations. Many examples can be cited from quantum theory (regarding the nature of reality) and from thermodynamics (concerning the nature of time). Conceptually there is no unique genetic order of the three: science, theology and the world-view or metaphysics.

Consonance is open to the reality of pluralism: a song can be accompanied in a variety of ways. However, part of this openness is due to vagueness. Given sufficient ingenuity in constructing world-views, almost every religious conviction can be made compatible with almost every scientific theory. If consonance is to be useful, it needs criteria that distinguish between genuine consonance and *ad hoc* constructions - like the criteria for distinguishing between scientific progress and *ad hoc* adaptations (Lakatos 1970).

Consonance is based on epistemological realism about both science and theology. Many leading persons in science and theology have defended a critical realist view of both science and theology (e.g. Barbour 1974, McMullin 1981, 1984, Peacocke 1984, Polkinghorne 1986). The philosophical literature describes a variety of forms of realism (Leplin 1984, McMullin 1986), some based on the 'approximate truth' of theories, others on the 'reference' of the central theoretical terms to reality. However, each specified form of realism has its troubles (e.g. Laudan 1984a,b, Fine 1984)[3]. I share the realist attitude, recognising both that there is an external reality (ontological) and that science is telling us something about that world (epistemological). The same should hold for theology, if faith is to be true and comforting. But both enterprises also have a *genuinely constructive side* that accommodates a significant distance between our ideas and reality.

So far we have not met objections of a theological nature. In fact, the pursuit of consonance fits well with the protestant rule of *sola Scriptura* (Scripture as the only norm for theology). However, this rule is itself problematic. We always approach persons and texts equipped with our prior assumptions. This problem is, of course, a well-known aspect of 'hermeneutics': how do we bridge the gap between a text and ourselves when we cannot get away from ourselves, when we have 'glasses' that shape and distort our view of the text? This question amounts to a reformulation of the first objection given above: we cannot first take the two as entirely independent, then look with an open and clear mind to see if there is consonance. Clearly, consonance is not merely descriptive. For something has been built in from the very beginning by the language we use and by the way we interpret our concepts.

2.5 Constructive consonance[4]

In order to understand the intellectual side of science and theology, and in line with what was expressed by Hefner and Peters, I propose to use consonance as a constructive principle, as a methodological assumption, operating not only for the construction of world-views, but also within theology, and to a lesser extent within science too. We use it in the interpretation of abstract concepts, be they theological, scientific or philosophical.

By assuming that consonance exists between a theological view and a specific scientific theory, one implies that one should search for a suitable interpretation of the concepts involved. Probably such a search places both sets of concepts in a (not necessarily complete) metaphysical perspective. As this search does so, it is not only the world-view or the metaphysics that changes. The terms at the theological and scientific levels can also change meaning. Precisely what gives way and what remains unchanged depends on the relative importance of the various elements and on their reliability. In general, the science is considered to be the most reliable. In such cases, my proposal resembles an interpretation of the world as known through science: we reflect upon the knowledge provided by science and develop contemporary concepts to express our faith.

However, science allows for different interpretations, e.g. in quantum theory. Moreover, science is always changing. In fact, Pannenberg appealed directly to the possibility of change with his question about inertia, thereby showing that the corresponding theological element was very important to him. At the frontier, where science is dealing with unsolved problems, there is a variety of ways to go. In such cases, a metaphysics informed by a religious perspective might determine the criteria for theory development and appraisal. I am not suggesting that theologians should be directly involved in the development of science. There is already ample ingenuity within the scientific community without them and, in any case, a serious contribution has to be based upon an understanding of the technical details. What I mean is that there are within the scientist certain convictions - informed by a wider perspective, to which the 'theology' of that person contributes - that occasionally play a role in the development of scientific theories. Not only in the context of discovery, but also in the choice of criteria. And people involved in 'science and religion' could make this role more visible and thereby much more open to analysis. For example, the cosmologists of the Universities of Oxford and Cambridge, Roger Penrose and Stephen W. Hawking, differ considerably on issues such as time-asymmetry and the nature of quantum reality. Here there is no direct theological influence, but there is a metaphysical influence that also has some bearing upon the theological issues, for instance, upon the nature of history.

My notion of constructive consonance has some similarity to the *interanimation theory of metaphors* (Soskice 1985). Metaphors are neither mere substitutions of one term for another nor direct comparisons. Similarly, my aim with constructive consonance is not substitutions of scientific terms for theological ones or direct comparisons. When linked by a metaphor, the two terms with their 'different networks of associations' (Soskice 1985, p. 49) interanimate one another as the search for consonance adds to or changes interpretations of the concepts used. By putting the terms from different networks together something happens to them. So the claim that has been made for metaphors also applies to constructive consonance: it 'can produce new and unique agents of meaning' (Soskice 1985, p. 3).

Theology today wrestles with two problems: (i) Is it true? e.g. Does God exist? and (ii) Is it intelligible? e.g. What does it mean to talk about God or *creatio ex nihilo*? A solution to the second problem, intelligibility, does not imply truth. We can communicate concerning the question whether the 'Universe' is open or closed without knowing which is correct. These concepts might not even be applicable in future theories. By focusing on theories that are assumed to approximate reality from the outset, one might attack both problems at the same time with an interpretation or a world-view that is intelligible and that approximates truth. The requirement of constructive consonance is more modest. It is primarily suitable for working on the second problem by showing the possible meanings of concepts. By aiming at an interpretation in the context of a specific scientific theory, it is parasitic on the intelligibility of the scientific theory. Hence in so far as scientific theories are intelligible, the method is useful. A ridiculous exaggeration, of course, would be the objection that in this way the concept of 'heaven above' can be understood in the context of a flat earth, a false but nonetheless intelligible idea. With this type of treatment the method would be reduced to a mere play with words, as if 'anything goes'.

Evidently constructive consonance is not pursued for its own sake but as the first step towards a credible view of the world. Through its achievements science has gained considerable credibility, whether philosophers of science credit this gain to its approximation of truth or to its method of testing (e.g. Laudan 1984b), or just do not explain it at all. Now, fortunately, it is not necessary to solve the age-old problem of how to relate ideas to reality prior to relating the ideas of science to those of religion. For the primary task in science and theology is to relate them using, as one source of bricks, the best science available. In conjunction with criteria for acceptable forms of consonance, this approach might prove quite restrictive on the selection made from the possible theological and metaphysical views. However, a genuine pluralism remains because different, metaphysical and theological contributions are always possible.

The acceptance of the plurality does not bring the discussion to an end, even if there is agreement about the science. In principle, it is still possible to analyze and to discuss other criteria that partly determine the credibility of any proposals that integrate theology and science. Several questions come quickly to mind. How well do they satisfy one's religious convictions and metaphysical intuitions? And how do science, theology and metaphysics fit together? Hence, the need arises for notions of simplicity, elegance and beauty.

Mary Hesse (1981, p. 287) stated the case admirably: 'the problem is essentially not one of scientific 'realism', but one of communicative strategy'. I agree. Arguing for the truth of religious convictions on the basis of scientific theories has failed far too often. In the dialogue between science and theology, it is much more promising to focus on intelligibility than to concentrate on truth. If there is a plurality of scientific views, for instance, on the interpretation of quantum theory, one should attempt to present the core of Christianity within each and every one of those frameworks in the same way as it has been presented in many different languages and cultures. However, the question of intelligibility is followed by one of credibility, as a step towards truth. The credibility of any theological position, of course, will be strengthened both by a clarification of the criteria for acceptable forms of consonance and by the use of credible science and philosophy.

3. Theology in the context of astrophysical cosmology

Recent understanding of the Universe confirms that we are an integral part of the cosmos. Almost every atom in our bodies has been involved in the nuclear processes within a star. Cosmology also shows an impressive coherence of large and small. Superclusters - clusters of clusters of galaxies of billions of stars - have arisen out of fluctuations that once were smaller than a proton. This coherence makes it possible to discuss the Universe as a single entity, and not as a mere collection. Hence, there are grounds for interpreting it as Creation. More specific theological claims related to the Big Bang theory have been made. For example, Big Bang theory indicates that the Universe had a beginning in time that resembles an initial act of creation 'out of nothing'. Also, the Big Bang theory shows the contingency of the Universe. The Universe could have been different (e.g. in density). Its specificity, therefore, indicates that somehow a choice was made at the beginning - a choice

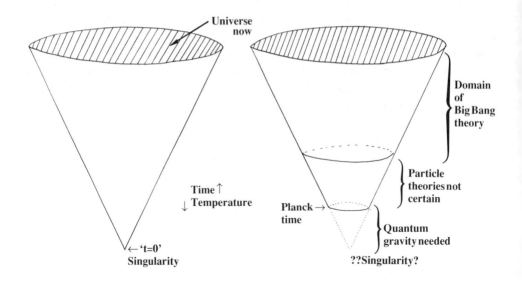

Universe
now

Domain
of
Big Bang
theory

Particle
theories not
certain

Time ↑
↓ Temperature

Planck →
time

Quantum
gravity needed

← 't=0'
Singularity

??Singularity?

fig. 1
The Big Bang model.

fig. 2
Limits of the Big Bang model.

unexplained by science but explained by faith. The Big Bang theory also discloses a dynamic, evolutionary Universe. These three issues are discussed in the following sections.

3.1 A beginning?

3.1.1 Limitations of the Big Bang theory

The Big Bang theory describes our Universe as expanding from an infinitely dense and hot point, 'the Singularity'. As expressed in the title of Steven Weinberg's popular exposition, *The First Three Minutes*, it would appear that the Universe had a beginning, and that we can describe the relevant processes right from the start (see figure 1). As the latter claim is a widespread misunderstanding, we cannot be certain about the former claim either. The Big Bang theory has *three limits* that arise on combining two important theories: general relativity theory relating to *space-time* and quantum theories dealing with matter. The theories relating to matter are only known up to a finite density and temperature, that is, they are known not up to the 't=0' moment but only up to a fraction of a second later. Closer still to the Singularity there comes a moment, presumably the Planck time (10^{-43} seconds), when general relativity theory needs to be superseded by a quantum theory of gravity. And the Singularity itself is a third limitation, *if* there is such a thing as a Singularity in theories that describe the Universe before the Planck time. The first two restrictions are clearly limits to our knowledge, while the third appears to be the edge of reality. But the Singularity is hidden behind the other two limits to our knowledge (see figure 2) and in fact might be non-existent.

The Big Bang theory *assumes* some *initial conditions*, for instance, large-scale homogeneity peppered with just the right amount of inhomogeneities to produce galaxies. This theory also assumes that the Universe has certain general features: the laws of physics, three spatial dimensions and one dimension of time, and the very existence of the Universe itself. The great challenge for physicists has been to explain those assumptions and to extend the domains of validity of the various theories in question. A particular concern has been the development of more complete theories (to be discussed in section 3.2). First, we will focus our attention on the initial conditions and on the Singularity as an (apparent) origination event.

3.1.2 Diversity at the frontier

1. Initial conditions
Some scientists defend a *chaotic cosmology*. They point out that the initial conditions of the Big Bang theory might be irrelevant. In this case, almost anything goes. It is like a sandy beach: almost any initial conditions - with or without sand castles - will result in a similar smooth beach after the lapse of sufficient time. In its most recent forms this approach is based on so-called inflationary scenarios (Andrej D. Linde, Allan H. Guth).

No boundary conditions, and therefore the absence of choice, is the proposal of the Cambridge cosmologist, Stephen Hawking. 'It would mean that we could describe the Universe by a mathematical model which was determined by the laws of physics alone' (Hawking 1984, p. 358f). This proposal will be discussed in some detail below (section 3.2.2). According to him, physics is fundamentally time-symmetric. His acceptance of the so-called Many Worlds Interpretation of Quantum Theory means that, for a given probability distribution, there is no choice left: all possibilities are actual.

The initial conditions were special according to the Oxford cosmologist, Roger Penrose. Our kind of universe is very rare among the set of all possible initial conditions. Penrose described this rarity using the image of the Creator picking one of the possible initial conditions (Penrose 1981, p. 249; it seems that the religious vocabulary is used only as imagery). He combines this selectivity with a strong emphasis on time-asymmetry. Moreover, he argues for a change in quantum theory that does away with the 'interpretation' problem, thus bringing this theory closer to a notion of 'objective reality' (Penrose 1987).

The differences between these three approaches are partly due to various metaphysical ideas about time and the (dis)similarity of future and past, about reality and potentiality, influencing the science especially in its criteria for theory choice.

2. The origination event
All current discussions of the 'origination event' use the recent conclusion that *the Universe might be equivalent to a vacuum*. There are no conserved physical quantities that have a non-zero sum over the whole Universe. Either the sum is zero (e.g. electrical charge) or the quantity is not conserved (e.g. baryon number which makes the distinction, for instance, between protons and anti-protons). Even the total energy is zero, or not conserved or not a meaningful concept.

Discussions about the origination event have to go beyond the first two limits sketched above, so they need to propose some ideas about quantum gravity. But most proposals are

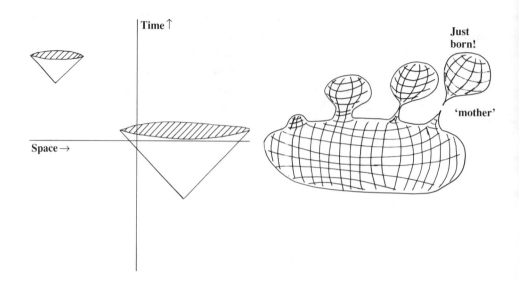

fig. 3
'Baby-universes' within an embedding space-time.

fig. 4 'Baby-universes' which become
spatially disconnected from the 'mother'.

not too dependent on the details: they are more like visions guiding current research. There is always, of course, the idea of an *eternally oscillating universe*. According to the Russian cosmologist M.A. Markov, the major advantage of this model is that it involves 'no problem of the origination of the world' (Markov 1983, p. 353).

The Singularity might be something like *birth or conception*, being, as it were, the beginning of time from the perspective of the baby or an event in time as seen by the mother. As 'conception' the Universe is like a bubble within an embedding space-time (Brout *et al* 1980, Gott 1982) (see figure 3). However, such babies tend to fill (and exhaust) their mother's womb (Linde 1983b). The model of 'birth' fares better: a mini-universe appears as a bubble on the 'surface' of the mother and, after evaporation of the connection, it becomes spatially disconnected (see figure 4). Andrej Linde has recently proposed an inflating universe consisting of bubbles, some of which inflate to sizes far larger than our observable Universe. As, in this kind of universe, there would be no first or last bubble, there would be for the whole no beginning or end of time either - although each bubble would have a beginning, and some of them also an end.

Such ideas might be formulated in terms of vacuum fluctuations, similar to the sudden short-lived appearance of an electron, an anti-electron and a photon together. As creation theories, such ideas are 'incomplete' because they assume the pre-existing spacetime framework in which the fluctuations occur. Other ideas attempt to evade this difficulty, basically by embracing the concept that 'time' is part of the created order, not prior to it. *Appearance out of nothing* has also been discussed repeatedly within the last few years (Vilenkin, Hartle and Hawking, Zeldovich and Starobinsky). Even if one disagrees with the philosophical *ex nihilo* interpretations of such theories, they do relate to traditional metaphysical questions, e.g. 'Why is the Universe as it is?' One of the most promising proposals of this kind will be outlined below (section 3.2.2).

3.1.3 Five implications for science and theology

1. The temporal cosmological argument (e.g. Craig 1979), which argues for the existence of God on the basis of a beginning of the Universe, is *not* univocally supported by science as it goes beyond the Big Bang theory. It is not too surprising that theologians and philosophers are not well informed about current research, but it is a serious failure on their part to neglect the limits of the theories they do use.

2. Many contributions to 'science and religion' concentrate on the methodological issues, but science is also theologically relevant for its content. For instance, Hawking has quite a different view of the nature of time from Penrose, a difference that has an important bearing on many theological issues.

3. Many people active in 'science and religion' restrict themselves to those areas where science shows a consensus. In the examples given the interesting issues lie clearly not in the Big Bang theory, but just beyond its limits in current research. What then is the actual relevance of established scientific theories for the science-and-theology dialogue?

4. If we leave the domain of consensus, we must face the variety of approaches at the frontier of research. Should we then on pursuing 'science and theology' restrict ourselves to the most promising ideas, pick the one that fits best our personal view, or wait until there is a consensus? If we look primarily for intelligibility, as I have advocated, we can take a look at as many approaches as are feasible in order to learn from each what we can and cannot say meaningfully about theological concepts.

5. Metaphysical influences on scientific research are also worthy of discussion. The differences between Hawking and Penrose on the nature of time, on the interpretation of quantum theory, and on many other issues are associated with metaphysical convictions about the nature of reality and about the relation between the potential and the actual. I think that 'the positive heuristic' is the place to locate such metaphysical influences (cf. Lakatos 1970).

3.2 Complete theories of everything, contingency, and God

3.2.1 The challenge: complete theories of everything

Stephen Hawking entitled his 1980 inaugural lecture for the Lucassian chair (Newton's Chair) in Cambridge 'Is the End in Sight of Theoretical Physics?' He considers it quite possible

> 'that the goal of theoretical physics might be achieved in the not too distant future, say, by the end of the century. By this I mean that we might have a complete, consistent, and unified theory of all the physical interactions which would describe all possible observations'.

Complex phenomena might be beyond our calculative capacities, but we would have a complete and unified theory. In his view, a complete theory contains both the laws and the boundary conditions. The laws might be superstring theories. As far as understood today, the number of possible consistent theories is very limited. As regards the boundary conditions, Hawking (1980) says that many people

> 'would regard the question of initial conditions for the universe as belonging to the realm of metaphysics or religion. (...) I think that the initial conditions of the universe are as suitable a subject for scientific investigation and theory as the local physical laws. We shall not have a complete theory until we can do more than merely say that 'things are as they are because they were as they were'.'

The challenge was put more polemically by Peter W. Atkins (1984, p. 17):

> 'I am developing the view that the only way of explaining the creation is to show that the creator had absolutely no job at all to do, and so might as well not have existed. We can track down the *infinitely lazy creator*, the creator totally free of any labour of creation, by resolving apparent complexities into simplicities, and I hope to find a way of expressing, at the end of the journey, how a non-existent creator can be allowed to evaporate into nothing and to disappear from the scene.'

As God becomes unnecessary to the explanations, 'the hypothesis can be dropped'. Many theologians would be willing to accept the disappearance of such a creator, since Atkins' 'Creator' is too much of a 'God-of-the-gaps', that is, of the not-yet-explained. But some other well-known theologians object to the complete disappearance of God from the explanatory scene. Wolfhart Pannenberg (1981, p. 4), for instance, said:

> 'If(...) nature can be appropriately understood without reference to the God of the Bible, then that God cannot be the creator of the universe, and consequently he could not be truly God and could not be trusted as a source of moral teaching either.'

Pannenberg refers to the *intelligibility* of the natural order. But the *contingency* of that order may be involved as well. Thomas F. Torrance (1981, p. 85) emphasizes contingency alongside order. He holds that there is a contingency implied not only 'at the beginning', but also when order as orderliness is discerned:

> 'Today natural science assumes both the contingency and the orderliness of the universe. The universe is contingent for it does not exist of necessity; it might not have been at all and might very well have been different from what it is.'

Would a complete theory of everything do away with those two kinds of contingency, thereby making God superfluous and so denying God's reality?

First, I will say something about Hawking's quantum cosmology without boundary conditions. Next, I will point to three inadequate responses to modern cosmology: Richard Swinburne's non-temporal version of the cosmological argument for the existence of God, Stanley L. Jaki's use of the limitations of science, and the anthropic principles (section 3.2.3). Then I will describe types of contingency, emphasizing the mystery of existence

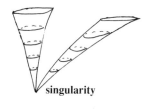

singularity

fig. 5a
The state of the Universe at t_2
'arises out of' the state at t_1.

fig. 5b
More than one possible universe
starts off with a singularity.

(section 3.2.4). I will also stress the importance of retaining a notion of transcendence contrary to much modern spirituality (section 3.2.5).

3.2.2 Quantum cosmology without initial conditions

The present discussion of this theory is not an attempt to defend it as a reasonable physical theory. That is not the job of someone who is interested in 'science and theology'. In any case, this theory has elicited many positive responses within the specialized literature. I accept, therefore, that it is a theory that deserves to be taken seriously. For present purposes this theory functions as a premise in a thought experiment: if one accepts this theory, what would that entail for theological reflection?

In the Big Bang theory, the state of the Universe at one time (the three dimensional geometry and matter) can be calculated using the equations *and* - as boundary conditions - its state at another time. In this sense one could say that a certain state 'arises out of' - or 'is created out of' - another state (see figure 5a). In the Big Bang theory the limit of such previous states is the initial Singularity. It is impossible to specify data at the Singularity; many different possibilities may start off with one-and-the-same initial Singularity (see figure 5b).

In quantum cosmologies a similar procedure holds. The Wheeler-DeWitt differential equation governs the evolution of a wavefunction. If one specifies the wavefunction at a boundary, it is possible to calculate it at other moments. In this way one could still look upon it as describing an evolutionary Universe. The disadvantage of this approach is that one needs to specify an initial or boundary condition. This problem is solved by the Hartle-Hawking proposal. They found a way to calculate the probabilities of the different states of the Universe, the three-dimensional geometries and matter configurations, without

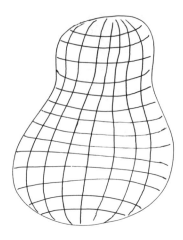

fig. 6a
An open surface has a boundary.

fig. 6b
A closed surface has no boundary.

having to refer to other states or to evolution from such other states. This procedure is highly technical, but the essential idea is that one takes, not open 'surfaces' (or super-surfaces, for instance, three-dimensional spaces in an abstract four-dimensional space), but *closed* ones. These closed 'surfaces' (or closed three-dimensional spaces), which are the 'resulting' states, form the only boundary present in the calculation (see figures 6a and 6b). That is the precise sense in which this description can be taken to describe *creatio ex nihilo*: a calculation for one state does not require the prior specification of other states.

However, ordinary time together with the notion of 'becoming' disappear through the device of taking one closed 'surface' (or space) instead of an initial state at t_1 and a final state at t_2 (compare figure 5a). Therefore, expressions like 'tunnelling from nothing' do not adequately describe the basic idea of this theory. Tunnelling* denotes a temporal process, while the 'from nothing' applies to a kind of time-independent actuality. This anomaly, of course, affects the understanding of the word 'creation', if it is used in this context. One might say that the Hartle-Hawking theory does without initial conditions, but one could say equally well that it is a proposal for the specification of a boundary condition. The proposal is so interesting because it appears to be an elegant way of specifying the boundary condition. It is a choice that avoids a total arbitrariness.

There is no external time parameter in this theory. Time arises as a phenomenological construct out of the specifications of the geometry and matter (fields). Therefore, this theory

---

* The term 'tunnelling' is applied, originally in quantum theory, when two given states influence each other while the penetration of the (energy) barrier separating them cannot be understood using the concepts of classical physics.

fits well with the idea of Augustine (*Confessiones,* Book 11), and centuries earlier, of Philo of Alexandria (*On the Account of the World's Creation Given by Moses* [section 26]), that time was created *with* the material creation and, therefore, that it makes no sense to talk about a before. The approach clearly has consequences for the 'beginning', 't=0'. For small spaces, one would expect to approach this interesting moment (compare figure 5b). However, in this scheme the internal phenomenological time becomes more and more unlike our ordinary time, although the calculation can be done without problems. In this sense, there is *no initial singularity where the theory breaks down.* Only our interpretation in terms of the usual notion of time breaks down. To put it differently, there is no edge to reality, only an edge to our description (see figures 6a and 6b). By way of explanation Stephen Hawking referred on a number of occasions to the North Pole: the degrees latitude end there, one cannot go farther north. However, as a point on the surface of the Earth, the North Pole is not different. from other points: it is not a special edge to the Earth. In the context of the Big Bang theory, it is possible to have space with a finite volume but without edges, like the surface of the Earth which is a finite surface without edges. Due to their approach to 'time' Hawking and Hartle are able to achieve the same in four dimensions, i.e. a space-time without edges.

Traditional theological ideas about *creatio ex nihilo* have two poles. They refer to *cosmogony,* the coming into being of our Universe. And they denote an eternal *sustaining* by God, an ultimate dependence at each and every moment, the Universe having its Ground in God. It seems to be widely held that the latter pole 'is somewhat decoupled from modern scientific thought' (Isham 1988, p. 376). In point of fact the theory presented here lends itself much more readily to an interpretation in terms of sustaining than of making. The basic entities are the three dimensional spaces together with their material content. They are, in this context, the primary products of creation, the 'what' that is created. Their relative probabilities can be calculated at the timeless level. Viewed from the timeless perspective, they are all coeternal, that is, created 'timelessly'. Hence, all are equally related to the Ground of Being. Another route to the same conclusion is to argue that this scheme does not have an initial event with a special status. There is no way to pick one space as the first of a sequence. All moments, therefore, have a similar relation to the Creator. Either they are all 'brute facts' or they are all equally created.

To summarize, this theory allows a precise interpretation of the term *ex nihilo,* and it accommodates better the idea that every space (with content) is created by God than the idea that God created 'in the beginning'. Consequently, this theory is more consonant with theism than deism.

A final word of caution: this theory is not to be taken as *the* indubitable conclusion of science today. It is only one example taken from the many ideas discussed in the current literature, although it is one of the most elegant and coherent. Some of its features are typical of most quantum cosmologies. The special feature of the Hartle-Hawking proposal is its emphasis on the 'timeless' calculation without other boundaries, hence the 'from nothing' which can be understood as doing away with the related contingency too - and thus with God? This point brings us back to the main line of thought in this section.

3.2.3   Three inadequate responses

1.   Richard Swinburne's non-temporal cosmological argument.

A non-temporal version of the cosmological argument, maintaining that the whole (possibly infinite) series of states needs an explanation, not just the initial state, has been defended by Richard Swinburne and by others too. The present research does not affect his argument that we have to face ultimately two possibilities: 'The choice is between the universe as a stopping-point and God as a stopping-point' (Swinburne 1979, p. 127). His argument for preferring God as stopping-point rests on the claim that 'God' is a much simpler assumption than the Universe alone with all its complexities. This claim is not in line with contemporary research. Scientific theories of the Universe gain progressively in elegance and simplicity - if not in the calculations at least in structure and assumptions - suggesting that these theories might provide a simpler stopping-point than 'God'. *Simplicity* is not the proper basis of an argument for transcendence.

2.   Stanley Jaki's limitations of science

Complete theories seem to do away with mysteries. But Stanley Jaki (1982, p. 258) has followed the opposite course in arguing for the persistence of mysteries. Even a perfect scientific cosmology

> 'can never pose a threat to that cosmic contingency which is intimated in the scientific portrayal of the specificity of the universe'.

All specific entities - specificity being a sign of limitation - find their explanation in the creator, who is the totality of perfections.

> 'The cosmologist disdainful of metaphysics will be left with a formidable if not frightening array of singularities, and the only scientific thing he can do about them is to trace them to another array of singularities' (Jaki 1978, p. 273).

Such scientists do not reach a final explanation, but instead commit 'the fallacy of infinite regress'.

Swinburne argued for the greater simplicity of a theistic explanation, but he acknowledged the possibility of two stopping points: either the existence of a God who created the Universe or the existence of the Universe itself. Jaki seems to assume that only the first option is a sound metaphysical position; the second is discarded as incomplete and frightening. His approach does not do justice to the actual discussion. Those who argue from a non-theistic perspective might well assert on metaphysical grounds, invoking criteria of completeness, simplicity, beauty and coherence, that a certain explanation is satisfactory.

3.   The anthropic principles

Standard cosmology assumes what is called the Copernican principle: we do not have a privileged position in space. Nevertheless, in the last few years, there have been rumours circulating that there is something special about us as expressed in the anthropic principles (Barrow and Tipler 1986). Those principles are related to a number of 'observed' features of our Universe. Because those features are thought of as necessary for the development of our kind of life, I prefer to call them 'anthropic coincidences'. For example, three dimensions of space appear to have significant advantages over two or four dimensions. Also, if the expansion rate of the Universe had been slightly greater or only a little less, there would not have been stars or there would not have been sufficient time for biological evolution, respectively.

The simplest version of the anthropic principle is the Weak Anthropic Principle (WAP), which states that what we see must be compatible with our existence. We see a Universe where there is carbon - because we depend on carbon, etcetera. Imagine the existence of many planets at different distances from their star and, therefore, with different temperatures. Since life depends on liquid water, life will only be found on planets with surface temperatures between zero and one hundred degrees centigrade. Well, there is nothing mysterious about that. There is no reason to call it 'a Principle'. It is standard use of evidence: we have A, we know that it needs B, hence there is B. This usage does not explain why A and B are there. In my example, it does not explain why there are such planets or why there are such living beings. It only repeats the rule used in the inference: the two go together. The WAP does not explain anything - whether combined with many 'worlds' (in my example, planets) or not. It is not wrong, but irrelevant. However, those who assume the existence of many 'worlds', for example, Andrej Linde with his idea of bubble-universes, generally combine the WAP with the metaphysical principle: everything that is possible must be actual. If that additional assumption of *plenitude* is introduced, one might then explain observations by appealing to the selection effect embodied in the WAP. The interesting issue, however, is not the WAP but the view of the relation between the possible and the actual.

The more interesting, but perhaps also more repugnant, version is the Strong Anthropic Principle (SAP): the Universe *must* have the properties that will allow life to develop at some stage in its history. If by 'life' is meant 'life as we know it', the principle is of course quite strong in its predictions about possible universes. However, that conjecture is plainly untestable as we do not have access to other universes. Besides, it is somewhat *post hoc*, and it uses something (life), which in all its richness is only partly understood, in order to explain other things. Perhaps other forms of life will develop zillions of years from now at completely different stages of the Universe. SAP explanations are also vulnerable with respect to the future developments of scientific theories. According to the history of science, subsequent theories have generally fewer and fewer independent and unexplained parameters (constants, boundary conditions). Indeed, this erosion of assumed evidence for the anthropic principles has already happened a number of times (Pagels 1985, Gardner 1986). If applied on a smaller scale, say 'planets must have the properties which allow for the development of life at some stage in their history', then the principle is surely wrong. This example shows the true character of the SAP. SAP is like the old *teleological* argument that everything must have a function, and so the moon must be populated - as the ancient philosopher Plutarchus argued (Raingard 1934).

There is another version of the Strong Anthropic Principle labelled the Participatory Anthropic Principle (PAP), which is based on an interpretation of quantum theory that ascribes enormous significance to the actual act of conscious observation, an act which gives reality to the past. According to John A. Wheeler, a universe needs to develop conscious beings who can observe their early Universe. Otherwise it will not come into existence. This conjecture might be accommodated readily by a metaphysics which gives 'minds in the Universe' priority over matter. As I find such metaphysics strange, PAP does not appeal to me.

From this sketch, I conclude that the strong anthropic principles are actually expressions of metaphysical principles in contemporary scientific language. As such they illustrate constructive consonance: different components are brought together and thereby develop certain meanings. One uses them only if one finds the implicit metaphysics compelling.

3.2.4 Types of contingency and the mystery of existence

The Hartle-Hawking quantum cosmology without boundary conditions does remove some contingency. For example, inflation* might turn out to be a necessary phenomenon within this scheme. But there are other kinds of contingency, so we have to see which kinds of contingency disappear.

1. Contingency of the initial conditions.

Most theories have a large set of initial conditions. Within the context of the pertinent theory they are all equally likely, if considered a priori - otherwise one would have an extra law and a different set of initial conditions would then be required. This kind of contingency disappears if physics and cosmology come up with a theory in which the set of possible initial conditions is empty (there is no need of initial conditions) or the set consists of only one element (which amounts to the same thing). In this sense, the Hartle-Hawking cosmology is a package deal: there can be no negotiations about details (like initial conditions) once the scheme is accepted.

Even if initial conditions are necessary, there might still be a second kind of contingency.

2. Contingency of the laws.

Why are the laws of physics what they are? Why is the Hartle-Hawking cosmology preferred and not another proposal, say Penrose's twistors? This line of inquiry seems safer ground for contingency. Complete theories of our Universe, as described by Hawking, need not be unique: there might be more than one (aside from trivial reformulations) which fit our observations. It is even more likely that there might be more than one consistent way to

---

*   In order to solve problems in Big Bang theory it has been proposed that the very early Universe has known an inflationary phase of extremely short duration; inflation might explain, for instance, the absence of anti-matter in our universe. This *inflation* should not be confused with the *expansion* of our universe, which continues until the present time.

set up a universe without the restriction that it is like our own. This likelihood is the contingency of the laws or the theories. In order to rule it out, one would require some kind of overview of all possible candidates for such theories, demonstrating that there is only one. That seems too strong a requirement. However, there might be only one theory which is consistent in all respects. Superstring theories are among the latest novelties of theoretical physics*; they are the best candidates available today, and their number is quite small. Six such theories are known to satisfy the required conditions of consistency, and perhaps three of them are actually equivalent. Additional conditions might reduce further the number of consistent theories. 'Ideally it will turn out that there is only one' (Schwarz 1987, p. 654).

Aside from all that, the contingency of theories is different from that of initial conditions. All possible initial conditions are equally good candidates a priori, but that does not hold for theories. For instance, there are variants of Einstein's theory of General Relativity that are compatible with present day observations. However, they are not considered to be as good as General Relativity itself. The criteria used in such evaluations include coherence, simplicity, and elegance. If one accepts such aesthetic criteria in addition to the requirement of consistency, the contingency of the laws might actually disappear in the not-too-distant future.

I am not sure that the two forms of contingency just discussed will ever disappear. However, even if it were to happen, there is no good theological reason for objection. It would do away, of course, with the fundamental role of experiments in science, and this would do away, in turn, with the argument that theology and science should remain friends because the theological idea of contingency made science possible in the first place (advocated by Jaki *et al*). It would do away also with the role of experiments in science as an argument for contingency (e.g.Torrance 1981). Thus we would lose certain arguments, but we still might be grateful for the things that we would understand. It would show that the Creator had only one type of universe available - given the rules of logic and mathematical consistency as well as certain aesthetic preferences. In a way this is similar to the theological dispute between Leibniz and Spinoza. Had God a choice among possible worlds? Or does God's nature imply that God creates the best possible world? (Hubbeling 1987, p. 148) As far as I see it, God's personhood is not dependent on these kinds of contingency. The personhood of God is more expressive in relation to individuals and in the will to have a creation - which reflects the goodness of creation as a free gift. However, this expression is not dependent on these two forms of contingency, but leads us to a third.

3. The contingency of existence.

Why is there anything that behaves in accordance with the mathematical rules written down in the Physical Review (a famous journal of physics, read world-wide)? Some people, like Atkins, hold that chance phenomena are sufficient explanation; others simply identify their mathematical ideas and what they consider to be the actual universe[5]. But as I see it, probabilities alone are not enough; they need an input of actuality. The probability of throwing a number below seven with one die is one, it is certain, but *only if* there is a die which is thrown

---

*   In a string theory the basic elements are not mass points but vibrating bodies that extend in one
       dimension: strings.

-hence, only if there is an actual die and a die factory, as well as a throw. Quantum fluctuations might do away with the throw - they happen all the time - but not with the need for some input of actuality. This kind of contingency lies beyond the limits of physics.

For a long time, I have considered this to be a stop-gap, a last resort for the theologian if there is nothing else left to claim. I still doubt whether it is useful in an argument for the existence of God. Nevertheless, this issue is related to a sense of wonder that, in my case, has increased steadily throughout my study of cosmological ideas. It has been aptly described by the physicist Charles W. Misner, who said that 'God blessed one formula in some creative act' (1977, p. 96). Whether or not it was the only beautiful formula available to God does not make any difference. Quoting Misner again,

'To say that God created the Universe does not explain either God or the Universe, but it keeps our consciousness alive to the mysteries of awesome majesty that we might otherwise ignore'.

To see the Universe as grace, as a gift, is a way of interpreting this sense of amazement and of relating it to an understanding of God. In this context a difference between theism and pantheism is clearly visible.

'We might perhaps define theism best by understanding it as that conception of God where the world is the product of God's free, self-conscious, creative and maintaining activity. This definition involves that God does not require the world for the realization of his being, because God creates the world *freely*' (Hubbeling 1963, p. 10).

3.2.5 The relevance of transcendence against holism
There is a new spirituality to which I alluded in the introduction, and which is variously labelled the New Age, holism, cosmic spirituality, etcetera. It offers a different answer to the last kind of contingency, namely, the mystery of existence: we can accept that the Universe just happens to be and still feel religious. Without attempting an exhaustive description and criticism (Restivo 1984), I respond to the challenge that it poses. As I see it, the challenge is against the transcendental component of Christianity, against the appeal to a God *beyond* the Universe. Why not instead label the whole 'God'? Or use that label for the final state? Or use it for the spirit or mind that pervades reality? There is surely something interesting and sympathetic about it. Often holistic views go with a responsible attitude towards nature and man together with an openness to poetry. Indeed, pantheistic systems can have great beauty and coherence.

I have two basic theological objections. Firstly, most holism neglects the brokenness of creation with its emphasis on wholeness. Too often, the only barrier seen is one of thinking, of knowledge. But the symbol of the cross expresses an element of *realism* about this world. The wholeness should be a vision rather than an unrecognized presence; it is more of a 'not yet' than of an 'already'. As a vision it transcends the actual universe. Secondly, holism tends to overemphasize the mystical ideal of the unity of the individual with the divine. Aside from having a mysticism of encounter in Christianity, that stresses the differences between the individual and the divine, there is also the prophetical side. In the prophetic tradition there is scope for criticism, because the God who is the source of the norms is not identical with the reality that surrounds us. Prophetic criticism rests upon a metaphysics which has a notion of *otherness*, an idea of *transcendence*. We need a difference between the Universe and the Beyond as the basis of the critical tradition that we have inherited, and that we require to preserve whilst changing.

3.3 A dynamic or a timeless universe?

Stephen Hawking said recently (*Time*, February 8, 1988, p. 60) about his own quantum cosmology:

> 'The universe would not be created, not be destroyed; it would simply be. What place, then, for a Creator?'

The Big Bang theory has often been understood as showing the dynamic, expanding and evolutionary nature of the Universe. I have no objection to that understanding other than that I think that it is a one-sided incomplete presentation. In physics there are often two descriptions, as we have seen in the Hartle-Hawking quantum cosmology: one can calculate the states not only by using a differential equation and an initial state, but also at a timeless level without referring to previous states at all. This theory is exceptional in that the timeless level of description involves individual spaces, that is to say, individual moments of 'now'. That raises some questions of its own, especially about the continuity of our experiences. However, the presence of two descriptions is not restricted to this exceptional (and still preliminary) theory. For instance, General Relativity, which is often understood as describing a dynamic expanding universe has as its most fundamental entity a four-dimensional spacetime. At that level of description, all moments are equally copresent. There is no way of talking at that level of description about things moving, changing, evolving and so on. The picture is completely 'static', because it makes no sense to talk about four-dimensional spacetime changing in time. A similar double description is also applicable to other theories, in which one can describe systems evolving in time also by their trajectories in phase space. Such trajectories represent whole histories at once. Theories formulated in that kind of language are not evolutionary. Instead, the theory is about different possible 'packages', complete histories, whereas the term 'evolutionary' is appropriate to another kind of description that is not timeless.

Almost all contemporary theologians who take science seriously opt for a dynamic picture. Scientists have discussed the problem of time extensively, and they have attempted to understand the arrow of time, the flow of time that is experienced. Theologians have always hoped for a favourable outcome of this discussion, since theology has an intense interest in history and, therefore, both in changes and in directionality (e.g. Griffin 1986, Russell 1984, Pannenberg 1981). I think that the presence of a double description in physics together with the differences between physics and biology provide theology with a welcome opportunity. This double description offers theology a valuable means of expressing different interests and of reflecting upon those insights, while their interrelation might be clarified by analogy to the correlation of its scientific counterparts. Here I cannot deal in great detail with this matter, so I will present only short summaries of the two descriptions - which are more like members of a family than two precisely circumscribed unities.

A description *within time* takes history and evolution (including cosmic, stellar, geological, biological and cultural elements) as basic. This kind of description resonates with a theological emphasis on 'Heilsgeschichte'- the 'history of salvation'. It leads to questions about causality and about the origin and purpose of processes. *Creatio continua* is the theological doctrine that deals with God's relation to the processes of change, especially God's relation to the emergence of novelty. This description also stresses the issue of contingency, as the things of today were different yesterday, and they will be different again tomorrow. *Value* is related readily to the future - what is produced by something shows its qualities. This is related to a teleological or utilitarian understanding of ethics. God's relation to the world is most easily formulated in terms of immanence or transcendence in a temporal sense.

A description *beyond time* might be understood as a view from God's perspective, *sub specie aeternitatis*. The whole of history is present at once. This raises far less questions about origins. Instead, the corresponding question is about the ground of everything. There is less emphasis on novelty - there can be nothing new if everything is presented in one overview - and more on permanent structures. Rather than emphasizing contingency, it pushes the idea of necessity- the eternal laws which are the same for all moments. Consequently, the sustaining element in traditional concepts of *creatio ex nihilo,* that is, the *conservatio*, has more emphasis. *Value* must be understood as belonging to every element by virtue of it being a part of the whole web. Transcendence is much more radical, completely outside the space-time description.

One could perhaps relate the two descriptions to emphases on God's activity and being respectively, or to the two different types of biblical literature, the historical and the prophetical within the history of Israel and the more distantial wisdom strand, which reflects on the way things are, will be and always have been.

4. Down to earth: the integrity of creation

I have looked at theology and science from an academic perspective. But what about its relevance for church and society? As a recapitulation and localization of my ideas, let me briefly point to some issues that have been discussed in recent WCC documents on the Justice, Peace, and Integrity of the Creation process.

1. Method
There is as much confusion about the relation between theology and ethics as in academic discussions about theology and science. Sometimes, it is claimed that an 'understanding [of the relationships between God, humanity and nature] is necessary to provide a framework for formulating value decisions on environmental issues' (WCC 1987c, p. 1). We must 'attempt to have a theocentric perspective of nature and this should be the basis of any Christian environmental ethic' (WCC 1987b, p. 41). This sounds as if theology is taken as the basis and ethics is derived from it. However, throughout the documents, it is amply clear that the ethical issues are incentives to reformulate the theology, and that theological approaches are also judged by their ethical implications.

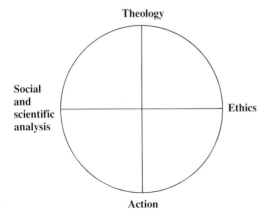

fig. 7
The 'Bossey circle': a frame for a pictorial evaluation of four aspects of a report or programme.

I have argued that natural science, theology and metaphysics mutually influence each other with different emphases placed on what is kept fixed in different cases. Something similar might be applicable here: theological and ethical reflection and ideas about 'how society works' come together. There is neither a unique temporal order nor one of priority. Each of them, theology, science, and metaphysics might change, but it also might be the core that is protected. Something similar might be read into the so-called *Bossey circle* (WCC 1987b) (see figure 7). It seems to be a tool for the description of the work done by others. But it is also a statement about what should be done (i) to cover those four issues indicated in the diagram, and (ii) to relate them and, if necessary, change them in order to give a consonant whole. The advantage of this approach would be its openness to the diversity of contributions from different sides - as present in the World Council and in society - while aiming at a wider perspective.

2. Sciences
There is a strong emphasis on biology - in line with the emphasis on environmental problems - in the documents of the World Council of Churches. Astrophysical cosmology is mentioned, but basically only as one of the many contributions to the overall picture of an dynamic and intelligible Universe[6]. Quantum physics is used partly to argue for a certain ontology (not substantial; subjectivity even for electrons, according to Charles Birch; relationality of everything), and partly to argue for freedom and responsibility. This discussion is stimulating and, perhaps, what should be put forward for a broader audience. However, as argued above, there are other aspects of current science that do not fit well. Especially troublesome in this respect are time, determinism, and creativity. Quantum

theory allows for more than one interpretation, and some interpretations are deterministic, e.g. the so-called Many Worlds Interpretation.

Of course, there is an impressive coherence among the different sciences. But plurality is there too in the form of the different disciplines, e.g. biology and physics, and within each discipline itself. There is no consensus on some crucial issues. As yet, there is no theological response to the plurality of and within disciplines. The WCC documents seem to be based upon choices that already lie beyond the domain of science itself. That is not wrong, but the choices made are not beyond dispute either.

3. Theologies

Those elements of a theology of nature that are developed in the WCC documents seem mostly concerned with an emphasis on God's immanence, e.g. 'how the scientific perspectives of the world interact with this traditional concept of God's immanence in the world' (WCC 1987b, p. 38). In the documents transcendence is also affirmed, but 'immanence' seems to be the attribute that calls for development today, both in relation to science and as a basis for ethics. This emphasis on immanence leads to an identification of 'sustaining' with *creatio continua*: 'The traditional picture of God 'sustaining' the universe can now better be seen in terms of God's continuous creative action' (WCC 1987b, p. 40). However, I argued earlier (in line with Pannenberg's question about inertia (1981, 1988)), that sustaining also has the meaning of *conservatio*, even if there is no change. This meaning links it more with *creatio ex nihilo* than with *creatio continua*. God can be seen as the permanent ground of everything, whether there is anything changing or not. I have also defended the theological importance of *creatio ex nihilo* in expressing the graciousness of creation, a notion that is played down in the WCC documents, because it does not fit well with the process-theological input.

Besides, I hold that the ethics should be based, at least partially, on God's transcendence and not on God's immanence. The WCC documents seem to look for a theocentric ethics through an emphasis on God's immanence in nature, e.g. 'God's *presence* in all creation reveals to us that in addition to human beings other creatures are also subjects that have a claim upon us' (WCC 1987b, p. 41; emphasis added). In contrast, I see as the source behind the criticism of the prophets not God's presence in the business of everyday living, but God's otherness.

I feel a little uneasy about my criticisms of the approach in those recent reflections on the Integrity of Creation. I agree that 'Justice, Peace and the Integrity of Creation' are major issues in the world today, issues with which Christians have necessarily to be involved. However, I must disagree with some of the theological ideas used without disagreeing about the other elements in the 'Bossey circle'. There is a plurality of acceptable theologies in today's world. But we need not let the matter rest there. We should find ways of clarifying further the nature of the differences and the agreements as well as methods of assessing which approaches are the most credible.

4. Realisms and constructions

One final reflection and comparison. The WCC documents are based on 'critical realism' both through Peacocke's influence and through the process-theological contributions (e.g. J. McDaniel in WCC 1987b, p. 106). This influence fits the more general mood in the churches. We accept that we do not know God completely, but we still claim that our concepts refer correctly and our descriptions are approximately true. However, I have expressed my doubts about such epistemological realism. I believe there is a reality (ontological realism), but also that a genuine distance exists between reality and theory. We have lost our naive belief in an immediate correspondence between our ideas and reality. We went through a period of criticism. Consequently, we know that our ideas are fallible. Nevertheless, we can still try to work with them. As Ricoeur (1967, p. 351) stated, 'it is by interpreting that we can hear again'.

Acknowledgements

I want to express my gratitude to Robert Russell and Phil Hefner, who contributed much to the development of my ideas as presented in this lecture. The contacts with them made my stay in the U.S.A. particularly fruitful, both at the Center for Theology and the Natural Sciences at the Graduate Theological Union in Berkeley (in the Fall of 1987) and at the Chicago Center for Religion and Science at the Lutheran School of Theology in Chicago (in the Winter and Spring of 1988). Also, I am very grateful that correspondence with Chris Isham has proved so valuable, especially to my understanding of the Hartle-Hawking theory.

These investigations were supported by the Foundation for Research in the field of Theology and the Science of Religions in the Netherlands, which is subsidized by the Netherlands Organization for Scientific Research (NWO). The period of study in Berkeley and Chicago was also supported by a Fulbright scholarship and additional financial support from the following Dutch organizations: Haak Bastiaanse Kuneman Stichting, H.M. Vaderlandsch Fonds, Vereniging van Vrijzinnig Hervormden te Groningen, Genootschap Noorthey, Fonds Aanpakken, and Groninger Universteits Fonds.

Notes

1. The ideas presented in this article have been developed in more detail in my *Beyond the Big Bang: Quantum Cosmologies and God* (to be published by Open Court, La Salle Ill. and London, 1990).
2. At the First European Conference on Science and Religion Viggo Mortensen expressed such a concern with respect to Ralph Burhoe's programme: 'When (...) God can be explained by genetics, then religion becomes nothing but words - words that we could just as well do without' (Mortensen 1987, p. 197).
3. The title of Ernan McMullin's book, *Construction and Constraint* (1988), suggests a very moderate form of realism - if one would still call it that - emphasizing the two elements I present below for science and theology. Perhaps, through the many qualifications (e.g. McMullin 1986), the author would not be that vulnerable to the philosophical criticism of realism.

4. The formulation is my own, but I share many of the basic elements with Robert Russell in Berkeley, who influenced my ideas through many conversations and articles. Robert Russell analyzed, for instance, finitude and other elements of contingency in relation to the different possible Big Bang cosmologies. One of his conclusions was: *The particular elements of contingency in a given cosmological model both interpret and limit the theological claim that creation is contingent* (Russell 1989, p. 192). Another influence, more in the background, is H.G. Hubbeling's work, which combined an openness for different views with a quest for rational assessment of the merits of different opinions (Hubbeling 1963, 1971, 1987).

5. An intriguing empiricist argument for an idealist identity of mathematical ideas and the actual universe has been put forward by Barrow and Tipler (1986, p. 154f.). If the Universe is simulated with a computer programme, we can 'equate the Universe with its simulation': '(...) If a simulation is perfect, then those subprogrammes which are isomorphic to human beings in the general Universal Programme act the same in the simulation as humans do in the actual Universe (....). A rational subprogramme inside the Universal Programme cannot by any logically possible operation distinguish between the abstract running of the Universal Programme and a physically real, evolving Universe. Such a physically real Universe would be equivalent to the Kantian thing-in-itself. As empiricists, we are forced to dispense with such an inherently unknowable object: the Universe must *be* an abstract programme, or Absolute Idea.'

6. The Glion report (WCC 1987b) combines 'Nature is intelligible' (p. 38) with 'Nature is ultimately mysterious. We do not know what matter (e.g. a quark) is 'in itself''(p. 39). Clarification is needed whether or not this is the kind of persistence of mysteries Stanley Jaki claimed, and how it fits with intelligibility. Besides, it is not an element of the scientific consensus, but rather a philosophical (Kantian?) position. As such, there is a tension with the choice for critical realism.

References

Atkins, P.W.   1981. *The Creation,* Oxford & San Francisco: W. H. Freeman.

Barbour, I.G.   1974. *Myths, Models, and Paradigms,* New York: Harper and Row.

Barrow, J.D., Tipler F.J.   1986. *The Anthropic Cosmological Principle*, Oxford: Clarendon Press.

Brout, R., *et al*   1980. 'Cosmogenesis and the origin of the fundamental length scale',
                        Nuclear Physics B 170: 228-264.

Craig, W.L.   1979. *The Kalām Cosmological Argument,* London: Macmillan.

Drees, W.B.   1990. *Beyond the Big Bang: Quantum Cosmologies and God,* La Salle
                        Ill.: Open Court; as thesis (University of Groningen, 1989) available in
                        academic libraries in the Netherlands.

Fine, A.   1984. 'The Natural Ontological Attitude', in *Scientific Realism,* ed. J.
                        Leplin, Berkeley and Los Angeles: Univ. of Calif. Press.

Gardner, M.   1986. 'WAP, SAP, PAP & FAP', *The New York Review*
                        (May 8): 22-25.

Gott, J.R.   1982. 'Creation of open universes from De Sitter space',
                        Nature 295: 304-307.

Griffin, D.R., (ed.)	1986. *Physics and the Ultimate Significance of Time: Bohm, Prigogine, and Process Philosophy,* Albany: SUNY Press.
Guth, A.H.	1982. '10^{-35} seconds after the Big Bang', in *The Birth of the Universe,* eds. J. Audouze, J. Tran Thanh Van, Gif sur Yvette: Éditions Frontières.
	1983. 'Phase Transitions in the Very Early Universe', in *The Very Early Universe,* eds. G.W. Gibbons, S.W. Hawking, S.T.C. Siklos, Cambridge: Cambridge Univ. Press.
Hartle, J.B., Hawking, S.W.	1983. 'Wave function of the universe', *Phys.Rev.D* 28: 2960-2975.
Hawking, S.W.	1980. *Is the End in Sight for Theoretical Physics?,* Cambridge Univ. Press; reprinted in J. Boslaugh, *Stephen Hawking's universe,* New York: Quill/William Morrow, 1985.
	1984, 'Quantum cosmology', in *Relativity, Groups, and Topology II,* eds. B.S. DeWitt, R. Stora, Amsterdam: North Holland.
	1988. *A Brief History of Time,* New York: Bantam Books.
Hefner, P.J.	1984a. 'Creation: Viewed by science, affirmed by faith', in *Cry of the Environment: Rebuilding the Christian Creation Tradition,* eds. P. N. Joranson and K. Butigan, Santa Fe New Mexico: Bear & Company.
	1984b. 'God and Chaos: the Demiurge versus the *Ungrund*', *Zygon* 19: 469-486.
Hesse, M.	1975. 'Criteria of truth in science and theology', *Religious Studies* 11: 385-400.
	1981. 'Retrospect', in *The Sciences and Theology in the Twentieth Century,* ed. A. R. Peacocke, Notre Dame: Univ. of Notre Dame Press.
Hubbeling, H.G.	1963. *Is the Christian God-conception philosophically inferior?,* Assen: Van Gorcum.
	1971. *Language, Logic and Criterion,* Amsterdam: Born.
	1987. *Principles of the Philosophy of Religion,* Assen: Van Gorcum.
Isham, C.J.	1988. 'Creation of the universe as a quantum process', in *Physics, Philosophy, and Theology: A Common Quest for Understanding,* eds. R.J. Russell, W. R. Stoeger, G. V. Coyne, Vatican: Vatican Observatory (distr. outside Italy by Univ. of Notre Dame Press).
Jaki, S.L.	1978. *The Road of Science and the Ways to God,* Chicago: Univ. of Chicago Press.
	1982. 'From scientific cosmology to a created universe', *The Irish Astronomical Journal* 15: 253-262.
Lakatos, I.	1970. 'Methodology of scientific research progammes', in *Criticism and the Growth of Knowledge,* eds. I. Lakatos, A. Musgrave, Cambridge: Cambridge Univ. Press (Reprinted in I. Lakatos, *Philosophical Papers, Vol.I,* eds. J. Worral, G. Currie, Cambridge: Cambridge Univ. Press 1978).

Laudan, L.	1984a. 'A confutation of convergent realism', in *Scientific Realism*. ed. J. Leplin, Berkeley and Los Angeles: Univ. of Calif. Press.
	1984b. 'Explaining the success of science: beyond epistemic realism and relativism', in *Science and Reality*, eds. J. T. Cushing, C. F. Delaney, and G. M. Gutting, Notre Dame: Univ. of Notre Dame Press.
Leplin, J.	1984. 'Introduction', in *Scientific Realism*, ed. J. Leplin, Berkeley and Los Angeles: Univ. of Calif. Press.
Lindbeck, G.A.	1985. *The Nature of Doctrine*, Philadelphia: Westminster.
Linde, A.D.	1983a. 'Chaotic inflation', *Physics Letters B* 129: 177-181.
	1983b. 'The new inflationary universe scenario', in *The Very Early Universe*, eds. G. W. Gibbons, S.W. Hawking, S.T.C. Siklos, Cambridge: Cambridge Univ. Press.
	1987a. 'Inflation and quantum cosmology', in *Three Hundred Years of Gravitation*, eds. S. W. Hawking, W. Israel, Cambridge: Cambridge Univ. Press.
	1987b. 'Particle physics and inflationary cosmology', *Physics Today* 40 (Sept. 9): 61-68.
Markov, M.A.	1983. 'Some remarks on the problem of the very early universe', in *The Very Early Universe*, eds. G.W. Gibbons, S.W. Hawking, S.T.C. Siklos, Cambridge: Cambridge Univ. Press.
McMullin, E.	1981. 'How should cosmology relate to theology?', in *The Sciences and Theology in the Twentieth Century*, ed. A.R. Peacocke, Notre Dame: Univ. of Notre Dame Press.
	1984. 'The case for scientific realism', in *Scientific Realism*, ed. J. Leplin, Berkeley and Los Angeles: Univ. of Calif. Press.
	1985. 'Evolution and creation', in *Evolution and Creation*, ed. E. McMullin, Notre Dame: Univ. of Notre Dame Press.
	1986. 'Explanatory success and the truth of theory', in *Scientific Inquiry in Philosophical Perspective*, ed. N. Rescher, Lanham N.Y.: Univ. Press of America.
	1988. 'The shaping of scientific rationality: construction and constraint', in *Construction and Constraint,* ed. E. McMullin, Notre Dame: Univ. of Notre Dame Press.
Misner, C.W.	1977. 'Cosmology and Theology', in *Cosmology, History and Theology,* eds. W.Yourgrau, A.D.Breck, New York: Plenum Press.
Mortensen, V.	1987. 'The status of the science-religion dialogue', in *Evolution and Creation*, eds. S. Andersen, A.R. Peacocke, Aarhus: Aarhus Univ. Press.
Pagels, H.R.	1985. 'A cozy cosmology', *The Sciences* 25 (2): 34-38.
Pannenberg, W.	1981. 'Theological questions to scientists', in *The Sciences and Theology in the Twentieth Century*, ed. A.R. Peacocke, Notre Dame: Univ. of Notre Dame Press (also in *Zygon* 16: 65-77).
	1988. 'The doctrine of creation and modern science', *Zygon* 23: 3-21.

Peacocke, A.R.   1979. *Creation and the World of Science*, Oxford: Clarendon.

                        1984. *Intimations of Reality*, Notre Dame: Univ. of Notre Dame Press.

Penrose, R.   1981. 'Time asymmetry and quantum gravity', in *Quantum Gravity 2*,
                        eds. C.J. Isham, D.W. Sciama, R. Penrose, Oxford: Clarendon Press.

                        1987. 'Newton, quantum theory, and reality', in *Three Hundred Years
                        of Gravitation*, eds. S.W. Hawking, W. Israel, Cambridge: Cambridge
                        Univ. Press.

Peters, T.   1984. 'Cosmos and Creation', *Word and World* 4: 372-390.

Plomp, H.R.   1987. 'Het heelal als hemel-en-aarde? - Kosmologie en theologie', in
                        De plaats van aarde en mens in het heelal, M.A. Maurice, J.W.
                        Hovenier, H.J. Boersma, P.P. Kirschenmann en H.R. Plomp, Kampen:
                        Kok.

Polkinghorne, J.   1986. *One World: The Interaction of Science and Theology*, Princeton:
                        Princeton Univ. Press.

Raingard, P.   1934. *Le Peri tou Prosopou de Plutarque,* Chartres.

Restivo, S.   1984. *The Social Relations of Physics, Mysticism, and Mathematics*,
                        Dordrecht: Reidel.

Russell, R.J.   1984. 'Entropy and evil', *Zygon* 19: 449-468.

                        1988. 'Contingency in physics and cosmology: a critique of the
                        theology of Wolfhart Pannenberg', *Zygon* 23: 23-43.

                        1989. 'Cosmology, creation and contingency', in *Cosmos as Creation*,
                        ed. T. Peters, Nashville: Abingdon.

Schwarz, J.H.   1987. 'Superstring unification', in *Three Hundred Years of Gravitation,*
                        eds. S.W. Hawking, W. Israel, Cambridge: Cambridge Univ. Press.

Soskice, J.M.   1985. *Metaphor and Religious Language*, Oxford: Clarendon Press.

Swinburne, R.   1979. *The Existence of God*, Oxford: Oxford Univ. Press.

Thiemann, R.F.   1985. *Revelation and Theology*, Notre Dame: Univ. of Notre Dame
                        Press.

Torrance, T.F.   1981. 'Divine and contingent order', in *The Sciences and Theology in
                        the Twentieth century*, ed. A. R. Peacocke, Notre Dame: Univ. of Notre
                        Dame Press.

Updike, J.   1986. *Roger's Version*, New York: Alfred Knopf.

Vilenkin, A.   1986. 'Boundary conditions in quantum cosmology', *Physical Review
                        D* 33: 3560-3569.

WCC   1987a. *Reintegrating God's creation,* Church and Society Documents
   (World Council   No. 3 (September 1987), Geneva: WCC.
   of Churches)   1987b. *Report and Background Papers: Meeting of the Working Group
                        Glion, Switzerland, September 1987*, Geneva: WCC.

                        1987c. *Church and society newsletter,* No. 8, December 1987.

Weinberg, S.   1977. *The First Three Minutes*, New York: Basic Books.

Zeldovich, Y.B.,   1984. 'Quantum creation of a universe with nontrivial topology', *Soviet
   Starobinsky A.A.   Astronomy Letters* 10: 135-137.

J. Van der Veken, philosopher,
Professor of metaphysics and the philosophy of God, Hoger Instituut voor Wijsbegeerte
(Institute of philosophy), Katholieke Universiteit Leuven,
Leuven, Belgium

God's world and man becoming: how can science possibly help us transcend dogmatism?

Jan Van der Veken

'You cannot shelter theology from science, or science from theology; nor can you shelter either of them from metaphysics, or metaphysics from either of them'(*RM* 76-77)*.

This is a clear statement made by Alfred North Whitehead in his *Religion in the Making*. In order to understand it fully, we must first see how, according to Whitehead, science, religion and metaphysics are related and interact. Then we will have to turn to the meaning of dogma and dogmatism. So we are preparing ourselves to see how the metamorphosis of science, which is taking place before our eyes, may help us to transcend a certain kind of dogmatism, i.e. to transcend a certain way of expressing what is disclosed in religious experience in a dogmatic formula, which by necessity is borrowed from a metaphysical and cosmological framework that is no longer our own. Finally I will give a contemporary, concrete example, which is more illuminating than bare methodological assertions.

1. The interpenetration of human interests

Whitehead recognizes that there are various human interests: science, aesthetics, ethics, religion. Each of these interests 'contributes its own independent evidence, which metaphysics must take account of in framing its description' (*RM* 76, where the statement is specifically applied to religion). He stresses that 'Religion, ... while in the framing of dogmas it must admit modifications from the complete circle of our knowledge, still ... brings its own contribution of immediate experience'(*RM* 77).

So it is obvious from the start that religion for Whitehead is in no way *based* upon scientific evidence or upon evidence derived from a scientific outlook on reality. Rather, the heart of the religious experience, according to Whitehead, is the 'direct intuition of a

---

*   In this article the general use is adopted of referring to the works of Alfred North Whitehead by standard abbreviations, such as AI, RM, SMW, directly followed by the relevant page number(s); see works cited at the end of this article.

righteousness in the nature of things'(*RM* 62), 'the recognition that our existence is more than a succession of bare facts'(*RM* 77).

I think that it is important to begin by stressing Whitehead's recognition of the relative autonomy of religion, since very often Whitehead is interpreted as basing belief in God on some cosmological proof of God's existence. That such a proof could still be considered possible in our age seems an awkward suggestion to those philosophers who have learned from Kant the difference between the phenomenal and the noumenal worlds. They hold that science is solely concerned with the world of phenomena, where sense experience is always implied but God never appears, since - if he exists - he is in principle a noumenal reality. And those philosophers inspired by the later Wittgenstein would be even more surprised - and even upset - to hear someone speaking about the influence of science on religion, since Wittgenstein has taught that science and religion are quite different language games and that the worst that can happen to philosophers is that they confuse languages.

And this is why it is important to emphasize that Whitehead takes account of the independent evidence of religious experience, as he stresses several times. He recognizes that the various human interests suggest a cosmology or a view of the world. Our outlook on reality is in fact a joint production, arising out of these varying sources. Each human experience suggests its own outlook and tends to be totalitarian unless it is put into balance by the evidences derived from our other interests. As we shall see, it tends to make a dogmatism out of its dogmas.

Religion, more specifically, tends to encompass all spheres of life. This is even truer in a primitive culture, where religion has an overriding importance (as Durkheim has argued), and where the various human interests are not yet clearly differentiated. But this feature is in no way only characteristic of primitive cultures. It may be said that the most salient characteristic of modern culture is an all-encompassing - and thus an almost religious - belief in the theoretical worth and the practical possibilities of the sciences. 'The mentality of an epoch springs from the view of the world which [has been], in fact, dominant in the educated sectors of the communities in question'(*SMW* vii). There is no doubt that, for Whitehead, the dominant mentality of modern times has been a boundless respect for the newly discovered (Newtonian) science. Whitehead considers this an example of a successful 'provincial' limitation.

The task of philosophy is to harmonize, refashion and justify our divergent intuitions about the nature of things. For Whitehead, the proper task of philosophy is to scrutinize the ultimate ideas that are used by every epoch to frame its overall outlook on reality - what we call cosmology - and to criticize any onesidedness in order that the whole of our evidences may be retained. 'Philosophy ... is the critic of cosmologies'(*SMW* vii).

The result of all this is that 'you cannot confine any important reorganization to one sphere of thought alone'(*RM* 76). And this is why 'You cannot shelter theology from science, or science from theology ....'(*RM* 76). As we will see, this is also why important developments in the sciences necessarily have some impact upon our dogmatic religious frameworks. But it is the heart of dogmatism not to open itself to such conceptual revision.

Thus, a religion that shelters itself from all other evidence - that is, limits itself to one specific sphere of experience and remains within its own language game - produces in the end only 'pleasing emotions and agreeable conduct'(*RM* 74): such would be merely an 'aesthetic' religion.

2. Dogma and dogmatism

And what is the role of dogma in religion? Dogma is not a very popular word. It should not be identified, however, with dogmatism. Whitehead remarks: ' .... it is natural for sensitive thinkers to minimize religious dogmas'(*RM* 74). But such pragmatic reasons are dangerous guides. Whitehead stresses the importance of dogma which for him 'is the precise enunciation of a general truth, divested so far as possible from particular exemplification'(*RM* 122). A religious dogma is an attempt 'to formulate in precise terms the truths disclosed in the religious experience of mankind'(*RM* 57). But dogma is a term of very broad application, in no way limited to religion: 'In exactly the same way the dogmas of the physical sciences are the attempts to formulate in precise terms the truths disclosed in the sense perception of mankind' (*RM* 57).

There seems to be a tension, however, between the direct apprehension of a basic truth about the universe and its formulation in precise terms. 'We know more of the characters of those who are dear to us than we can express accurately in words'(*RM* 123). 'A one-sided formulation may be true, but may have the effect of a lie by its distortion of emphasis'(*RM* 123). Therefore, 'an ill-balanced zeal for the propagation of dogma bears witness to a certain coarseness of aesthetic sensitiveness. It shows a strain of indifference - due perhaps to arrogance, perhaps to rashness, perhaps to mere ignorance - that is, a strain of indifference to the fact that others may require a proportion of formulation different from that suitable for ourselves. Perhaps our pet dogmas require correction: they may even be wrong'(*RM* 123-124).

Here we see how the pejorative term 'dogmatism' emerges: 'The modern unfavourable implications of the kindred words, dogma, dogmatic, dogmatist, tell the story of some failures in habits of thought'(*RM* 124). Of necessity, a dogma is expressed within a framework; it is borrowed from a definite sphere of thought and cannot be detached from that sphere of thought. In order to understand it, 'you must also understand the system of thought to which it is relevant'(*RM* 125): 'You cannot claim absolute finality for a dogma without claiming a commensurate finality for the sphere of thought within which it arose'(*RM* 126). Hence a 'dogma - in the sense of a precise statement - can never be final; it can only be adequate in its adjustment of certain abstract concepts'(*RM* 126).

'Progress in truth - truth of science and truth of religion - is mainly progress in the framing of concepts, in discarding artificial abstractions or partial metaphors, and in evolving notions which strike more deeply into the root of reality'(*RM* 127).

To summarize the meanings of the notions we are employing: a dogma is a general truth that by necessity is expressed in words and schemes borrowed from an overall conceptual framework. Dogmatism is the excessive trust in the adequacy of *any* conceptual framework to account fully for the concrete richness of experience.

3. Strange alliances

Now we are much better equipped to tackle the most basic religious dogma: 'Today there is but one religious dogma in debate: What do you mean by 'God'? And in this respect, today is like all its yesterdays'(*RM* 66). From all that has been said so far, it follows that - and without doubt Whitehead would agree - any contemporary philosophical understanding of God will be seriously inadequate insofar as it refuses to consider what contemporary science has to tell us about the world and about man's place in the cosmos. The following quote from Maurice Merleau-Ponty could have come just as fittingly from Whitehead: 'Whatever one's conception of philosophy, its business is to elucidate experience, and science is a sector of our experience ....'('the Concept of Nature, I' in *Themes from the Lectures,* p. 84). I propose to illustrate, therefore, the above-stated theoretical, epistemological framework by examining a concrete problem that clearly shows that a new understanding of man's place in the universe bears directly upon the way the relationship between God and the world may be adequately conceptualized.

A curious and intriguing 'reversal of covenants' has taken place. In the modern cosmological framework bequeathed to us by Descartes and Newton, there is no ontological continuity between man or world and God. The world is a mechanistic whole. God imposes his laws upon matter simply because he has chosen to do so. He intervenes to prevent the planets from collapsing into one another due to their own gravity, and from time to time he adjusts their trajectories. A God who must function in such a cosmology is, in fact, an a-cosmic God who occasionally 'intervenes'. This idea of a two-level universe is borrowed in fact from Greek philosophy, and the new findings of science were uncritically integrated within this framework. Newton takes for granted that two different spheres of reality exist: the mechanistic universe and the purely spiritual God (who has, nonetheless, this universe with its space and time as his 'sensorium', or seat of sensations).

What can possibly be the place of life, of consciousness and of man *in this universe*? Given such a framework, the origin of life is, for the believer, the result of divine intervention. For the nonbeliever, it is nothing other than the result of chance. Now, although the believer and nonbeliever are clearly opposed insofar as their ultimate interpretations of reality are concerned, they do hold one very basic assumption in common, and therefore we may consider them as 'allies': they both assume that life arose unexpectedly, that it came as a surprise. For both the believer and the nonbeliever, a lifeless universe is far more plausible.

According to the believer, the emergence of life, with all its rich complexities, from the inorganic, mechanistic world is clear evidence that a supra-cosmic creator is at work. He can conceive of no way that inorganic matter could generate life. Louis Pasteur attempted to prove the impossibility of 'generatio spontanea' - an attempt that had clearly religious overtones. A nonbeliever in God, who in fact is a believer in a mechanistic universe, accepts the same premise as the religious believer so far as cosmology is concerned. But because he has recourse to no other ontological level, he offers as his solution an appeal to chance, however implausible such a solution may seem. Jacques Monod, in his much discussed book *Chance and Necessity: An Essay on the Natural Philosophy of Modern Biology*, offers just such a solution. The emergence of life is the most improbable event that could occur. Rejecting in principle as a scientific explanation any directedness towards an aim (be it more complex structures or consciousness or whatever else), there is only one way out: this whole, impressive cosmic adventure is *nothing other* than the result of chance.

Thus, although their conclusions differ greatly, Descartes, Newton and Monod form a strange alliance: all are mechanists, while some are also other-worldly spiritualists. And Monod finds, as his opponents, both Teilhard de Chardin *and* dialectical materialists. Again, what a strange alliance!

What divides the two camps, then, is clearly not belief in God - since believers and nonbelievers are found in both camps - but cosmology. In the cosmologies of Newton *and* Monod, life is unexpected, improbable. Newton and Monod, as allies, share the same worldview. What separates them is the belief in the existence of another world, as held by Newton. But because he holds a mechanistic worldview, Newton (or any deist) must believe - if he believes - in an a-cosmic, wholly transcendent God. In the end, the common world of everyday experience must be such that it can be explained without any recourse to (such a) God. Pierre Simon de Laplace has drawn this conclusion with respect to the trajectories of the planets, Monod with respect to the emergence of life. Newton, like all deists, is a dualist; Monod is a materialistic monist. The problem with dualism is that it contains within itself the seed of materialistic monism. For if God is not at all present in the world, then the world, in the end, will be conceived without God.

4. A rewarding dialogue

As I said, Teilhard de Chardin *and* dialectical materialists are Monod's opponents, since they share another, non-mechanistic outlook on reality. (Monod belittlingly calls their view 'animistic'.) According to Teilhard, the world is permeated through and through with consciousness, so that the emergence of complex structures does not come as a surprise at all; rather, given the fundamental 'law of complexification', this emergence is to be expected. More complex structures are indeed probable, and hence not merely a matter of chance.

Of course, dialectical materialists do not believe in the intervention of a divine creator; but they equally reject a mechanistic conception of matter, since a nondialectical mechanism cannot account for the emergence of qualitatively new levels of organization. Dialectical materialists enrich the notion of matter by projecting onto it all that is necessary to account for the emergence of more complex structures, including life and consciousness. For them, as well, the emergence of life is a probable event. Again, what a strange alliance! An alliance between a God-believing Jesuit, who was not allowed during his lifetime to publish his seemingly revolutionary insights, and atheistic DIAMAT, dialectical materialism, the keeper of the official doctrine of the Soviet Communist Party. How are we to understand such a strange situation?

The word 'alliance' holds the key. In the context of this lecture, alliance, indeed, has a third meaning - a meaning essential to an understanding of Monod's position, and essential as well to an understanding of the real importance of a work that has sometimes been called the 'anti-Monod': Ilya Prigogine and Isabelle Stengers entitled their work *La nouvelle alliance. Métamorphose de la science.* It is a pity that the word 'alliance' has been stripped from the titles of the English and Dutch translations. For the meaning of the book's title is: yes, there is between man and nature an alliance in the literal sense of the word. Such a view is an important break with the positions of Newton, Laplace and Monod - in short, with any mechanistic conception of the universe. Since mechanists conceive of no alliance between the universe and man, their only possible explanations for the emergence of life are either chance or the intervention of an a-cosmic God. Those who conceive of an alliance between the universe, consciousness and man - Teilhard, dialectical materialists, the authors of *La nouvelle alliance*, and of course Whitehead - have less difficulty understanding how life could emerge from matter, or consciousness from the lesser forms of life. After all, life and consciousness permeate the whole universe. Thus the God of such a religious believer is far more immanent than the wholly transcendent God of Newton, who intervenes in an inconceivable way. Nonmechanists have moved beyond the dogmatism of a two-stage universe which, in fact, is nothing other than the superposition of a wholly transcendent God upon a mechanistic and material universe. But nonbelievers, such as dialectical materialists, have equally moved beyond their form of dogmatism and have rejected a wholly mechanistic universe as completely inadequate to account for the emergence of qualitatively different structures. For this reason a dialogue between dialectical materialists and, say, 'holistic God-believers' would be far more rewarding than a dialogue between either of these and those who, for dogmatic reasons, stick to a bygone form of scientism!

Conclusion:

And so we have come, full circle, back to our point of departure. Although science itself cannot determine whether belief in God is justified or whether, say, a dialectical conception of matter contains the whole solution to the problem of the emergence of life, a certain scientific outlook on reality - as it becomes more probable - may help us to overcome those conceptualizations of religious belief that are tied up with a particular, bygone cosmology.

It seems to me that a scientific outlook that favours continuity between so-called inorganic nature and life, between organized matter and consciousness, and between other forms of life and man has indeed become highly probable. And if man is the best 'image' of God that the religious believer finds in this world, then it is obvious that God cannot be conceived as a complete stranger to the cosmic game either. Rather, God should be conceived as the 'counteragency' at work in reality itself that accounts for a directedness towards higher forms of order.

Of course, the believer will want to say much more about God - and this, on the basis of his religious experience. He will, above all, recognize God's face where he is summoned to practice justice and to obey ethical claims. This is well beyond what science can possibly investigate. But in *conceptualizing* his belief in God, the believer cannot proceed as if he lives in a world completely different from the one disclosed by contemporary science. Hence, he should not shelter his religious faith from science or metaphysics. And he might well have to transcend certain kinds of dogmatism that are remnants of a conception of the universe that is no longer his own: 'The progress of religion is defined by the denunciation of gods. The keynote of idolatry is contentment with the prevalent gods' (*AI* 11).

Works cited

Maurice Merleau-Ponty, *Themes from the Lectures at the College de France, 1952-1960*, translation by John O'Neill, Northwestern University Press, Evanston 1970.

Jacques Monod, *Chance and Necessity: An Essay on the Natural Philosophy of Modern Biology*, translation by Austryn Wainhouse, Collins, London 1972.

Ilya Prigogine and Isabelle Stengers, *La nouvelle alliance. Métamorphose de la science* (2nd. ed.), Gallimard, Paris 1986.

Alfred North Whitehead, *Adventures of Ideas,* The Macmillan Company, London/New York 1933, 1961; abbreviation *AI*.

Alfred North Whitehead, *Religion in the Making*, The Macmillan Company, London/New York 1926, 1954, and the World Publishing Company, Meridian Books, New York/Cleveland 1971; abbreviation *RM*; 7th edition quoted.

Alfred North Whitehead, *Science and the Modern World*, Lowell Lectures 1925, The Macmillan Company, New York 1925, 1953; abbreviation *SMW*.

O. Pedersen, physicist,
Professor of the history of science, Aarhus Universitet,
Aarhus, Denmark

Historical interaction between science and religion

Olaf Pedersen

1. Introduction

The present talk about the divorce of science and religion takes very much for granted. It presupposes that there is such a thing as religion without further qualifications just as it assumes that there is such a thing as science pure and simple. Moreover, it postulates that these two entities are not only distinct and separate, but even divorced through a process upon which we can look back in retrospect as something that took place in a more or less distant past. Here the underlying assumption must be that there was a time when science and religion could have been said to be happily married, or at least living together in some kind of intimate relationship. So many hidden presuppositions might easily give the impression that this whole subject is utterly confused and in great need of both philosophical and historical clarification. It goes without saying that this cannot be achieved within the compass of a brief contribution. In consequence the purpose of the following paper is only to present a few comments on the notions of science and religion, followed by a consideration of some of their principal interactions throughout history, before we decide whether a divorce must be granted on the grounds of an ineradicable incompatibility of spirit, or if there is a simple case for annulment because there never was a valid marriage, or finally, if the relationship can continue without foundering on the rocks of the unequal development of the two partners.

On the term 'religion' a mere historian of science cannot have much to say except that it seems to be a very loose-fitting one, and that it is not clear what it stands for in the sense in which it is conjoined with the term 'science' in our present subject. There are a great many religions in the world; some of them are even world religions that have been able to appeal to many different ages and varieties of human civilizations. Is the religion of the title of this paper a kind of common denominator of the doctrines spread over the whole of this grand religious spectrum? Or is it a hypothetical, common religious attitude that pervades the actual religious communities regardless of specific creeds or concrete beliefs? Or is it perhaps the ghost of the fictitious natural religion of all human kind so beloved by the philosophers of the Enlightenment? Unfortunately, I have to set aside all these questions, being familiar only with the the Christian religion, and also seriously doubting that one can gain appropriate insights into a religion, the faith and practice of which one has never shared. In consequence I must restrict my contribution to the topic of science and Christianity. However, I do not consider this to be a damaging restriction. For even if it is true - as I think it is - that, for instance, ancient Indian science was closely connected with Indian religion, this does not alter the fact that today the whole world is adopting a specific scientific system which grew to maturity within the pale of Christendom. It follows that, from a purely historical point of view, it would be apposite to speak of a 'Christian science' in analogy to the generally recognised concept of 'Islamic science', were it not for the fact that Christian Science has become the name of a new religion and is disqualified as a generic term. Of course, the rather bleak 'Western science' is but a poor substitute. This narrowing down of the perspective is not to say that the development of science has not been influenced from outside the Christian world from where it has indeed received many important stimuli, just as it originated in the Greek world long before the advent of Christianity. But it shows that to investigate the development of science against the background of the religious system in which it grew up, that is, the Christian Faith and its concomitant theological expressions as they, too, have developed over the ages, is undoubtedly to tackle a problem of special interest.

It seems to become more and more necessary to adopt a very broad view of the notion of science. Many of the difficulties in coming to terms with the problem of science and religion appear to stem from a concept of science that is too narrow and too clear-cut, and that describes science as a well-defined activity that is directed towards a single purpose and approaches its goal using a single method of investigation. This picture of science does not agree with that of the historian of science who must recognise the existence of several types of scientific discourse, each of which gives rise to its own problems when confronted with the religious discourse of different historical periods. To get a clear picture of the principal modes of scientific discourse we could do much worse than go back to the very infancy of science.

2. The linguistic birththroes of science

All ancient civilizations have left evidence of a stage of intellectual development in which the discourse about nature was framed in the ordinary language of interpersonal communication between human beings living together in societies. In consequence nature was conceived as a kind of state or society, ruled by more or less powerful gods possessed of intelligence, free-will and emotions, often of a very human kind. Each of them governed a specific part, either of the natural world or of human society, by his or her personal decisions. The arbitrary will of the gods was behind everything and served as an intelligible explanation of natural phenomena. For example, the low sun in wintertime was explained among the Greeks by saying that the sun god, Helios, had gone away to the southern land of the Ethiopians, as Hesiod tells us[1]. Thus, the discourse on nature became a discourse on the gods in the form of mythical stories which Plato named 'theologia' in the only place where this term appears in his writings[2], just as Aristotle mentions Homer, Hesiod and the mythical Orpheus as 'the ancient writers who were concerned with theology'[3]. One immediate consequence of this mythological discourse on nature was that the story about the origin of the world took the form of a genealogy of the gods. Cosmogony became theogony and creation was explained in terms of procreation.

The mythological discourse on nature made man familiar with its forces. Whether they were benign or malign they could be described in ordinary human language and approached like human beings through supplications, gifts, or by forcible means (i.e., magic). Nature and society formed a whole. And the same language served this whole; there was no other. Nevertheless, there came a time when this unified, or rather non-diversified, discourse was deemed unsatisfactory, presumably because it could provide no reason for the regularity of many natural phenomena: if winter came because the sun-god had decided to take a holiday in the south, who could be certain that he would also decide to return when the farmers needed him? Thus the essential freedom of the gods became problematic. The priests who tried to persuade the gods to behave through prayer and sacrifice, together with the augurs who tried to divine their secret decisions, were challenged by a new kind of 'philosopher' who tried to explain the regularity of nature by a new idea of an inherent necessity in nature that forced the phenomena to appear without divine assistance. The story of this intellectual revolution forms one of the principal chapters of any history of science or philosophy and need not be repeated here, where there is time for only two general observations. First, notwithstanding all the information provided by the history of science on the mathematics, astronomy and medicine of earlier cultures, there is no doubt whatsoever that the first scientific revolution originated in the Greek world. Secondly, it met with purely linguistic difficulties of a very serious nature which were solved in different ways that have marked the discourse on nature ever since.

The first philosophers were groping with a dawning insight into an inherent necessity in nature. But how could this insight be expressed in a personalistic language that was tuned to reflect the essential freedom of divine and human beings? In fact, the new philosophic or scientific insight would seem to be homeless in ordinary language. One way out of this difficulty was to use words from ordinary language, forcing them to serve metaphorically in the new sense that was imposed on them, and that was by no means obvious. For example, Herodotus launched a theory that the annual inundation of the Nile was due neither to the god of the Nile nor to the Ethesian winds blowing from the north. It had the annual motion of the sun, as a physical body, as its 'aitia'[4]. In ordinary language the word aitia meant the guilt that a criminal brought upon himself by committing his offence, so what Herodotus seemed to say was that the sun was a criminal and a habitual one at that. What he really meant was that the sun was the cause of the inundation; naturally, it would take some time before this philosophical meaning of the word would be recognised along with the new conception of nature as an impersonal whole governed by laws of necessity. Even the fundamental notion of necessity was expressed by the word 'ananke' which also had judicial connotations as denoting the forcible means by which an accused person was made to confess[5]. Examples of such transformations of the old ordinary language into a new scientific medium are legion; a whole catalogue of such metaphorical terms was published by Aristotle in the *Metaphysics*[6].

A quite different solution to this linguistic problem was found by the so-called Pythagoreans, as Aristotle called them[7]. There is no reason to doubt the tradition that the Pythagorean philosophers performed real acoustic experiments with string and wind instruments, discovering that the harmonic intervals of the musical scales could be represented by mathematical relations between small integer numbers such as 2:1 for the octave, 3:2 for the fifth, and 4:3 for the fourth. The significance this discovery is not just that it resulted from perhaps the first physical experiments on record in history. It is much more significantly that here two classes of phenomena, in this case the length of strings and the pitch of sounds, proved to be connected by a relation that could be stated in purely mathematical terms without the use of any metaphorical language at all. This was one of the most consequential discoveries of all time; as such it has also impressed the philosophers who have always had a tendency to consider any use of mathematical language in discourse on nature as a Pythagorean characteristic. But this view is simplistic, for already among the early Pythagoreans mathematical discourse had taken two very different forms. The experiments in acoustics led to a new insight that could be obtained and expressed only by using mathematical language *a posteriori* to the empirical evidence. But when the Pythagoreans went further with the assumption that the velocities of the planets in their orbits could also be described by the harmonic ratios previously known from acoustics, they obviously used the language of mathematics in an *a priori* way by forcing a given mathematical structure upon a department of nature in which there was no evidence of its applicability.

Here there is no need to go into the details of the subsequent discussion about the proper way to account for the phenomena of nature using linguistic tools of one kind or another, tools that could accommodate the fundamental scientific assumption of the inherent necessity in nature. Generally speaking it established three major epistemological traditions, each of which was connected with a distinct ontology and implied special relations between science and religion.

3. Three great traditions

The Platonic tradition appeared as the inheritor of one of the two trends of the Pythagorean philosophy of nature. Plato argued, for instance, for the existence of no more than, and no less than, four material elements. He did this in two ways, both of which had as the point of departure an already known mathematical structure, viz., the theory of proportions or the geometrical properties of the regular solids. These structures were applied to nature in a purely *a priori* manner, as if the material world must be structured according to mathematical principles such that mathematical relations between phenomena can be stated without reference to experience, at least in principle, and notwithstanding the evidence that at least some acoustical experiments were carried out in the Academy. Plato's view was intimately connected with the ontological theory that the mathematical forms belong to the invisible, immaterial and unchanging world of ideas which is the only real and permanent world, in contradistinction to the ever-changing world of phenomena. In the course of time, this tradition often degenerated into pure numerology or number mysticism.

The Aristotelian tradition continued and developed the approach of the Ionian philosophers, adopting their metaphorical discourse on nature, and framing it in metaphysical terms such as matter and form, substance and accident, and cause and effect, the latter pair being most fundamental of all. For Aristotle all '(intellectual) knowledge deals with causes and principles'[8], and the object of scientific research is 'the causes of the phenomena'[9]. No scientific account of a natural phenomenon can be complete until it has disclosed all four types of causes that have produced it - the material, formal, efficient, and final causes. The search for a final cause presupposes that nature operates to a purpose; yet there are numerous fortuitous events of which no final cause seems to exist, although they certainly have an efficient cause; an example is an eclipse of the moon or the sun[10]. The Aristotelian conception of science is dependent on an ontology of substances that differs sharply from Plato's ontology of ideas. Individuals do not belong to the same species because they participate in the same separate idea, but rather because they are constituted by a uniting of matter with the same form. This form does not exist in a separate world but resides in the substances themselves; from them it can be known through sense experience processed, as it were, by abstractive and integrative reasoning. Consequently, all natural knowledge presupposes sense experience.

While the Platonic and the Aristotelian traditions have always been recognised by philosophers, there arose also a third tradition which has been much more neglected. Although in reality it goes back to the *a posteriori* trend of Pythagorean philosophy, it is more convenient to call it an Archimedeian tradition, partly in order to avoid confusion, but partly also because its epistemological characteristics and cognitive power are best illustrated in Archimedes' two extant treatises on the mechanical problems of the equilibrium of solid bodies. These treatises were shaped in a precise mathematical form resembling that of the *Elements* of Euclid, in contrast to the ordinary language of the discourse of both Plato and Aristotle. In consequence they have often been relegated to the realm of mathematics, although they have obviously an empirical point of departure. They belong, therefore, to a class of sciences which Aristotle called intermediary, that is, one lying between physics and mathematics, since they describe relations between physical phenomena by means of mathematical relations. While Aristotle was strongly opposed to Platonic numerology, he admitted that such sciences were authentic because of their empirical presuppositions. But, at the same time, he considered them to be incomplete since the relevant mathematical discourse was unable to reach out to the final causes. It seemed to follow that this incipient mathematical physics could have no ethical implications and was irrelevant to the ultimate purpose of philosophy, considered as the guide to the good life of man and society. Nevertheless, these sciences must be of very special interest since they have proved capable of producing truths that have resisted the course of time much better than the statements resulting from the metaphorical and metaphysical discourse of the Aristotelians. Aristotle, who could not foresee this, was unable to find any form of wisdom in them. All the same, the overwhelming success of the Archimedean approach in all subsequent times calls for our careful consideration before it is branded as irrelevant to a proper understanding of the human situation. To this problem we shall have to return on several occasions.

It goes without saying that the new scientific discourse on nature made the old gods of nature obsolete. In fact, the philosophical movement in Hellas went hand in hand with a critique of the Olympic religion. Already Heraclitus found that many of the doings of the gods were shameful, and Xenophanes ridiculed the anthropomorphic concept of the gods of the popular religions. Here we meet with the first instance of a crisis between religion and science in which each of the three major traditions participated in significantly different ways, but always with the same result: as explanations of the phenomena of nature the old gods of nature had to go. To the extent that this explanatory role had been their one and only function, they were removed from the discourse on the universe. To the extent that they survived the scientific revolution, they fulfilled other functions. This explains the motley picture of Greek religious thought from the fourth century onwards. We now meet various schools of sceptics who denied any links between the gods and the world. At the same time, however, old and new mystery religions became more popular, being more concerned with the personal religious life than with the running of the universe.

Thus the scientific movement seemed to create a religious vacuum which its protagonists tried to fill by various attempts to accommodate the idea of God to the new discourse on nature. In Plato this led to a theory of the creation of the world by 'God'. But this God is not the highest principle or origin of the universe, only its architect and as such only a servant of the idea of the Good. Creation proceeds in steps; first, a number of lesser gods are created as assistants of the demiurge; they are responsible for making the various parts of the world, beginning with the four elements. Among these lesser gods we find some of the traditional Olympic deities, although without their earlier function as guardians of individual classes of natural phenomena.

Placing the concept of God in a very different perspective, Aristotle regarded the world as an eternal and uncreated structure of substances, the changes of which could be scientifically analysed in terms of cause and effect, all causes depending in the end on the ultimate cause which is itself uncaused and unchangeable and as such outside the material world of the elements. This first cause is 'God' who is thought to reside in the outermost sphere of the universe as an immaterial force that keeps the whole world going so that the various purposes of nature are fulfilled. So where Plato had used the idea of God to explain the origin of the world, Aristotle used it to explain its unity and continuous existence. In both cases the discourse on nature and God used the notion of causality as its logical tool. This explains why the Archimedean tradition with its lack of causal explanations was unable to make any independent contributions to this debate.

4. The advent of the gospel

When Christianity began to spread from Israel into the Mediterranean world, it was in some ways in a situation similar to that of the Ionian philosophers six hundred years earlier. It tried to convey a fundamentally new insight which the established language was unable to express in adequate terms. This time it was not an insight into the operations of the natural world but the conviction that the fundamental relations between God and the world had been radically influenced by the birth, life, death and resurrection of Jesus. But how this had come about was a mystery that could not be expressed fully. In consequence, the first theological language became just as metaphorical as the first scientific language had been. Thus St. Paul tried to describe the achievement of Christ as a salvation of the world, borrowing a word that originally belonged to medical language where it signified that a crisis had passed, and the patient was on the way to recovery. Alternatively he might use a term from the social institution of slavery, speaking of the world as being redeemed from slavery under sin, Jesus having paid the ransom demanded by law. St. Paul seems to have been fully aware that all such linguistic experiments were inadequate and metaphorical; he was speaking 'in a human manner'[11], and the Christian message must seem a 'scandal to the Jews and foolishness to the Greeks'[12]. Therefore, the new insight must remain a mystery - not because it was not public or had to be kept a secret, like the rituals of the Pagan mysteries, but because no human language was able to express it fully.

The public character of the Christian proclamation as addressed to both Greeks and Barbarians made it necessary to enter into some kind of dialogue with the intellectual world outside the early Church. It began very slowly. There is no cosmological treatise in the New Testament. This might be construed as a conscious rejection of science in favour of the one thing that was necessary: the proclamation of the Gospel. However, one can safely assume that, if there had been a radical incompatibility between Christian insight and scientific discourse, it would have left clear traces in the Apostolic writings. The very absence of a sustained polemic against Greek science shows that there were no serious objections to its basic assumptions. In fact, only such special features as magic and divination (in particular astrology) were attacked as idolatrous remnants of the old religions of the gods of nature.

Nevertheless, the New Testament contained a number of passages that were destined to become points of departure for that interaction between theology and science which would inevitably occur when the Church made proselytes among the educated; and so much more so, when the Church began to provide its own Christian education in a world that had not come to the quick end that was originally expected. First of all there was the belief that there is NO IDOL IN THE WORLD*, and (that) THERE IS NO GOD EXCEPT ONE[13], which Christianity had inherited from Judaism. This meant that Nature was demythologised just as radically as in Greek philosophy, although in a different way. In consequence, Christianity had no dissenting comments on the basic presupposition of Greek philosophy of nature; they agreed on the belief that natural phenomena were not arbitrary effects of the old gods of nature that simply did not exist. Science was perfectly compatible with a monotheistic religion that recognised in some way or other the existence of laws of nature as instituted by the one and only God, and as upheld by His providence.

Secondly, the One God was the LORD OF HEAVEN AND EARTH [WHO] HAD MADE THE WORLD AND ALL THINGS THEREIN[14]. This belief in creation expressed the insight that the world was wholly derived from and dependent upon God, or, in negative terms, that man had no part in its establishment and no share in the glory of its creator, just as both the Book of Job and many of the Psalms had explained. This meant that the doctrine of creation had

---

*   'No idol is *anything* in the world' or 'no idol has a real existence'.

no immediate cosmological consequences; St. Paul and other New Testament authors were singularly uninterested in questions about the physical origin of the universe which the Greek philosophers had so eagerly discussed. Their approach was entirely theological and intimately connected with the belief that the redemption in Christ meant a 'new creation'. As time went on it became increasingly difficult to uphold this soteriological understanding of creation against the desire to be informed of what really happened 'in the beginning'. The result was a long series of discussions, all through the Patristic age, of whether or not the question of the physical origin of the world could be answered on the basis of the creation stories in Genesis 1 and 2. Thus, much of the time of the Fathers was occupied by disputation, for instance, of whether the six days of creation were ordinary days or symbolic expressions for longer priods of time.

The relations between God and the world were further illuminated by two other seminal ideas of the New Testament. When St. John stressed: 'No man has ever seen God'[15], he said not only that God is invisible, but that He is not to be identified with any natural phenomena at all. There is nothing divine in the things we see around us, however great an impression they make upon our senses or imagination. God is transcendent and no created being shares His essence, a doctrine which clearly separated Christianity from Neo-Platonic ideas of the world as an emanation from the Godhead, and which, at the same time, made it possible to study nature scientifically without any fear of intruding upon the precincts of its Creator.

But this radical separation between God and the world was not the whole story, for St. Paul claimed: 'what may be known of God is manifest ... from the creation of the world, being understood by the things that are made, even His eternal power and Godhead'[16]. Time and again this passage has served as the point of departure for a Christian theology of nature as scriptural evidence that in some way God has made Himself known in His created works. This led to long discussions on the *vestigia Dei* - the vestiges of God - which in many ways provided a theological legitimation of the study of nature. Here two different ideas were brought into play. Since St. Paul had maintained that even the Pagans were without excuse for not knowing God from His works, this knowledge must be open to all men, and it is not a distinctly Christian mystery, a conclusion which led to the Scholastic distinction between the *prolegomena* of faith and Faith itself. Secondly, the passage from St. Paul seemed to imply that, if there is a road from nature to God, it must follow the path of our knowledge, not that of our ignorance; gaps in knowledge cannot be loopholes for faith.

Finally, perhaps the strongest and most far-reaching interaction between theology and science was caused by St. John's doctrine of Christ as the logos of the world. When the fourth Gospel begins by saying: IN THE BEGINNING WAS THE LOGOS[17], it sounds like the opening of a Greek philosophical treatise on the 'arche' or principle of the universe. This principle or unifying substratum had already been called 'logos' by Heraclitus and had become prominent in Stoic philosophy as a universal principle of rationality which was immanent in nature, in contradistinction to the rationality which Platonism derived from the separate world of ideas. Now the term 'logos' may mean both an inward reason or an outwardly spoken word. This had enabled Philo of Alexandria to connect the Greek logos with the many passages in which the Old Testament speaks of God's word as the creative force in the universe, and thus to draw the strange conclusion that much Greek philosophy had originated with Moses and the Prophets. It would have been tempting to regard the logos of St. John in much the same way, that is, as a creative power, since 'all things were made by it', just as Hebrews maintained that 'the worlds were framed by the logos of God'[18]. However, the assertion that the logos is not only *with God* as His spoken and creative word, but that it *was God* from the beginning, was a new idea. In fact, the identification of the divine logos with Christ was another Christian mystery which ordinary language was unable to express adequately. Without going into all the problems that arise from this idea, it is sufficient to note here that it made it possible to connect in a fundamental way faith in Christ with the quest for understanding the inherent rationality of nature, or even to see this rationality as a sign of God's immanence in the world.

5. The world of the Fathers

The story of how the seminal ideas of monotheism, creation, *vestigia Dei* and Christ as the *logos* influenced the theology of the Fathers, as well as their attitude towards the scientific discourse on nature, is too complicated to be summarised in a few paragraphs. Here we shall consider only the general setting of this first interaction of theology and science, and two special points on which conflicts were unavoidable. In general Patristic theology dealt with these questions within an overall Platonic framework, not only because this was the general tendency of contemporary Greek thought, but also because the Platonic discourse on nature had an immediate appeal to Christian thought. Plato began his account of the universe with a god in the form of a demiurge who had shaped the world in a process called creation. Christian revelation seemed to be more in harmony with this approach than with the Aristotelian discourse in which God did not appear at the outset, but only at the end and after much philosophical speculation on the problems of knowledge and the chain of causality. 'This is why we prefer the disciples of Plato', said St. Augustine, 'to those other philosophers who toil with their reason in order to search for the cause of things, the guidelines for knowledge, and the rules of life. ... [The Platonists] have, as soon as they have known God, found in Him the cause of the existence of the world, the light in which truth becomes accessible, and the source of all happiness'[19]. There seemed to be more wisdom in Platonism than in Aristotelianism. What wisdom there might be in the Archimedean approach was a problem that the Fathers never really discussed, although Origen, for instance, seems to have been better informed of the latest astronomical ideas (on precession) than most contemporary astronomers and philosophers.

Now the Platonic theory of creation had supposed that the demiurge had shaped the cosmic order out of an original chaos of unstructured matter. This idea was also adopted by early Christian writers like St. Justin, Clement of Alexandria and the unknown author of the *Letter to Diognet*. But already in Origen the idea of pre-existing matter was found to be incompatible with the belief in one God. For, if matter was eternal it would, at least according to Greek thought, also be divine, with the consequence that there would be two eternal beings, i.e. two gods. To avoid this idea it became necessary to develop the doctrine of *creatio ex nihilo*: creation was not construed as an act by which a chaos was shaped into a cosmos, but as an act by which the world was called into being from a state of nothingness; this was another example of the philosophical foolishness of the Faith. It also implied that space must be regarded as created together with matter, since space in the Greek philosophy of nature was construed as that which confines material bodies. But, if there was no space before creation, one had to ask, 'Where was God before the world began?' - a problem with which many of the Fathers toiled without really finding an answer that made it possible to describe the infinity and omnipresence of God in cosmological terms.

The problem of time was even more difficult, and it was also more important, since the Greek philosophy of time directly offended the doctrine of creation. The generally accepted definition described objective time as the 'number of motion'. But , as St. Augustine had said, '(if) time cannot be without motion, who is able to realise that time could not have been before some movable thing was created, by the motion and successive change of which time would go on?'[20]

Consequently the idea of a *creatio ex nihilo* implied that time must have come into being together with matter and space. The world was not created *in* time, but time was created *with* the world. This notion created difficulties in theology with respect to the immutability and eternity of God: what did God do before the world began? Origen had tried to answer this question on the assumption that God had been occupied with another world, different from ours and preceding it in time, just as God would be busy with yet another world when the present one had come to its inevitable end - in agreement with the Aristotelian principle that the generation of a subject entails its ultimate corruption. This idea of a succession of worlds owed something to the common theory that time was cyclical, a theory that the Pythagoreans had imported from the East and that most later Greek philosophers had adopted. As this theory was clearly incompatible with the belief that Christ had died and risen to die no more, St. Augustine was not the least active of those who fought extremely hard to liberate Christian eschatology from the grips of the Greek theory of generation and corruption. In the end, he cut through the problem by a radical separation of the concepts of time and eternity: 'the extent of time is produced by nothing other than the succession of many moments which cannot pass simultaneously. On the contrary, there is nothing successive about eternity: everything is present, while time cannot be present all at once'[21]. In other words, eternity is not a temporal category. It denotes a particular form of being which is the prerogative of God, and it is quite different from the notion of infinite time, or *sempiternitas*; in the words of Boethius, eternity is *the perfect possession of unlimited life all at once*[22].

Thus the first great interaction between Christian theology and natural science had remarkably little to do with the concrete doctrines of Greek science. There were those who objected to the spherical form of the earth like Lactantius who had very few followers; but in general the established view of the cosmos was accepted without reservations, as was also the theory of matter as composed by the four elements. This Greek universe had been born out of a revolt against the gods of nature, and Christian thought had no serious comments upon it. By and large one must say that Christianity left Greek science in peace, thereby no doubt contributing to its own survival. Nevertheless, the interaction was both profound and consequential, and it went both ways. The doctrine of creation *ex nihilo* implied a new conception of the fundamental notions of matter, space and time which greatly extended the possibilities of future scientific investigation. In theology it certainly helped to clarify the problems of belief in God as an eternal Being outside the course of time as we know it. At the same time, it liberated eschatology from the idea of a world that was doomed to destruction by its own nature. Behind all this was the great and immensely fertile idea of Christ as the logos of the world. This was undoubtedly one of the inscrutable mysteries of the Faith; but it was also of extreme importance to science as a revealed assurance that Faith in Christ and belief in the rationality of creation are intimately connected in the total Divine economy.

6. The sanctification of the universe

If the work of the Fathers had established the fundamental principles on which natural science could be integrated into the Christian view of the world, it took a long time before these principles bore visible fruits. One of the reasons was that the scientific revolution of the Greeks had been accomplished by a small elite of philosophers, while the large majority of the population of the ancient world continued to regard nature as the battleground of the gods and the spirits of nature. In the theoretical domain the process of demythologisation of nature was complete; but there was still a long way to go before it was followed by a general change of attitude. That such a change came about was the result of a second interaction between theology and the discourse on nature. This interaction was much slower and more inconspicuous than the one which had taken place in earlier centuries. It was not brought about so much by an expertise in theology as by the popular proclamation of the Gospel, which resulted not only in the conversion of the peoples of Europe to the Christian Faith, but also in the conversion of the faithful to a new attitude towards the natural world, producing a change in the intellectual climate of immediate importance for the general acceptance of the scientific discourse.

There were several elements in this movement. When in the 9th. century, John Scotus Erigena introduced the pseudo-Dionysian writings to the West with their insistence on the negative theology of the *via remotionis*, he also taught his contemporaries how to read the phenomena of nature as symbols and signs of an invisible reality behind them, or as pointers to central tenets of the Faith. Medieval art became imbued with this symbolic approach to nature. The mystery of the Eucharist could be represented by the picture of the pelican which feeds its young on its own blood; or the Virgin Birth of Jesus could be illustrated by the simple worm which is formed directly by the earth without sexual intercourse. Of course, such interpretations may be branded as naive and unscientific; but in actual fact they did encourage people to regard the phenomena of nature as interesting and relevant to the daily life of the believer. When in the 12th. century the amount of concrete knowledge of nature began to increase due to the recovery of the Greek sources of science, a new understanding of the unity of nature made itself felt. The old Platonic soul of the world made a brief reappearance only to be replaced by the idea of the Spirit as the unifying force which penetrates all creation and unites it with God, as the learned St. Hildegard of Bingen expressed it so beautifully in her sequence *O Ignis Spiritus Paracliti*. And not long afterwards, St. Francis of Assisi wrote the *Canto del Sol,* in which the old deities of the sun and the moon together with the base elements of fire and air and water and earth were praised as good creatures of the good God. Clearly nature had now become a safe place and a lovely abode for man, made by God and penetrated by the Holy Spirit. Magic and witchcraft might still thrive as occult practices, and Manichaean distrust in the material world would still raise its head in heretical movements, but it is difficult to deny that at long last a watershed had been passed and that the old and dangerous forces of nature had been cast out from the Christian conscience.

7. God and the Aristotelian discourse on nature

Similarly there is no doubt that this change of attitude towards nature prepared the way for the great intellectual revolution of the thirteenth century when Aristotelianism conquered the schools and universities, turning the traditional view of the relations between the natural and the theological discourse on nature upside down. Christian theology remained what it was in so far as it still took revealed truth as the point of departure for the light it tried to shed upon the world. But Aristotelian metaphysics captured the mind with its attempt to explain the world in terms of substances connected by a network of causal relations which terminated in God as the supreme cause and first mover of everything. This made it possible not only to separate theology from philosophy, but also to establish the *prolegomena fidei* by a philosophical reflection on the material world. This made the study of nature even more relevant to theological enquiry than ever before. And at the same time, we can observe how the Aristotelian philosophy of science helped natural scientists to understand and to apply the principle of experience, even by way of physical experiments; in this manner the study of magnetism became a new branch of physics, just as research in optics resulted in the understanding of lenses and the eye, and led to the invention of spectacles. In all this there was a feeling that the investigation of nature and its causal relations was of immediate relevance to the understanding of the world as God's creation; the metaphor of the Book of Nature as in some ways parallel to the Book of Scripture expressed this idea. That the 13th. century also saw a great expansion of the Archimedean mathematical discourse on nature is well known today; but as it happened, this did not really engage the attention of philosophers and theologians who were still unable to find any road to wisdom in this approach.

Such spectacular developments in both theology and science did not mean that Aristotelianism reigned supreme and unquestioned. Already Albertus Magnus had emphasized that 'Whosoever believes that Aristotle was a god must believe that he never erred; but if one believes him to have been a man, then without doubt he could err just as we can do'[23]. In fact, there was more than one point on which Aristotelian doctrines seemed to prejudice the integrity and purity of Christian theology, and in January 1277 Pope John XXI complained to the bishop of Paris about the heresies that were reported to be rampant in the university. After a rather hasty investigation Bishop Étienne Tempier published a list of no less than 219 propositions that were condemned as heretical, none of them being ascribed to any particular scholar. The list is not too systematic, but it is easy to pick out a number of specific targets for criticism by the bishop; some of them are genuinely Aristotelian doctrines while others refer to a motley of other ideas. A number of the condemned propositions state the astrological belief that everything in the elementary part of the world is governed by the stars, human actions included. Others express the Aristotelian doctrine of the celestial spheres as living beings animated by intelligent souls. Yet others maintain the eternity of matter, motion and time, or the cyclical character of history. One particular proposition states that philosophers may deny the novelty of the world, while believers may deny its eternity - an example of the theory of double truth which was actually held by some Parisian scholars. But the majority of the propositions are concerned with limiting the power of God; God could not have created prime matter without the assistance of the heavenly bodies; He cannot act in nature except through secondary causes; He cannot move the planets in another way than that in which they now move; and God must make of necessity what is immediately made by Him.

The condemnation of 1277 had very far-reaching consequences. First and foremost it taught theologians to be very careful with statements beginning with words like 'God cannot ..'. But this emphasis on the divine omnipotence had to be reconciled with the belief in the world of creation as governed by an inherent necessity which was the fundamental assumption of science. This led to a better understanding of the laws of nature as contingent. The necessity inherent in nature is indubitable since God has created the world in a definite way. But it is not an absolute necessity since He would have been free to create it in another way and with different laws. This view permeates the theology of Duns Scot; but it also lies behind the efforts of William of Ockham to remove all philosophical barriers to God's freedom and power, helped by the new suppositional logic and the ruthless attack on the belief that universal concepts are more than mere names for individual things. In science the condemnation led to the insight that the laws of nature are not necessarily valid in the form in which they have been stated by Aristotle or by any other philosopher: God could have made them otherwise so it would be better to investigate them anew.

In this way arose the critical attitude of the 14th. century, in which the principal tenets of the Aristotelian philosophy of nature, physics and cosmology were subjected to a searching analysis, often with direct reference to the condemnation of 1277. Ockham's nominalistic logic has often been seen as the principal tool of this critical movement, but this is only part of the truth. For instance, Ockham's attempt to do away with the notion of motion as such did not win the approval of the physicists. In fact, a variety of intellectual tools were applied to produce the very spectacular ideas that now emerged. The most conspicuous among them was the idea of an infinite and imaginary space outside the firmament that was proposed by Thomas Bradwardine in order to account for the infinity and omnipresence of God; it was identified with the very 'immensity of God' and had to be 'imaginary', i.e. devoid of the usual three spatial dimensions, since God is not a dimensional being. Another result was the insight of Nicole Oresme that all astronomical phenomena produced by the daily rotation of the heavens might also be explained on the assumption that the firmament is at rest and the earth is rotating around its axis, an hypothesis that could be disproved neither by observation nor by Scripture, since the Biblical talk of an immovable earth is just ordinary language without cosmological implications. It was also Oresme who destroyed the Aristotelian theory of the natural places of the elementary world, doing away with the distinction between the gravity and the levity of bodies, and paving the way for a new conception of gravitation as an *inclinatio ad similes,* a tendency to what is of the same kind. Last but not least, the Archimedean tradition became more outspoken; it led to the insight that motion could be described both *quoad causas* and *quoad effectus,* that is, with respect to its cause and with respect to its effect, and that much could be said about its kinematical aspects even if the causes of motion were not investigated; thus motions with a constant acceleration were treated mathematically in a way that Galileo would make use of later.

All things considered, one has to admit that here we witness an authentic interaction between theology and science. More than anything else it was the belief in God as omnipotent, omnipresent and infinite that helped scholars to explode the Aristotelian universe, in conjunction with genuine elements of the Aristotelian philosophy of science, such as the principle of experience, together with an Archimedean endeavour to find mathematical relations between phenomena regardless of what the philosophers might think about their causes. This complex situation served as the background to the renaissance of science which, in this perspective, is not simply identical to the science of the Renaissance, as the traditional historiography of science would have us believe. However, this is not the place to go more deeply into this question. Instead, we must briefly consider the intense interaction between science and theology that marked the period when so-called modern science emerged from the rich forest of ideas that had grown up in the later Middle Ages. Here much of the discussion centred around the metaphor of the Book of Nature, which now rose to prominence after a long period of gestation going back to the time of the Fathers. If nature could be likened to a book, several questions had to be investigated. In which language was this book written? What did it say? And who was its author?

8. The Archimedean discourse and the scientist as a priest

One of the first to answer these questions was Kepler who occupies a conspicuous place in the history of science because all the three major traditions of discourse on nature combined in his fertile brain. He began in a purely Platonic way with an abortive attempt to explain the distances of the planets from the sun in the Copernican system by the purely mathematical properties of the regular polyhedra. His later work on planetary motion began in the Archimedean way as an attempt to extract general kinematic laws from Tycho Brahe's observational data. Unable to do this to a sufficient degree of accuracy, Kepler turned to Aristotelian speculations on the forces that might produce these motions; it is one of the many ironies of the history of science that, even if these speculations proved to be wrong, they certainly helped him to state both the second and the first of the three famous laws that still bear his name. The third law was also found in an Archimedean way directly from observational data, but the procedure is disguised as a Platonic-Pythagorean attempt to apply the mathematical theory of music to the motions of the planets. Through these changing methodologies runs the constant conviction that the Book of Nature is written in the language of mathematics. According to Kepler this is because the mathematical structure of the world 'was written in the divine essence before it was present in matter'[24]. Consequently, to disclose this structure is to know something in God himself; in fact, Kepler does not hesitate to describe himself as a *Priest of God the Creator with respect to the Book of Nature*[25], and to present one of his books to the emperor as *a sacred hymn to God the Creator* and *a kind of poetry which is new and yet attuned to the most ancient and perhaps primeval lyre of the Samian philosophy*[26]. (Samos was the island where Pythagoras was born.) This new poetry is the mathematical, non-causal discourse on nature. Kepler makes this quite clear when he says that the author of Psalm 104 is 'far removed from speculations about physical causes, for he is completely content with the greatness of God who made all this [world], and has composed his hymn to God the Creator in whom the phenomena of the world roll on in order'[27]. This is presumably the first attempt by a scientist, who had himself demonstrated the power of the Archimedean approach, to explain why there is wisdom to be found in it.

Galileo presents a different case. He spent his life demolishing one Aristotelian tenet in cosmology and physics after another, so it may seem paradoxical that, towards the end of his life, he described himself as a better Aristotelian than most others. What he meant was that he, like Aristotle, regarded sense experience as the foundation of all natural knowledge. But in other respects he proves to be more of an Archimedean than an Aristotelian. Thus it is significant that his epoch-making research into the free fall of bodies was based on the explicit assumption that the problem of the physical cause of the fall could be postponed until the mathematical relations describing it as a mere phenomenon had been found. Also Galileo spoke of the Book of Nature as a mathematical treatise written by the finger of God. But, where this metaphor had been used sporadically in Kepler, Galileo subjected it to a systematic analysis in his *Letter to Mma. Christina*, Grand Duchess of Tuscany, which gave its author a place of no mean importance in the history of theology. Here Galileo maintained that 'the Bible and the phenomena of nature proceed alike from the divine Word, the former as the dictate of the Holy Spirit, and the latter as the observant executrix of His will'[28]. It follows that *every truth is in agreement with all other truths*, and that apparent contradictions between the Holy Scripture and 'solid reasons and experiences of human knowledge'[29] mean that we 'cannot have penetrated the true sense of Scripture'[30]. This is followed by an historical argument which shows that the exegetical tradition from the Fathers onward has always respected this principle, admitting that the Bible uses ordinary human language in order to show ordinary people the road to salvation, and that one cannot draw specific cosmological consequences from the literal sense of the text. Coming from a scientist this was an important reminder to theology of the danger of compromising the Bible by abandoning an age-long exegetical tradition in favour of a new tendency to fundamentalism -

if one is allowed to use this term in an anachronistic way. As such it was a genuine interaction between science and theology.

The *Letter to Mma. Christina* was written in 1615 on the occasion of the process against the Copernican system which the Holy Office had started at the instigation of Galileo's scientific enemies in the so-called 'Liga'. The climax of this process came in February 1616 when the theological experts of the congregation branded the idea of the motion of the earth and the immobility of the sun as heretical, after only one week of deliberation. Ever since, this condemnation has been taken as evidence of the hostility to scientific progress on the part of a Church which had committed itself to an Aristotelian cosmology as a dogmatic truth. However, this simplistic explanation is wrong. Aristotelian cosmology had never had any dogmatic status, and the reservations about it, expressed in 1277, were still valid. Moreover, the judgment of 1616 did not refer to Aristotle at all, but to the theological opinion that Copernicanism (the motion of the earth) 'explicitly contradicts the words of Holy Scripture (....) both in the verbal sense and according to the common interpretation and understanding of the holy Fathers and the doctors of theology'[31]. Behind this was the exegetical decree of the Council of Trent which had declared that concrete points in Scripture should be interpreted according to the consensus of the Fathers, if such a consensus existed. However, it had never decreed that the literal sense was the only possible one! In his *Letter* Galileo had agreed to this decree; but he had also pointed out that the apparent consensus of the Fathers on the immobility of the earth was no true argument, since they had never discussed the question. Unfortunately the *Letter* was never considered by the tribunal, which contented itself with superficially establishing the fact that the Fathers had never spoken of a mobile earth. Previously, a question of similar importance would have been referred to the Catholic universities and discussed in both theological and scientific detail before any conclusion would have been drawn. Unfortunately this did not happen in this case; the Holy Office was much too busy to await the outcome of a proper discussion. That the condemnation of 1616 had fatal repercussions on the image of the Church is undeniable, but it is difficult to regard the affair as an authentic interaction between theology and science. In spite of the great damage it did, this encounter took place in waters too shallow to be profoundly significant.

9. Loopholes in nature

A more genuine encounter began around the middle of the 17th. century when the discussion of a possible infinite space outside the world flared up again. The old argument that there can be no empty space in nature proved to be untenable in the light of the results of the experiments on vacuum physics by Torricelli and Von Guericke. Von Guericke drew the conclusion that the universe was indeed infinite, but he refrained from ascribing dimensions to outer space, which he still seemed to regard as an attribute of God. This reservation vanished in Newton's *Principia* (1687) in which space was described as infinite, as having the ordinary three dimensions, and as absolute in the sense that it existed independently of matter. These revolutionary ideas seem to have escaped the attention of the theologians until 1706, when Newton happened to describe absolute space and time as the sensorium of God[32]. This caused Berkeley to protest, and Newton had to explain that 'God is not duration or space, but He endures and is present forever and everywhere'[33]. Also, Leibnitz expressed his anxiety about rumours that there were philosophers in England who described God as a three-dimensional body. Without going into unnecessary detail, it is enough here to say that the debate ended with the insight that the theological discourse on the omnipresence of God could no longer be framed in a language derived from the physical account of the universe.

This skirmish was not Newton's only contribution to theology. In the *Principia* he had read the Book of Nature as a mathematical treatise in a way that integrated into a single theory almost all known terrestrial and celestial phenomena in mechanics; but he himself drew attention to the fact that his account was not complete. There were phenomena for which no natural explanation was at hand. One such phenomenon was the fact that all the planets move in the same direction and almost in the same plane. This cannot be a law of nature, since comets behave differently. In consequence Newton described it as something the Creator had arbitrarily arranged according to His own will. Similarly, Newton's assumption of a universal gravitation as a mutual attraction of all particles in the universe would in the long run result in what is now known as gravitational collapse. In order to prevent this and to ensure the stability of the universe, Newton also assumed that God would counterbalance the gravitational force in such a way that the world remained stable, something that, on one occasion, he described as a 'permanent miracle'[34]. In this way he became one of the founding fathers of that natural theology which, in the century of the Enlightenment, represented one of the most spectacular interactions between theology and natural science.

The new Natural Theology had several strings to its bow. One of them was indicated by Newton when he introduced the direct intervention of God in order to explain phenomena for which his scientific theory was unable to give any reasons. This meant - bluntly speaking - that God was used to stop a gap in the scientific discourse on the world. The omnipotence of God was repairing the impotence of science - a very dangerous theological argument that would loose its force as soon as science developed and became capable of doing its own repairs. Other arguments seemed to be more positive in the sense that they inferred the existence of a deity from what was known instead of from what was unknown or incomprehensible. The great progress of natural history, due to the invention of the microscope, and due also to the study of new animals and plants in the new world, opened new vistas in biology and anatomy, and pious naturalists began to write books on Physico-Theology demonstrating the existence of God from the marvels of nature. Here the old arguments of design and providence appeared with the support of all that the new science could give. The eye was clearly designed to see with, and it was indeed an optical instrument of such perfection that it must have been designed by an intelligent designer. Similarly, the whole universe was an intricate but harmonious construction that testified to the existence of an intelligent creator, just as a watch testified to the existence of a watchmaker, an argument developed in the beginning of the 18th. century by Bernard

Nieuwentyt, and exploited with great virtuosity by William Paley towards the end of that century. Finally, the apparently rational behaviour of animals in their natural environment would be quite incomprehensible unless they were either endowed with reason - and we know that they are not - or directed and acted upon by a superior intelligent Cause.

Thus the natural theologians held some good cards. But what was the game? In the beginning of the movement, it was both to argue for the existence of a sage, powerful and benevolent creator, and also to demonstrate the certainty of the Christian religion as revealed in the Bible. But, as time went on, the existence of a deity became the principal object, while the argument for Christianity as a religion of salvation receded into the background. Otherwise expressed, theology became more occupied with the *prolegomena fidei* than with Revelation. One cannot but wonder at such attempts to discourse on Christianity without mentioning Christ as its central core! Today, this seems preposterous. It was also dangerous, for from the almost exclusive preoccupation with natural reasons for the existence of a deity there was only a short step to a natural religion - that gentle but chimeric construction which was supposed to be common to all mankind and to be a sufficient basis for the good life, perhaps with the mild, kind figure of Jesus as one teacher of morality among many. Behind this was no doubt a serious theological aberration with respect to the dogma of creation. When Baron von Holbach in 1770 spoke up for atheism with the argument that 'to produce from nothing, or the Creation, is a term that cannot give us the least idea of the world'[35], he was of course correct. But he was wrong in supposing that the dogma of creation implied a physical account of the formation of the universe. In this, however, he could be excused, in view of the intense preoccupation of the theologians of his time with the formation of the universe and all its marvels as the foundation of belief.

10. Nature as history

Looking back upon the period of natural theology, one is impressed by the fact that there was a time when new scientific discoveries were eagerly welcomed by theologians as new evidence for belief. But if this was true, it was also a fact that science provided much information that seemed to disturb this apparent idyll. The common feature of these alarming discoveries was that they were all concerned with time. While space had been discussed on several occasions, the problem of time had not really been on the agenda since the time of the Fathers. Even at the time, when the new natural theology arose, it was generally believed that the world was more or less as it had been constituted in the beginning, about 6000 years ago, apart from trivial events like the birth and death of individuals. In particular, the biological species had remained fixed since God created plants and animals according to their species, as we are told in the Book of Genesis. And, even if the Flood had ravaged the earth, God had taken care to preserve the species from destruction in the Ark of Noah.

The first scientific discovery to start the break down of this static picture of the world was the correct interpretation of aquatic fossils by Niels Stensen who was able to prove that the present landscape of Tuscany must have been formed in six geological phases, during two of which it had been covered by the sea. His correctly stated principles of stratigraphic geology were soon able to reveal many more such distinct geological periods in which successive layers of sediments deposited in water, and plutonic rocks formed from molten material, testified to great upheavals and catastrophic changes over the face of the earth. To find room for all these cataclysms within 6000 years proved increasingly difficult, and first Buffon, and then Lyell, took the decisive step of rejecting the geological catastrophes in favour of a slow and gradual change produced by the well-known forces that are still operative in nature. The obvious implication was that the geological time-scale had to be vastly extended.

The new stratigraphic geology put the incipient science of palaeontology on a sure footing by making it possible to place fossil remains in a relative chronological sequence. This showed, firstly, that there had been forms of life that were now extinct, or that had not been there from the beginning, and secondly, that it was difficult to uphold the notion of distinct and invariable species. Here Lamarck drew the conclusion that species were not fixed but rather subject to change through a long period of evolution under the influence of changes of the environment. Immediately this idea proved offensive to theology, both because it presupposed a very long time, and because it denied that the actual species were as God had made them. If the theory were true, it would be necessary to deny the historical truth, at least, of the first few chapters of Genesis. But if the Bible was not true in its beginning, how could one be sure that it was true at its end: as Joseph Townsend had already asked in 1813, 'If we cannot trust Moses, how can we believe in the story of Christ?'[36]. The following half century is marked by the efforts of Christian geologists and theologians to answer this question in a way that both science and Faith could accept. This work was interrupted, as it were, when Darwin published the *Origin of Species* (1859), in which the evidence for a long organic evolution was clearly presented. At the same time, the driving force of evolution was identified as the struggle for existence and the survival of the fittest without special divine intervention. This theory contradicted blatantly one of the favourite arguments of natural theology by explaining the marvels of nature on purely natural grounds.

We shall not go into details here of the enormous theological storm that arose in the wake of the theory of evolution and seemed to separate natural science and the doctrine of creation totally and for ever. We only reflect upon some of its more general features. In the evolutionary camp Darwin himself never attacked theological doctrines, but retired more and more into a private lack of belief. His supporters were less reticent. It is true that Huxley coined the word agnosticism for his own conviction that the theory of evolution was purely scientific and neither more nor less theistic or anti-theistic than the *Elements* of Euclid. But John William Draper in New York, followed by Ernst Haeckel in Germany, started a concerted campaign to convince the educated that evolution and creation were incompatible and contradictory, a view that was expressed in somewhat specious terms by John Tyndall in Britain. Among theologians there were several reactions. Thus, it is worth noting that Newman found no serious reason to object to the theory of Darwin and that he found no more Scriptural evidence against it than against the Copernican system. In fact, in his letters he took care to distance himself both from those who say that 'religion and science are on this point contradictory and (...) proceed dogmatically to conclude that there is no truth in religion'[37], and from those who opposed Darwin on theological grounds. The latter are of the same ilk as those who would not 'allow Galileo to reason 300 years ago', and whose 'notion of stability in faith is ever to be repeating errors and then repeating retractions of them'[38]. Unfortunately he did not speak up in public, but left it to others to wage the battle on this front.

A serious attempt to find a just balance was made by Frederick Temple in his Bampton Lectures (1884) on *The Relations between Religion and Science*. Here he admitted that 'the enormous evidence in favour of the evolution of plants and animals is enormously great and increasing daily'[39]. Apart from scientific details he recognised the whole of Darwin's theory as the most plausible account of the history of the living world. At the same time, he stated clearly his reservations against two of the principal tenets of the anti-religious camp of evolutionists: life could never have evolved out of inorganic matter, and consciousness could never be a product of organic evolution as such. In this way God became the now well-known 'god of life', as, at the same time, the moral consciousness and indeed religious faith were entrenched in that inner castle of the mind which science would never be able to conquer. Little did he know what problems psychoanalysis on the one hand and microbiology on the other hand would create for this attempt to define a *modus vivendi*.

10. Envoy

Must we conclude, then, that the coming of evolution meant the final divorce of natural science and Christian theology after the long period in which they had lived in constant interaction? Or is this divorce only an apparent phenomenon, a passing stage of an ongoing relationship that we do not experience as such because we are in the middle of it? Now a historian is occupied with the past, and even if he is concerned about the future, he has no means of predicting it. Nevertheless, it seems to me that we should not declare all future interaction impossible so long as we have not really considered all the aspects of the present situation. I can discern here three fields of particular importance. First, the pseudo-incompatibility of creation and evolution has become so entrenched in the public mind that it will be a very strenuous undertaking to remove it. This must imply, among other things, a profound study of the Christian notion of creation as a central mystery of faith that can only be translated into human language by the *via negationis*: creation is not a story about the formation of the world, but an assertion that man took no part in its coming into being and has no part in its glory. Secondly, it seems that theology has not yet really come to grips with the central and most general lesson of evolution, namely, that for better or for worse the mere *passage of time* has become an overriding factor in the human consciousness of anything. Never again shall we look upon the world as a stable structure or regard divine providence as a safeguard of stability. Evolution has taught us that this is not so, thereby reminding us, in the words of St. Paul, that the whole creation 'is groaning in labour unto this very day'[40]. It has also spread from the history of the earth to the history of the universe as a whole, reminding us that God is the Lord of the Universe and that '[in Christ] He has made his peace with everything both in heaven and on earth'[41]. As long as the implications of evolution for theology in these two fields have not been sufficiently investigated it is far too early to consider the interaction to be irrevocably interrupted. But, thirdly, apart from the concept of evolution, theology still has one other major problem to solve. On the one hand, it is a historical fact that philosophy and theology have really considered only the Aristotelian discourse on nature as partner in the debate. On the other hand, it is also a fact that, all through history, the Archimedean discourse has been able to produce the most solid truths of science, and that today it has not only survived all the crises of the Aristotelian discourse - such as the onslaught on the traditional concepts of cause and effect, matter, and space and time - but it has also drawn more and more fields of natural knowledge into its domain. This must have some importance for the understanding of the world in the perspective of the Faith. However, there seem to be very few theologians who have really addressed themselves to this problem. If in fact they did, we could be more certain that the divorce is truly apparent, and that there is going to be a genuine interaction in the nearby future.

References

1   Hesiod, *Erga* 527
2   Plato, *Rep.* 379a
3   Aristotle, *Meteor.* 353a
4   Herotodus II, 25
5   Herotodus I, 116
6   Aristotle, *Metaph.* Books IV-V
7   ibid. 985b
8   ibid. 1025b
9   ibid. 992a
10   ibid. 1044b
11   Rom. 6,19
12   I Cor. 1,23
13   ibid. 8,4
14   Acts 17,24
15   I John 4,12
16   Rom. 1,19f.
17   John 1,1
18   Hebrews 11,3
19   Augustine, *De civ. Dei* VIII,10
20   ibid. XI, 6
21   Augustine, *Conf.* XI,11
22   Boethius, *De cons. phil.* V,6
23   Albertus Magnus, *Phys.* VII, i,14
24   Kepler to Tanckius 1608, *Werke* XVI, 305f.
25   Kepler, *Epitome Astronomiae Copernicanae, Werke* VII, 9f.

26 ibid.

27 Kepler, *Astronomia Nova,* dedic., *Werke* III,31

28 Galileo, *Opere* V,316

29 ibid. V,320

30 ibid. V,322

31 Quoted in Galileo's *Opere* XIX,321

32 Newton in a Query added to the Latin translation of his *Optics* 1706

33 Berkeley, *Principles of Human Knowledge,* §117

34 In a conversation with David Gregory 1694

35 Von Holbach, *Système de la nature* (1770), 28

36 Jos. Townsend, *The Character of Moses vindicated* (1813)

37 Newman to David Brown 1874, in *Letters and Diaries* XXVII,43f.

38 Newman to W.G.Ward 1876, *Letters and Diaries* XXVIII,71f.

39 F. Temple, *Bampton Lectures* (1884) 195

40 Rom. 8,22

41 Col. 1,20

J.R. Durant, biologist,
Assistant director Science Museum
and visiting professor of public understanding of science, Imperial College,
London, England

Is there a role for theology in an age of secular science?

John R. Durant

1. The affinity between science and theology

Introduction

Science and theology are often seen as being in conflict with one another, yet in many ways they are strikingly similar intellectual enterprises. Above all, in spite of their many differences, science and theology share a common allegiance to a particular kind of natural knowledge. For both enterprises seek a knowledge of the world and of our place in it which transcends history. By speaking of a knowledge which transcends history, I mean that scientists and theologians formulate propositions about the world which purport to be true for any observer, and not merely for this or that individual, this or that society, or even (bearing in mind the possibility of intelligent life elsewhere in the universe) this or that species.

This universal character is clearest in the case of science. Faced with an alien culture (be it terrestrial or extra-terrestrial), the scientist will be inclined to ask questions such as: Have these aliens discovered universal gravitation? Do they understand the structure of the atom? and - rather important, this one, for practical purposes - What do they know that we don't? All of these questions are posed on the assumption that gravity, the structure of the atom, and innumerable other things as yet unknown to us, are objective truths about the world awaiting discovery by any sufficiently intelligent and suitably equipped beings. Of course, the scientist may concede that the aliens' history is a decisive determinant of how much they know; but he or she will not concede that their history is a decisive determinant of what they know, for this (the scientist will argue) is very largely given by the nature of the world. In this sense, therefore, scientific knowledge-claims may be said to transcend history.

It is not an entirely straightforward matter to show that what is true for science is true also for theology. This is because there is a far greater diversity of opinion amongst theologians than there is amongst scientists about the fundamental character of their discipline. While many theologians have defended the universality of theological knowledge-claims, many others (particularly in the modern period) have been more modest. Indeed, some contemporary theologians appear to have given up making knowledge-claims altogether in favour of purely ethical or existential discourse[1]. This last move, however, amounts to professional suicide. For there are many modes of discourse about ethics and existence; and a demonstration of the necessity of the theological mode, in contrast to any other, will surely require the making of at least some distinctively theological knowledge-claims. Fundamentally, this is because it is only if the world is a particular sort of place that we shall really need theology in order to make sense of it.

To be taken seriously, then, theology *must* make knowledge-claims. Furthermore, it must make universal knowledge-claims. Consider once again the thought-experiment of an encounter with an alien culture. Faced with such a culture, the theologian will be inclined to ask questions such as: Do these aliens acknowledge the divine authorship of the world? Do they recognize the continuing dependence of the world upon providence? and, Have they been granted a direct revelation of God? Posed by a social anthropologist, such questions may be taken to represent nothing more than an impartial inquiry into the alien culture's belief-system; but posed by a theologian, they will be taken to represent much more, namely, the attempt to ascertain whether the alien culture has discovered certain fundamental truths about the world. For what else could theology (in contrast to anthropology) possibly be about? As in science, so also in theology we are dealing with knowledge-claims that transcend history.

In the past, this fundamental affinity between science and theology has permitted the two to function together in single, more-or-less harmonious accounts of the 'world beyond history' (henceforth, nature). From the historian's point of view, it makes no sense to ask whether the medieval doctrines of a geocentric universe, circular motion in the heavens, macrocosm and microcosm, and all the rest were scientific or theological; for in reality they were both. Similarly, to the historian there is little point in asking whether the 18th. and early 19th. century doctrine of the fixity of organic species was scientific or theological; for at the time the distinction simply would not have been made. In each case, a variety of theological assumptions underpinned the scientific enterprise and served both to justify and to regulate the search for particular kinds of order in nature. The point to notice here is that only intellectual enterprises which have a great deal in common with one another can be made to dovetail as closely as this.

Naturalism versus historicism

The common commitment of science and theology to the establishment of universal knowledge-claims distinguishes them rather sharply from what may be termed the essentially historical disciplines. Most arts and humanities subjects, as well as many of the social sciences, are essentially historical. By this, I mean that they deal directly only with the social world - with particular people, places, institutions and cultures. Practitioners within the essentially historical disciplines treat the social world as *sui generis*. Rarely do they turn their attention from society to the larger context of nature within which it is set; and never, if they are genuinely historicist in outlook, do they attempt to explain the social in terms of a presumptively universal order of nature.

The gulf that separates science and theology from the essentially historical disciplines may be illustrated by returning once more to our thought-experiment of an encounter with an alien culture. Faced with such a culture, historians and anthropologists will be inclined to ask questions such as: How are they organized? What traditions do they have? and, By what fundamental values do they live? Significantly, they will *not* be inclined to ask questions such as: Have these aliens hit upon parliamentary democracy? Do they understand the

Geneva Convention? and, Have they discovered table-manners? These latter questions strike us as silly because the things to which they refer are not features of the natural world waiting to be discovered. Rather, they are features of the social world whose very existence can only be understood historically; and that, of course, is the *raison d'être* of the essentially historical disciplines.

The significance of this contrast is clear once we consider what tends to happen whenever some of the more enthusiastic practitioners of the essentially historical disciplines turn their attention to science and theology. Consider, for example, the currently fashionable sub-discipline of the sociology of knowledge. Sociologists of knowledge take for their task the explanation of belief-systems in exclusively historical terms. In doing so, they tend to disregard the objects of belief altogether, since by their very nature these lie outside history. Such disregard amounts to an implicit assumption that the objects of belief play little or no part in its production. Thus, over many decades, sociologists of religion have taken it for granted that God does not intervene decisively in human affairs in such a way as to cause religious belief; and more recently, some sociologists of science have adopted the analogous assumption that nature does not intervene decisively in such a way as to cause scientific belief[2].

The challenge of history

In the past, such historicism has been the basis of a succession of sociological challenges to theology so powerful that by comparison with them the much-vaunted challenges of science pale into insignificance. The seriousness of these sociological challenges is easy to appreciate. For it is difficult to see how theology can be sustained in any very serious way in the face of the claim that the objects with which it purports to deal are merely secondary elaborations of what are primarily historical realities. Historicist notions such as that God is a projection of human hopes and aspirations, or even that he is a symbolic representation of society itself, reduce theology to the status of a highly metaphorical branch of the humanities, and religion to the rank of a highly mystifying branch of psychotherapy or social work.

Some sociologists of knowledge have worked hard to protect the objects of their study from this sort of harm. The American sociologist, Peter Berger, for example, has argued for the strict separation (or 'bracketing') of the sociology of religion, on the one hand, and epistemological inquiry into the truth or falsity of particular religious and theological propositions, on the other[3]. Such bracketing, however, is scarcely possible. Confronted by an orthodox Freudian, a theist has every reason to feel threatened. For the Freudian claims to be able to account for the theist's belief in the existence of a personal God in terms that presume such belief to be without rational foundation. It was Voltaire, of course, who said, 'If God did not exist, it would be necessary to invent him'. The Freudian, however, has it the other way about: 'If God were an invention, it would not be necessary for him to exist'.

What is true for psychoanalysis is true also for the sociology of knowledge. In recent years, a number of historical sociologists have published case-studies purporting to show that neither nature nor reason have made really decisive contributions to the resolution of particular scientific controversies[4]. While this claim may be readily accepted in particular cases, any attempt to generalise it to most or all of science has the unfortunate consequence, either that there is some sort of pre-ordained harmony between history and nature, such that processes largely confined to the one domain miraculously yield genuine insights into the other; or alternatively, that the long-term course of science is arbitrary with respect to nature, in which case our intuition that science does indeed yield genuine insights is simply false. The perversity of both these options goes a long way towards explaining the very real discomfort that many scientists feel whenever they encounter enthusiastic proponents of the sociology of scientific knowledge.

Ironically enough, the general question at issue here is largely empirical: what are the relative contributions of history (in the form of biographical factors, social interests, etc.) and nature (in the form of empirical evidence, rational argument, etc.) to the contents of scientific knowledge-claims? If, on the one hand, the answer to this question is that history is overwhelmingly the most significant of the two influences, then we had better abandon the attempt to provide rational grounds for science and instead consign it for safe-keeping to anthropologists with an interest in the collection of esoteric beliefs. If, on the other hand, the answer is that nature is at least a significant contributor alongside history (for of course it is perfectly possible that both influences are simultaneously at work), then we had better clarify the rational residue which no amount of sociological analysis can dissolve, in order to justify continuing to accord privileged status to these knowledge-claims, in contrast with all the others in the anthropological museum[5].

Discerning theologians have long seen where the real challenge to their discipline lay. (It is no coincidence, for example, that the theological world was generally far less exercised about Charles Darwin's essentially scientific *Origin of Species* in 1859 than it was about the incipiently historicist *Essays and Reviews*, which appeared a year later.) For well over a century, they have wrestled with the problem of how to do justice to history while at the same time preserving the integrity of the theological enterprise. Scientists and philosophers of science, by contrast, have only very recently begun to face up to this particular issue, and many of them are as yet ignorant of the rules of the contest and uncertain about the prize over which it is to be fought. *In this situation, it is ironic indeed that so many scientists should continue to regard as potential adversaries the very people who might just be able to teach them a thing or two about how to meet the real challenge to the integrity of their subject: history.*

2. Secular science

The private domain of personal belief

Having begun by discussing the affinity between science and theology, it is necessary to acknowledge immediately that in the modern period the two enterprises have nonetheless moved rather far apart. Today, very few theologians are inclined to suppose that their training enables them to make direct contributions to science; and very few scientists are inclined to look to theology for guidance in the search for knowledge. Where once theological science offered the prospect of a truly unified world-view, the characteristic 20th. century view is that such an enterprise is hopeless. Rather than seeking a genuine union between theology and natural science, our fractured intellectual culture has tended to look for no more than a form of peaceful coexistence between the two.

In part, at least, this profound change of outlook has arisen as a consequence of the particular misfortunes of theological science. Repeatedly, the apparently secure and timeless constructions of theological science have crumbled with the passage of time and the discovery of new knowledge. Thus, for all its marvelous generality the medieval synthesis ran into difficulties over the motions of the heavens; and in the end, close attention to this problem undermined the entire structure. Similarly, in spite of its formal beauty classical natural history was fundamentally ahistorical; and eventually, the discovery of geological time - 'deep' time - led to its demise. In these and other cases, the progress of knowledge left not only old theories but also old theologies swirling in its wake. It is not surprising that in the end most theologians opted for a life in calmer waters, well away from the unpredictable course of the advancement of science.

With the retreat of theology, modern science has rapidly become thoroughly secular. Officially, at least, it has come to proceed on the basis of no distinctive theological premises of any kind; and what is more, it has come to accord no particular theological significance (or 'sacredness') to any of the objects or processes with which it deals. Of course, as individuals secular scientists are still free to hold whatever religious or theological views they please, just so long as these do not actually prevent them from pursuing their research; but it is generally understood that such views belong exclusively to the private domain of personal belief. Any scientist who dares to introduce overtly religious or theological considerations into his or her published scientific work risks incurring the wrath of the scientific community.

The evasion of secular science

Since at least the turn of the century, secular science has been orthodoxy and theological science has been heresy. Nevertheless, secular science has not been without its critics. Over the years, there have been many different attempts to evade the strict conventions of secular science, and it will be worth exploring one or two of them before moving on to consider a quite different approach to the problem of the relationship between science and theology.

Certainly the most popular way of evading the conventions of secular science (at least in the western world) is that of the Christian fundamentalists who seek to recover a long-extinct species of theological science in the form of so-called 'creation science'. Creation scientists claim to accept the canons of orthodox science, but at the same time they reject many of orthodox science's most important claims about the world and our place in it in favour of alternative views which - coincidentally, as it were - bear a striking resemblance to a literal reading of the first few chapters of the book of Genesis. There have been a number of more-or-less ingenious attempts to bolster this somewhat implausible position with argument and evidence; but none has even come close to removing the aura of anti-intellectualism which has hung about fundamentalist special creationism ever since the days of the Tennessee 'monkey-trial', when William Jennings Bryan tried to get the better of Clarence Darrow by claiming that he cared more for the Rock of Ages than he did for the ages of rocks[6].

Christian fundamentalism is by no means the only source of dissatisfaction with the conventions of secular science. From an altogether different quarter, for example, there has emerged in recent years a variety of so-called 'New Age' philosophies based on the reinterpretation of scientific knowledge in overtly religious or theological terms. Of especial significance here is the relatively esoteric field of quantum mechanics. Judging from the mass of semi-popular literature that has appeared on this subject in the past few years, the general reader could be forgiven for supposing that the phenomenon of wave-particle duality resolves the relationship between mind and body, while Heisenberg's Uncertainty Principle provides an answer to the problem of free will. As if this were not quite enough, in some quarters quantum mechanics has been trumpeted as some kind of scientific vindication of the age-old philosophical wisdom of the east[7].

I am not a physicist, but nonetheless I should like to suggest that for the most part this sort of metaphysical appropriation of quantum mechanics represents a form of beguilement with what are no more than superficial analogies and resemblances. There is nothing wrong with superficial analogies and resemblances, of course, so long as they are recognised for what they are. In his play *Hapgood*, for example, Tom Stoppard makes splendidly entertaining use of the superficial analogy between wave-particle duality and the confusing spy-catcher world of the double agent[8]. This is all perfectly innocent, precisely because *Hapgood* is a piece of theatre and not a piece of science. The trouble with books bearing titles such as *The Dancing Wu-Li Masters* and *The Tao of Physics* is that they offer little more than Stoppardian word-play as a basis for the most grandiose schemes of metaphysical reconstruction.

Finally, we turn from the rather dewy-eyed world of the New Age to the old-fashioned but strangely persistent attempt to fashion from secular science itself some kind of religion. Some scientists who have no particular religious or theological affiliations are nonetheless unhappy to operate within the confines of secular science. What they appear to want is all the benefits of genuinely theological science with none of the supposed disadvantages of genuine theology. An example, which I have discussed at greater length elsewhere, is provided by the writings of the American 'scientific theologian', R. W. Burhoe[9]. Over a period of several decades, and largely through the pages of his journal *Zygon*, Burhoe has developed an evolutionary religion according to which natural selection is God, genetic continuity is immortality and adaptation is salvation. For Burhoe, Christian theology is a metaphorical version of Darwinian science; the gospel, we are given to understand, finds its ultimate vindication in population genetics.

It is hard to take this kind of thing very seriously. Evolutionary humanists like Burhoe have always been in a position somewhat akin to the magician who startles his audience by producing a rabbit out of a hat. In the case of evolutionary humanists the hat is secular science and the rabbit is (variously) morality, social norms or even, as with Burhoe, the entire intellectual apparatus of Christian theology. The trouble is that, as with rabbits and hats so also with morality and science, it is impossible to extract the one from the other except by sleight of hand. Within the terms of secular science, events may be judged particularly interesting or noteworthy, as they bear upon major questions of scientific fact or theory; but they may not be judged particularly appropriate or good, since secular science possesses no moral framework within which to make such judgements meaningful, let alone valid.

The domain of secular science

Fundamentalism, New Age philosophy and scientific theology are very different attempts to build a theology upon the foundations of secular science. I have argued that all three are unsuccessful. In their different ways, they may be taken to illustrate the inherent difficulty (I should prefer to say, the impossibility) of this particular enterprise. Clearly, therefore, we require a rather different approach to the problem. If theology is not to be built upon the foundations of secular science, it must instead be constructed on territory of its own somewhere nearby. As a prelude to this task, however, we must first establish the boundaries of the domain of secular science; for unless we know where these boundaries are, how shall we know where to build theology? A clue to a correct approach to this problem is provided by what is often rather irreverently termed 'God-of-the-Gaps theology'.

From time to time, religiously inclined scientists have been tempted to invoke God's hand to explain particular aspects of the natural world that have appeared to them otherwise inexplicable. The list of things that have come in for this sort of treatment is very long, extending as it does from the orbital paths of the planets around the sun (Isaac Newton) to the existence of the human ability to do mathematics (Alfred Russel Wallace). Unfortunately for this approach, the progress of science has steadily removed items from the list of the otherwise inexplicable. Newton's problem of the planets' orbits passed into the domain of the straightforwardly explicable many moons ago; and though Wallace's problem of the origin of mathematical capabilities is certainly not yet solved, recent studies of the evolution of intelligence have made it appear a good deal less intractable than he supposed.

This, of course, is precisely the trouble with God-of-the-Gaps theology. As the list of things for which God is held especially responsible steadily dwindles, so too does our confidence in the idea that he is especially responsible for anything at all. More importantly (since our levels of confidence are more a matter of psychology than they are of philosophy), God-of-the-Gaps theology fails to do justice either to science or to theology. Scientifically speaking, it is absurdly defeatist continually to interpret the hitherto unexplained as the inexplicable; and theologically speaking, it is simply perverse to make human ignorance the criterion by which to judge the handiwork of God.

Learning the lesson of the God-of-the-Gaps tradition means coming to terms with what I shall term 'the principle of the *omnicompetence* of secular science'. By this, I mean that secular science is capable (or is to be presumed capable) of providing authoritative answers on all matters of empirical fact concerning objects and processes in the universe. Given the spectacular successes of secular science, this may be considered no more than a reasonably charitable extrapolation from the past. While of course the principle of omnicompetence can never be proved (it is always possible that we shall discover questions that we are unable to answer) it is certainly heuristically sound; and it has the added advantage that it acts as a perpetual safeguard against our succumbing to the temptation to transform the purely local and temporary failures of science into permanent victories for theology.

The limits of secular science

Some people have taken the principle of omnicompetence to mean that secular science can explain absolutely everything. For example, in his rather euphemistically entitled book *The*

Creation, the physical scientist Peter Atkins argues that science is on the verge of attaining a literally complete knowledge of the universe. Such a knowledge, he argues, will demonstrate that, 'ultimately, there is nothing to explain'. By this, Atkins seems to mean that once secular science has accounted for absolutely everything theology will become utterly redundant. 'My aim', he writes in his Preface, 'is to argue that the universe can come into existence without intervention, and that there is no *need* to invoke the idea of a Supreme Being in one of its numerous manifestations'[10].

Atkins is certainly right about one thing. If secular science can indeed account for absolutely everything then serious theology of the kind we have been considering is certainly redundant. For once it is granted that secular science possesses, or will eventually possess, a literally complete knowledge of the world, then there is simply no role left (beyond that of merely making us feel better) for the other great intellectual enterprise in our culture that offers universal knowledge-claims about the world. Therefore, the question is: Can secular science in principle account for absolutely everything? Atkins states repeatedly that it can. On the contrary, I suggest that it cannot.

At first sight, my suggestion appears to contradict the principle of omnicompetence. It will be recalled that according to this principle secular science is presumed to be capable of accounting for all matters of empirical fact concerning objects and processes in the universe. To be valid, however, Atkins' argument requires a great deal more than this. For in order to account for absolutely everything, and thus extinguish theology, secular science must be able (at least) to explain both the universe's existence and our subjective experiences of it; and neither of these things is an object or a process in the universe at all. The problems of existence and experience are not secular scientific knowledge 'gaps', like Newton's problem of the planets or Wallace's problem of the mathematical faculty. Rather, they are problems that lie wholly outside the domain of science.

Atkins appears not to accept this last point, for he attempts to sketch the outlines of what purport to be secular-scientific theories of existence and experience. On closer inspection, however, these outlines turn out to be mere shadowy illusions, lacking in both conceptual coherence and the potential for any improvement in the light of future scientific discovery. I shall briefly consider each of them in turn.

1. The problem of existence

Consider first the question: Why is there anything at all? This question has perplexed philosophers down the ages. Significantly, it remains totally untouched by any and all advances in scientific understanding. This is because by their very nature advances in scientific understanding consist of giving accounts of particular states of affairs in terms of other, prior states of affairs. Clearly, the chain of potential explanations of this kind is in principle endless. In one way this is a great comfort to physicists working on fundamental theory, since it means that they are never at risk of making themselves redundant; but in another way it is a great disappointment, since it also means that fundamental theory can never hope to explain the most fundamental thing of all, namely, existence itself. To have any content an explanation of existence must necessarily contain terms positing some prior state of affairs which results in existence; and then the question can always be asked: But why this prior state of affairs?

Given that the problem of existence is so manifestly insoluble, we may wonder how anyone can suppose that science will solve it. The answer is, I think, the ambiguity of one small and deceptively simple word: 'nothing'. Atkins tells us that science is on the verge of explaining how space-time comes into being 'out of nothing'. Apparently, then, we are being offered an explanation of existence itself. This explanation, however, is couched in enigmatic and elusive terms. What, exactly, is Atkins claiming? So far as I can see, the only remotely plausible candidate for the role of 'absolutely nothing' in Atkins' creation play is a quantum field capable of fluctuating in such a way that not just one but a whole host of (mostly extremely unstable) universes keep appearing from it, rather like bubbles bursting on the surface of boiling porridge. In one sense, certainly, a quantum field does look a bit like nothing (it is an awful lot less than empty space, for example, which is often referred to as nothing); but in the only sense that matters so far as the problem of existence is concerned, a quantum field looks much more like porridge. In the beginning, let it be granted, was the quantum field; but why, oh why was the quantum field?

2. The problem of experience

I conclude that the problem of existence is unsolvable by science (and, I might add, by anything else). Next, consider the question: Why is there subjective experience? It is a fact for me that I have subjective experience, and I presume that it is also a fact for you who are reading these lines. I am strongly inclined to think that it is also a fact for some other animals, though I am not certain quite how many. Now whatever else they may be, people and other animals are also objects and processes in the universe. Thus they fall within the domain of secular science. What does it mean, then, to say that secular science is inherently limited in face of subjective experience? It means that, while people and other animals may be known scientifically as objects, they can never be known scientifically as subjects. Even the secular sciences which deal with subjective experience - some branches of psychology, for example - deal with it only as (some other subject's) objective fact; always, in a scientific analysis, the strictly subjective point of view is written out.

This feature of secular science is closely related to the mind/body problem. Once again, this is a problem that has perplexed philosophers down the ages; and once again, the most significant thing to be said about it from our point of view is that it has remained totally untouched by any and all advances in scientific understanding. René Descartes thought the brain was a system of hydraulic tubes, and he puzzled over how such a machine could possibly have anything to do with thoughts and feelings. We know that the brain is a system of electrochemically interacting neurons, and we puzzle over how such a machine could possibly have anything to do with thoughts and feelings. From 17th. century plumbing to 20th. century neurophysiology is a gigantic leap of science, but it is a leap that has left the mind/body problem precisely where it always was.

As with existence, so also with experience, Atkins wishes to persuade us that science is on the verge of a satisfactory solution (pp. 35-37):

'At the deepest level decisions are adjustments of the dispositions of atoms in the molecules inside large numbers of cells in the brain .... That this motiveless, purposeless, mindless activity emerges into the world as motive and purpose, and constitutes a mind, is wholly due to the complexity of its organization. As symphonies are ultimately coordinated motions of atoms, so consciousness emerges from chaos.'

Atkins has a fine style, and this sounds all right until we stop and ask what it actually means. The proposition that consciousness emerges from chaos may be taken to mean simply that the neurophysiological machinery whose activity is associated with consciousness is an energetic system operating in ways that are consistent with the second law of thermodynamics. If so, well and good; but of course this proposition fails even to address, let alone to resolve, the mind/body problem. Alternatively, therefore, the proposition may be taken to mean that the activity of the neurophysiological machinery in question actually generates consciousness. This second proposition at least has the virtue of addressing the mind/body problem; but at the same time it has the fatal weakness that it does absolutely nothing to help resolve it. For what we wish to understand is precisely *how* the mere motions of atoms and molecules - however complex they may be - can possibly generate anything so utterly different from movement as an experience.

A television camera picks up an image, converts it into electrical signals and transmits the signals to a magnetic tape for storage. Complex atomic and molecular movements have taken place in ways that are satisfactorily predicted - indeed, demanded - by physical theory; and since that (so far as we know) is all that happens, there is no problem. Now contrast this with the following, apparently similar situation. An eye picks up an image, converts it into electrochemical signals and transmits the signals to a brain for storage. Complex atomic and molecular movements have taken place in ways that are (or at any rate soon will be) satisfactorily predicted - indeed, demanded - by physical theory; but this time, something else has happened as well. For the owner of the eye and brain has had a subjective experience of the image, and this is something that by its very nature physical theory neither predicted nor demanded.

Now we have a real problem, and it will not go away simply because we assert that molecular movements *must* generate experiences since we so obviously have them. The mind/body problem has not been solved by secular science, and I suggest that it never will be solved by secular science since it has to do, not with how much scientific knowledge we possess, but rather with what sort of thing scientific knowledge *is*. Science deals exclusively in objective knowledge. The fruits of successful scientific inquiry are clear and compelling accounts of what the Scottish communications scientist Donald Mackay has termed 'the outside story'. When it comes to certain objects, such as particular sorts of brains, we know that this outside story is incomplete; for alongside it there is an 'inside story' of subjective experience. The plain fact of the matter is that this inside story is totally inaccessible to scientific inquiry, even though it is immediately available to the subject of that scientific inquiry.

I conclude, therefore, that *both existence and experience* are problems that help define the limits of secular science.

3. A role for theology?

This is a conclusion which, if correct, deserves the attention of theologians. After all, the two foundational principles of Judeo-Christian theology are: first, that God is the ground of being and the creator of the universe; and secondly, that God stands in some sort of continuing and personal relationship with his creation. The first of these principles does not, of course, resolve the problem of existence. For as with scientific, so also with theological (or any other) explanations, we are always left with explanatory terms which themselves require explanation. In this case, to propose that God is the ground of being leaves unexplained - and, in principle, inexplicable - the fact of God's existence. This having been said, it remains the case that theology is perfectly free to explore the creation of the universe safe in the knowledge that this issue lies outside the domain of secular science.

Turning to the second foundational principle of theology, we find that this, too, is strikingly relevant to one of the problems which we have used to help define the domain of secular science. For at root Judeo-Christian theology has to do with subjective experience. It claims, minimally, that the universe has been personally brought into being; that it is personally held in being; and that human beings were made in the divine image in order to enjoy a personal relationship with their maker. Once again, we must note that these claims do not of themselves resolve the problem of subjective experience. Whether we accept the claims of theology or not, we have still to fathom the interconnections between the mental and the material in our universe. However, theology may surely take heart from the fact that here, for once (its foundational principles being personal and subjective rather than impersonal and objective), it is far better placed to make progress than is secular science.

Theology can retain its credibility in an age of secular science only if theologians are able and willing to claim that without its intellectual resources the universe as we know it must remain deeply mysterious. I have suggested two specific areas in which this claim may be pursued. In neither case, clearly, is the theological position free of its own peculiar difficulties; but in spite of this, the basic point remains that if theology is to survive at all it cannot retreat from the high ground upon which philosophers and scientists have always sought a better understanding of the world and our place in it. *If theology has nothing of substance to say on these most fundamental issues, then it certainly will not deserve a hearing on anything else.*

References

1. See, for example, D. Cupitt, *The Sea of Faith*, BBC Publications, London 1987.

2. See, for example, B. Barnes, *Scientific Knowledge and Sociological Theory*,
    Routledge and Kegan Paul, London 1974; B. Barnes,
    Interests and the Growth of Knowledge, Routledge and Kegan Paul, London 1977;
    and K. Knorr-Cetina, *The Manufacture of Knowledge. Towards a Constructivist and Contextual Theory of Science*, Pergamon Press, Oxford 1981.

3. P. Berger, *A Rumour of Angels. Modern Society and the Rediscovery of the Supernatural*, Penguin, Harmondsworth 1970.

4. See, for example, many of the essays in K. Knorr-Cetina and M. Mulkay (eds.), *Science Observed. Perspectives on the Social Study of Science*, Sage, Beverly Hills and London 1983.

5. The best recent historical study that addresses this question critically is M. Rudwick, *The Great Devonian Controversy. The Shaping of Scientific Knowledge among Gentlemanly Specialists*, University of Chicago Press, Chicago and London 1985.

6. For an account of Bryan's involvement in the American anti-evolution movement of the 1920's, as well as a review of contemporary 'scientific creationism', see the essays by J. Durant and E. Barker in J. Durant (ed.), *Darwinism and Divinity. Essays on Evolution and Religious Belief*, Basil Blackwell, Oxford 1985.

7. See, for example, F. Capra, *The Tao of Physics*, Wildwood House, London 1975; and G. Zukav, *The Dancing Wu-Li Masters. An Overview of the New Physics*, Collins, London 1979.

8. T. Stoppard, *Hapgood*, Faber & Faber, London and Boston 1988.

9. See J. Durant, 'Evolution, Ideology and World-view: Darwinian Religion in the Twentieth Century', in J. R. Moore (ed.), *History, Humanity and Evolution. Essays in Honour of John C. Greene*, Cambridge University Press, Cambridge and London (in press).

10. P. Atkins, *The Creation*, W. H. Freeman & Co., Oxford and San Francisco 1981.

J. Hübner, theologian and biologist,
Senior research fellow, Forschungsstätte der Evangelischen Studiengemeinschaft,
Heidelberg, The Federal Republic of Germany

Science and religion coming across*

Jürgen Hübner

In contemporary discussion on science and religion a variety of views are expressed and a diversity of models are used to describe their relation. Most of these contributions are very helpful in the dialogue between the different disciplines and areas of thinking. It must be borne in mind, however, that they are human constructions, attempts to understand, no more; they all present in essence a kind of particularity. That is, they discuss only aspects of reality, particular experiences of perception and of awareness, realization, not the comprehensiveness of reality itself. With respect to the question of the whole of reality, one cannot objectify, but only participate. Reflections in which the whole of things is considered must necessarily be particular, fixed as they are by the specific points of view of the different partners in the dialogue. Distinct cultural and biographical traditions, indeed, give rise to corresponding world-views. Their meeting, therefore, often results in confrontation and encounter as enemies. Consequently, a long process of conversation may be needed in order to come to true mutual understanding, and such understanding is the precondition for the reconstruction of old models, and the creation of new models, of the inter-relationship between science and theology.

One of the difficulties that are encountered arises from the clash between the different cultural traditions that play a part. It may lead to diverging identifications of our subject: Is it, for instance, a matter of dialogue between science and of religion or between science and theology? Which one is the partner of science, religion or theology? Generally speaking I think both, but why do some people address religion and others theology? What is the meaning of the notion of religion, and of that of theology? Do they bring to mind the same thing? If so, what is the connection between the two concepts and where does the difference lie? A similar question occurs on the scientific side: Who is the partner in the science versus religion/theology dialogue? Science itself or the scientist? And once again, physicists, biologists and physicians provide very different professions with specifically differing arguments during their dialogue with theologians. Are there arguments that are common to all disciplines of science, and that are specially relevant for the dialogue with theology?

---

* See general reference volume mentioned at the end of the text.

It is neither possible nor my task to develop here a system or a mere topology of the different relations in this field. For a typology I refer the reader to the lecture delivered by Dr. Drees. I myself only want to put some general questions of importance. Next I will try to describe a kind of scenario for the dialogue.

1. My first question refers to the difference between reality itself and talking or reflecting about reality, and to the relation between the two: What is the difference between, and the relation of, real life in nature, the biosphere, and life as considered by the life sciences, of true religious life and reflection about religion, of Christian faith and Christian theology, or of the reality of God and concepts of God? In the following paragraphs I will go into each of these sub-questions.

- It is clear that life in nature and what biology tells us about life are not the same thing. As A.M.K(laus) Müller points out, we learn only aspects of life from biological science as they are methodically obtained by rational constructions and carefully designed experiments. In extreme experiments, life must be destroyed before scientific knowledge of certain conditions of life can be obtained. Besides, nature must be prepared in order to obtain physical knowledge. The preparing subject with his aims, and even the institution to which she or he belongs and also its activities, are essential parts of the experiment. Moreover, the experiment gives not only some insight into the essence of the living processes of our world, it also changes nature at the very same time. For after the experiment, nature is no longer what it was before! This observation can be amplified in many respects. Expressed in an extreme way, the buildings of a research institute, for instance, have already changed nature even before the investigation has begun. Such changes, which obviously happen in the process of time, are part of the evolution; they are, so to speak, evolutionary steps at particular points in nature.

- Reflection about religion, of course, can take place apart from a religious life. Research into religion can develop its own dynamics, and the religious believer may change himself and his religion by such activity. In what sense, however, does the state of reflecting on religion differ from that of being religious? What kind of truth does the philosophy of religion provide if it only describes and analyzes religion that is practised? I think a religious man or woman meets in faith a truth other than that encountered by somebody (or even by himself or herself) who is only reflecting upon religious life. I think that meditation uniquely includes elements of both kinds of experience, but again in quite different ways. What then is the significance of this difference?

- The distinction between Christian faith and Christian theology runs in the same direction. Faith as a way of believing that generates the fullness of life or as theological argumentation are two different things. Theological reflection may arrest a living faith or it may stimulate it. What is the meaning of this ambiguity? It is, I think, a question of right thinking, of thinking in the right relation to the reality that is questioned.

- In this sense I also think that the understanding of what we mean by the word 'God' as expressed by many metaphysical conceptions needs further reflection. What is intended when using such phrases as 'God is doing', 'God acts', and 'God's activity in creation' - especially in a universe that is described as self-evolving, and in a life that is understood to be self-organising and to be proceeding without the 'hypothesis of God', as it is put so often? The problem of atheism must be thought through to its end and, therefore, the option of theism must be reconsidered. Is the theistic concept of God a religious concept or only a philosophical one? What relation does this concept have to Jahweh of the Jewish-Christian tradition in the Old Testament and to the Father of Jesus Christ? I think that the required answer is not - or is no longer - self-evident.

2. My second question is connected with the last (sub)question: it concerns the problem of realism and nominalism. This problem has to be posed in different ways by science and by theology, or by history and by the philosophy of religion.

- In what manner does science deal with reality? What does science do? Is it only describing reality, giving a picture, a model, a view of the world, or does it do more? Does it perhaps reveal reality or does it give a perspective of the world, and does it manifest in this way part of reality itself? Answers to these questions are extremely relevant for the concepts of natural theology. Natural theological concepts and reflections based on science are only meaningful if the implications of science itself at least refer to reality. At the conference many contributions presupposed either implicitly or explicitly a kind of realism, although there was a consensus that science has important roots and origins in the nominalistic tradition of the Middle Ages. Are the findings of our science realistic enough - in that philosophical sense - to serve as a foundation for a natural theology? At the very least, it will be necessary to account for fundamental findings that are permanently changing.

- Another question is whether or not the realistic option is common within the scientific community. I think that it is not. Most scientists look at the facts with which they work, not at their potential philosophical value. This tendency, however, lends no support to the argument against examining science in order to assess the feasibility of natural theology.

- The same problem of realism and nominalism should be discussed in theology. I think there is also a nominalistic option in Christian theology. This means that theology describes the events of faith, the manifestations of revelation, but only the believer himself or herself is aware of the reality of faith and of the revelation. What is the nature of the truth that is at work while reflecting upon faith as a phenomenon in theology or in philosophy? I think both activities have realistic implications when they are reflecting and re-thinking living faith.

- At the conference we had realistic options for theology as well as nominalistic ones. For instance, I think that Professor Torrance presents a realistic theology, whereas Dr.Drees advocates a nominalistic way of theological thinking. I think, however, that we need equally both ways of thinking, and, therefore, that it is important to reflect upon their mutual implications, that is, upon the nominalistic elements of a realistic theology and upon the realistic implications of a nominalistic theology. The former includes the contingent order of creation, the latter the commitment to the word of Christ. The accents are different, but they depend on and reflect upon the same truth of Christianity. In my opinion, this important ground shared by two different ways of thinking should be cultivated.

3. I want to put a third question: the question of human responsibility. This question was one of the serious omissions at our conference. We discussed the mystery of creation, its marvellous - cosmic - order and the possible harmony of science and religion. We also discussed the relationship of science and theology in order to harmonize them. But we did *not* discuss the consequences of modern science with respect to the world of today and tomorrow. The scientifically induced changes are not restricted to those of world-views. The world itself, the substance of nature, that is, the essence of our whole world and of our whole life will be thoroughly changed. The sophisticated communications technologies, and those of biotechnology and of genetic engineering, are surely the most important challenges of our day. Man is beginning to change the very order of nature that he has inherited. This profound change will also in turn change man's religion and his faith. What are the theological implications of this challenge? In the future, man will be responsible for completely new kinds of order, at least on our planet. I think that in this particular respect the theologian should be the critical partner of the scientist, also in the same sense that the scientist needs dialogue with the theologian just as much as the theologian does with the scientist. The main question will be: What must we do to preserve God's creation and, at the same time, cater for its further evolution? So we need right thinking on creation in science as well as in theology.

Let me illustrate the questions I have in mind in a rough scheme (see following page).The implications of this scheme can be explained as follows.

The basis of all scientific and theological thinking is real life, the life of human beings in nature, society and cultural traditions. Religion is a fundamental part of human life and it proceeds with a history of its own. Religious life - I now think especially of Christian religion - is characterized by faith and by the communion of Love, by diaconical service and worship. Christian worship is an authentic expression of Christian faith and life. Here God talks with men and men answer God in prayer and praise, as Martin Luther said. Men, women and children bring to God their afflictions and their joy, and God listens to his people, and strengthens and consoles them.

The presence of Christ in his word and sacrament is the central creed of Christians. It is the experience of their faith. In the interpretation and extrapolation of their spiritual life they confess: Jesus Christ is the Lord of all creation, and in the beginning of all things he already dwelt with God and was with God as God's Word, the 'Logos'. He opens the future to eternal life, to the Kingdom of God without harm and death. The Life of God embraces the life on earth, and Jesus Christ is the revealer of this new reality. So in Christian life and worship is revealed the way in which God himself in his creating activity attends his creation. The promise of eternal life gives a new perspective and a new sense to empirical life on earth. Biological dying is included in this view: death becomes the gateway to a new form of life.

Having dealt with the level of life itself, the reality of life as it happens every day, we turn to another level, that is, to reflection *about* life. Here life in its reality is intellectually reconstructed. This activity, of course, is part of real life, too. But intellectual reflections can be separated from their grounds - in order to understand these grounds better and to alter their conditions. I remember in the discussion of this level 'the context of discovery' as Hans Reichenbach has called it.

Reflections about life can be executed in well differentiated modes. One mode is science, another theology. Both have their own subjects and methodological frameworks: the empirical conditions are described and analyzed by searching for efficient causes

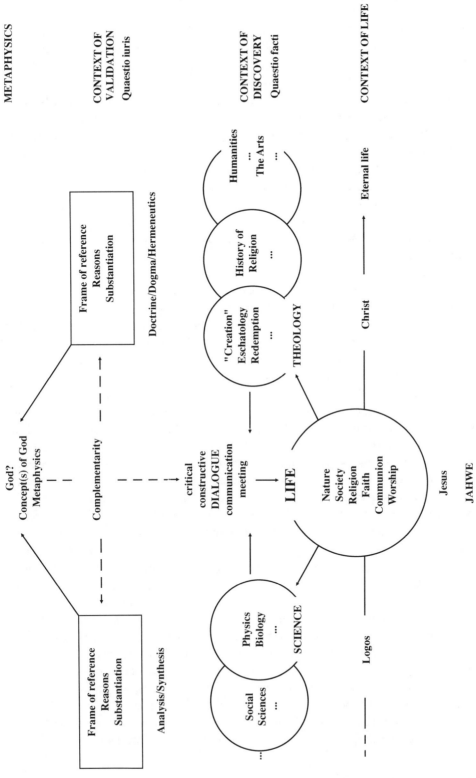

METAPHYSICS

CONTEXT OF
VALIDATION
Quaestio iuris

CONTEXT OF
DISCOVERY
Quaestio facti

CONTEXT OF LIFE

Frame of reference
Reasons
Substantiation

Doctrine/Dogma/Hermeneutics

God?
Concept(s) of God
Metaphysics

Complementarity

critical
constructive
DIALOGUE
communication
meeting

Frame of reference
Reasons
Substantiation

Analysis/Synthesis

Humanities
...
The Arts
...

History of
Religion
...

"Creation"
Eschatology
Redemption
...

THEOLOGY

LIFE

Nature
Society
Religion
Faith
Communion
Worship

Physics
Biology
...

SCIENCE

Social
Sciences
...

Eternal life

Christ

Jesus

JAHWE

Logos

(*causae efficientes*), and religious experiences of life are reflected upon by the retelling and reconstruction of personal and common stories and traditions. Therefore, science (physics, chemistry, biology...) can be characterized by the key words, 'analysis/synthesis', and theology by those of 'doctrine/dogma/hermeneutics'. Scientific knowledge is acquired by analyzing causal factors and synthesizing them by hypothesis and theory, and finally by the construction of new products. Theological insights represent the experiences of fulfilment and a good life, of goodness and love, of obligation, sin, judgement and grace. Science concentrates mainly on the present, whereas theology recounts history and stories from the past for the sake of the future. The social sciences follow the same causal-analytical method as the natural sciences, but the history of religions, the humanities, and the arts accompany in many respects the method of theology (with exceptions).

The methodological presuppositions of science and of theology are different. Lacking conformity at the functional level, they are not immediately comparable. The language of science cannot be translated directly into that of theology and *vice versa*. It is not possible, therefore, to harmonize them without further reflection and conceptualization. Science and theology cannot achieve a theoretical relation without philosophy!

This relation is established at the next level: the level of philosophy. The task of discovering and consolidating reasons for comparing and selecting the arguments of science and theology - in part as the 'context of validation' in Hans Reichenbach's sense - can be tackled from each side, and then it becomes possible to find ways in which they can approach one another. Nevertheless, it is also difficult at this level to come to terms that are acceptable to both sides. The traditional approach is that of classical Christian metaphysics, namely, the concept of the substantial harmony of nature and grace. Nature needs grace for fulfilment, and grace co-operates with nature. The problem is that the concept of nature required in this context is not the same as the one used in modern science: nature in the Ptolemaic world is not the same as nature in science which, according to Cartesian philosophy, is the objective field of inquiry by human subjects. In the latter case there is no point of contact with spiritual entities, with divine grace as expressed in terms of another nature.

Respectable attempts to find a new harmony between the nature of creation and the nature of the Creator are evolutionism and process thought. Both are new kinds of metaphysics, no longer based upon the paradigm of the Ptolemaic world, but founded in the new paradigms of the world in evolution and of process thinking. Professor Schmitz-Moormann champions the Teilhardian world-view, and Professor Van der Veken the philosophy of Alfred North Whitehead. The findings of natural science, embraced in the theory of evolution and their interpretation in terms of process-philosophy, are bound together here with a new interpretation of the theological tradition: God is not the monarch in residence beyond the sphere of the fixed stars, but the evolver and processor of the universe. The notion 'God' is no longer a transcendental concept, but a *panentheistic* one. Here the coordination of science and theology approaches something like a fusion. The price is, on the one hand, the necessity of a speculative philosophical interpretation of the theory of evolution, and, on the other, a need for an equally speculative change in the theological assertions.

A third attempt to specify the relation of science and theology at the level of philosophical interpretation is the concept of complementarity. Here the conceptual difference between both methodologies is conserved, but it is asserted that they still form a paradoxical unity analogous to that of the modern physical theory of light (which behaves controversially as waves or as particles). I think that the concept of complementarity describes the problem in an exact manner, but that it does not solve it. It is helpful, however, in discussing the relationship in ever new ways, as much from a scientific point of view as from a theological one.

Aiming directly for combination, the speculative, philosophical conceptions of science and of theology converge at any one time on a particular concept of God. There are several different concepts of this kind: God as supreme being, as evolver, as process itself, or as sovereign beyond all human understanding. All these concepts of God are metaphysical: they belong to the Greek-Roman tradition of the Christian Occident, they were used for the interpretation of the holy scriptures of both the Jews and the early Christians, and they have developed along with that tradition. Today, the problem is growing again: What kind of relationship is there between the concepts of God and the living God of the Christian experience, the Father of Jesus, Jahweh of ancient Israel? Can we address our prayers to the force of evolution or the process of the universe? In the interests of theology, the most important thing is that our concepts of God represent the reality of God and his manifestation in the word of the *Gospel*, in his Spirit, in the Spirit of Jesus Christ, and in the revelations recounted by the Holy Scripture, the Bible. The real danger is that our ideas of God may get in the way of God's living activity, that we may be confused or mistaken in our conceptions, and that we may become unfit to listen for the word of God in Jesus Christ.

There are two special dangers. One is that theological arguments become self-sufficient and self-complacent, without contact with the effective realities in the world, including the findings of science and scientific research. Theological thinking without dialogue with the sciences and with the humanities can become ignorant of the world and its actual problems, can become unworldly and ivory-towered, without relevance in the daily life of mankind. The conceptual preparation and isolation of theological problems from the context of common life is right, necessary and helpful. But the transfer of abstract solutions, isolated from the discussions of the sciences and the humanities, directly into the context of life may be considerably more destructive than constructive. The other danger is that the same thing may happen on the side of science and of the humanities. Scientific arguments that do not reflect contact with human and natural history, with biographical stories and physical events, and with philosophy and theology, may be destructive, resulting in the demolition and devastation of nature and of human life with it. Problems raised by the isolated application of scientific knowledge (e. g. environmental problems, questions about medical practice) involve ethical issues. Indeed, arguments from environmental or medical ethics are commonly added to those of science to compensate for the absence of those aspects in scientific method. But often ethical arguments come too late - when the damage is already done or, alternatively, when it is well on its way. The isolation of science and technology from their contexts in nature and in human history becomes extremely dangerous.

If scientific arguments and their applications, and likewise theological reflections, are isolated, the former can lead to destructive events, and the latter can remain inconsequential and uninspiring. But both, science and theology, arise from the same source: everyday life and its problems. By serving within this life-context, that is, the life-contexts that are their own, they must meet each other. So they need a dialogue that presents them as partners, simultaneously and mutually, in confrontation and criticism, and, equally, in cooperation and appreciation.

Questions arising in physics, biology, and the other sciences, that transcend the coherence of scientific research, should be discussed with the arts and the humanities, and with philosophy and theology. Also, theological statements should be confronted with arguments from the natural and social sciences. Thus, a critical dialogue in constructive communication is, I think, the essence of the relation of science and theology. A philosophical system for reconciling and harmonizing them is not the very first operational requirement. To begin with, we need a dialogue in order to establish the relevance of theology and to avoid dangerous developments in the sciences. When dialogue and communication are alive, systematic reflection on the relationship and its harmony can become helpful. The results of systematic thinking will then enter the actual discussion and promote it. Assuming they do open the discussion, they should not lead it into a closed system, as the latter will arrest living communication.

In my opinion, a true meeting of 'science' and 'theology' will be a happening more in the nature of an occurrence and of an experience than in the form of a rational systematization. Such a meeting may start with confrontation and an encounter of disputants from opposing camps or, on the contrary, with recollection and recognition. Rational discourse should be the second step. The bringing together of these two modes of human knowledge, science and theology, is a philosophical task which implies an important programme for finding arguments for the dialogue. But the dialogue itself is the principal instrument for finding solutions to the questions arising in everyday life. The realization of life-aspects in a suitably arranged dialogue will bear the mark of enlightenment or the stamp of illumination. In this medium, metaphysical constructions and conceptions become meaningful and, in the final analysis, concepts of God may become helpful. Concepts of God should serve the experience of God, and the communication of science and theology should be consonant with this happening.

The successful outcome of a meeting of scientists and theologians will help to make life meaningful within God's creation. The failure of such dialogue may heighten our fear of death. This is of enormous importance for the meaning of our lives, for our prospect of the future. The continuation of the evolution of life on our planet depends in large measure on the hope that our future is embedded in God's future, and that his grace to humankind may lead us to one another as participators and as partners in his creation.

References

In this lecture some points of view that were either held or put forward by speakers at the conference are considered. The pertinent texts can all be found in this volume with one exception:
The reference to K. Schmitz-Moormann concerns his contribution to the First European Conference on Science and Religion; the texts in question have been published in: Svend Andersen and Arthur Peacocke, *Evolution and Creation*, Aarhus University Press, Aarhus 1987.

The work of A.M.K(laus) Müller referred to in the text is his *Die präparierte Zeit*, Radius Bücher, Stuttgart 1972, and his 'Die Identität des Menschen und die Identität der wissenschaftlich-technischen Welt' published in: A.M.Klaus Müller (ed.), *Zukunftsperspektiven*, J. F. Steinkopf Verlag, Stuttgart 1976.

A general reference volume is:
Jürgen Hübner (ed.), *Der Dialog zwischen Theologie und Naturwissenschaft. Ein bibliographischer Bericht*, Chr. Kaiser, Munich 1987.

G. Vahanian, theologian,
Professor of theology and ethics, Université des Sciences Humaines,
Strasbourg, France

Creation and Big Bang:
the word as space of the creation

Gabriel Vahanian

Galileo has just been rehabilitated; it was on the news not too long ago. The event, however, seems to have been somewhat less newsworthy than the inter-religious gathering that took place in Assisi at about the same time. Be that as it may, by reopening the case of its relations with science, the Roman Catholic Church (together, for a change, with all the other Christian Churches) has paved the way for an intellectual renewal of even greater significance and, at the same time, still more radical.

To be sure, inter-religious dialogue deserves nothing less than inter-confessional discussion that it is spared all the deception of entrenched positions based on second-hand recollections of hitherto irreducible differences, the downgrading of which results not so much from a disenchanted world as from a world restored at last to a worldliness both proper to it and without make-believe or presuppositions. Whether we like it or not, with the successive scientific revolutions affecting our frame of mind, and with technology invading our life-style and even our dreams, such a dialogue can only take place amidst the ineluctable unfolding of a logic in the light of which all those disparities, that, through sheer force of habit, still manage to acquire the status of a postulate or even of a religious presupposition, appear as no more than cultural relics of the distancing past.

1. Science and faith

Both in view of the technological phenomenon and because of the concomitant scientific epistemology at work in all walks of human life, what is problematic today is no longer of the same order of magnitude as its correlate in all previous ages of human history. Even more important, nowadays, we become conscious of what is problematic by confronting science and technology rather than by apathetically taking note of the differences of our religious orientations or of the points at which they seem to converge. For instance, in order to show reverence to God, one can do so either by covering one's head or by taking one's hat off. By contrast, a computer works exactly the same way whether it is located in Geneva or Jerusalem, in Rome or Calcutta or Tokyo, in New York or Moscow. And, to be sure, a certain degree of conviviality and sharing, whether on the interconfessional or on the inter-religious level, is not to be dismissed out of hand much less frowned upon, if only because a new understanding of one's own faith may occur even while adding to the grounds upon which such encounters become possible. Indeed, no real or significant renewal of the intelligence of faith will occur until and unless this intelligence itself is, so to speak, cross-examined by being confronted with the canons of scientific knowledge as well as with the symbols or tenets of a cultural change that is subject both to scientific know-how and to the increasing impact of technology upon knowledge, even knowledge of one's self.

But then, as pointed out elsewhere, the crisis of our time is a spiritual one. It affects - and does so especially if with Paul Tillich we hold that religion is the substance of culture - not only theology but also no less significantly science itself, not to mention the social or political economy. From J. Robert Oppenheimer to Professor Testard, many a scientist would rise to the occasion and argue or show and assert that no scientific revolution can be said to respect what is human and, at the same time, be sheltered from conscience or spared the obligation to account for itself.

In Antiquity, science and wisdom went hand in glove. Perhaps, the part played by conscience was more evident, if not more important. I should not say that this part had necessarily grown smaller with the advent of modernity or since the rise of that *scienza nuova* so well depicted by Vico; nor should I say that it was sacrificed on the altar of the latest novelty. It has been given, however, quite a different role to play. At any rate, it has had to confront a new set of data, a new crop of facts as well as a new fiction (in the best sense of the term). Like Christopher Columbus who set out to discover the Indies but instead discovered America, we are in the process of discovering an America of the mind, a new world that leaves behind all the dichotomies of the subjective and the objective and of matter and spirit, and that builds itself indefinitely, if not infinitely, while remaining finite. This America gave Frantz Kafka the title of his novel and John Dos Passos the opportunity to dream of it. Ah, with all due respect to Karl Barth, if we had theologized with the Bible in one hand and the novel rather than the newspaper in the other, would the world of the Bible have turned today into a focus of so much nostalgia, or would theology now receive as much care as is taken while embalming a corpse?

Grace, that takes away the sins of the world but does not abrogate nature (the onto-logy of past days), remains no less an abstract entity for propping up, albeit in the name of human solidarity, an obsolete political vision of a responsible society even while the order of things has so shifted that traditional soteriology has lost its impact on reality and by-passes the enlivening experience of the people of today. At the Nuremberg trials, no question of God was ever raised. Theology, geared as it was to salvation, still kept aloof from the scene. By contrast, it is science, rather than or in spite of theology, that brings us back again to the question of God - but with a twist: the existential question 'Who am I?' is focused not so much on the God who saves as on the God who creates.

Indeed, we had become so accustomed to reading Genesis as kind of a preface to the Gospel that we managed to forget that the prologue of John also contains a cosmology. The world of matter is not foreign to the world of spirit. The God who saves is also the God who creates. Nevertheless, as *religious* as the notion of creation may be, it cannot be used in any shape or form as an alibi by an understanding of faith that would countenance by reason of some new-fangled *sacrificium intellectus* the hi-jacking of scientific discourse.

2. Scientific method and religious language

Whether the divorce of science and religion has come at last to an end or not, one thing is certain. There no longer exists between them any kind of no man's land. Nor are they confined within watertight boundaries. And whatever boundaries do exist, it seems that they disappear as soon as science and religion reach their respective peaks of ultimate concern. This can be verified in many ways. I will cite two of them in order to show, on the one hand, the extent to which science has pervaded the need for religion and subverted the latter's traditional vocabulary and, on the other hand, how science itself, in keeping with its own methods, is forced to raise questions that belong to the realm of the spirit, although it is not as a result diverted from its own goals or ends.

With respect to sociology, or simply the social problem, one can be satisfied, I think, with a reminder of phenomena such as the establishment of ethics commissions by governments or industry, or the practical behaviour (brought to light in a recent survey) of Roman Catholics who believe in heaven without believing in hell. Going out of their way to meet the Pope and adulate him, they queue up to hear him but do not listen to him. They only hear what they want to hear. They have given up Latin. But they have not lost their faith. It is as if, by switching from one language to another, from one worldview to another, their faith has acquired a new intensity, another resonance. It sounds different depending on whether it is said in the vernacular or Einstein's language, or in some Canaanite dialect or the language of Ptolemy. Indeed, different to such an extent that one begins to wonder if, for all practical purposes, faith is not already *reasoned out* quite differently.

With respect to knowledge and one's understanding of reality, the objectivity claimed for the so-called scientific method has been renounced, if not denounced, by science itself on its own grounds. Science calls for the imagination and nurtures it, no less than religion does. In any case, François Jacob is one scientist among many who writes things like 'with the advent of microphysics ... the border between observer and observed has become somewhat less clear. The objective world is no longer as objective as it seemed until quite recently'.

Besides, while matter and energy are one, light can be understood in terms of particles as well as in terms of waves. As for moral values, they are not fully sheltered either from scientific incursions that bring those values into question. And if physics and biology are not by themselves able to identify evil much less to prescribe the good, they do seem nevertheless remarkably keen on wandering into aesthetics, the ambit of which even encompasses natural catastrophes or cancerous cells alike, as though such things belonged to a realm other than that of evil. Indeed, nature knows no evil and cannot intrude on this question without submitting itself to the judgement of an authority beyond its control. This would mean that, surpassing itself, science would acknowledge and respond to principles and ends that lie beyond its recognised limits.

Be that as it may, the indicative mood characterizes the whole of science. But with the moral imperative, another mood altogether is representative of human reality in quest of itself. The whole issue comes down to the question whether science, because of its obligation to objectivity, can refuse to take account of this other dimension without incurring the very accusation of *sacrificium intellectus* so long levelled at theology.

3. Equation and metaphor

Data (or information) and knowledge are two quite different things, that must not be confused. While an electronic memory stores and processes data only, the human brain is always looking for what it does not yet know. As J. Bronowski has pointed out, science is not the business of insects and machines. It can no more do without symbols and metaphors than can poetry or theology.

All language is symbolic. And even $E = mc^2$ is no longer only an equation. By now, it has become a symbol - not unlike water that makes us clean and also cleanses us spiritually. To be sure, the primary goal of the scientific method is an equation, and mathematics correctly treats such symbols as *only* symbols. But then, though with Tillich one could deplore the fact, doesn't the same apply equally to religious symbols, if and when, so to speak, the language of the world and that of the church drift away from one another, and the language of faith, of belief, is one world behind the world of unbelief? However religious a symbol may be, is it not itself also only a symbol?

Anyhow, if the equation is basic to scientific method, metaphor is still more basic to religious language. But while an equation is reversible, the metaphor is not. Science is interested in what is, or in what was, and in a sense even in what will be. Faith, by contrast, is less concerned with what is than with the fact that whatever is, is ever and only *once for all*.

And just as God is equidistant from everyone, so is he at an equal distance from all things. Hence the universe postulates neither that God is necessary nor that he is superfluous. It can only posit itself in relation to God's radical otherness. It needs God no more than a utensil needs to be a pot or a pan. Even on the threshold of the creation, all is grace. And God - believe it or not! - can only be believed in. Though not necessarily through the language of an antiquarian. Faith is not inextricably bound up with any particular language, however ancient.

To begin with, and more important when it is a question of the creation, what we are dealing with is an exclusively religious understanding of reality rather than a scientific category. First and foremost, creation is and has always been an article of faith, although, even as such, it must also at some stage confront non-religious considerations, in particular, scientific ones. Still, the object of theology and the object of science must not be confused. For the very same reason, however, faith can have no other language than that of unbelief. Nor does the Word become a metaphor unless the latter is wrested from some kind of equation despite its nature. It is not necessary either that these two languages be *complementary*. They need only be *compatible*, in the same way that things - or a man and a woman - are that are not actually planned for one another. They are compatible, as in the story of Genesis, to the point of being *one*.

Expressed differently, an equation is a symbol, though it is *only* a symbol. By crossing over the symbolic threshold of language, it veers into metaphor (as formerly physics did into metaphysics), just as, conversely, the logic of faith irrigates everyday words and transfigures them (in the same way that poetry transfigures everyday prose). It is through words as well as through the Word that the world comes about, becomes present and is re-presented. The interdependence of words and the Word, of scientific discourse and religious discourse or, better still, of what makes them compatible, has no other warrant than the symbolic load specific to the language through which, whether scientifically or religiously, the world of things and beings is grasped.

4.   Quest of origins and the creation: the sacred and utopia

Such grasping, such re-presenting of the world is what, following Genesis, we call the *creation*. It differs essentially from what we call *emanations*. From the standpoint of the former, the world does not have its origin within itself, but it is not to be seen, as from the latter viewpoint, as an emanation of God either. Nor does it emanate from anything that came before it. On the contrary, before the world was, there was 'tohu-wabohu', that is, nothing that could be said to be *before* the world was. The world is an entirely new thing. Not to be explained by reference to antecedents, and not to be understood in terms of causation. Rather than a quest for origins, the creation is in fact an attempt to refute such a quest and, in particular, it constitutes a warning against the temptation that lurks behind all such quests, that is, the tendency to equate God and nature. Nor is that the only thing peculiar to the biblical story, a story that does not shrink, by the way, from borrowing quite substantially now and again from other myths of creation, the result being that they have much more in common than just a family resemblance.

The story of Genesis, however, evinces still another peculiar feature that makes it differ even more markedly, for instance, from Enuma Elish. In the Babylonian myth of Enuma Elish, we are faced with a sacral conception of the universe while the hierarchical structure of the latter, though it evokes some notion of transcendence, is expressive of a principle wholly immanent to it. By contrast, Genesis depicts a world called forth by God through his word. And to the extent that it is a world that comes about as a response to God's call, it is - we would say today - a disenchanted world, a world come of age: God is no personification of the forces of nature, but its ruler. He is no part of the world's make-up, but its maker. Whereupon Genesis moves into an Edenic, paradisiacal reading of the world. That is to say: evil, of which nature knows nothing, but which seems no less an alternative to the good that humankind must choose, is not in the least necessary. God is pleased with creation, not jealous of it. He finds that it is good. Indeed, the world is a world come of age in so far as evil can be overcome. Even more, it is God's own utopia: nowhere is God to be found, yet he *is here*, everywhere. Given along with the reality of the world, the reality of God is never a datum, whether on the natural, social or cultural level or, for that matter, on the religious level. Utopic, the creation thus gives a framework to the alliance, to the covenant between God and humanity, God and Israel, a covenant renewed by the Christ through whom God is tipped into the human, and the human into God, without either separation or confusion.

Finally, like the New Jerusalem of the Book of Revelation, at the other end of the spectrum, but unlike the Babylonian myth of Enuma Elish, in Genesis the Garden of Eden contains neither Temple nor sacred precincts. It is to chaos, to the tohu-wabohu, as the Promised Land is to Egypt. And this comparison becomes all the more significant when we recall that, in ancient mythology, chaos is considered as the absolute symbol of the sacred. Far from harking back to a sacral conception of the universe, the notion of creation militates against it. There is no creation but *ex nihilo*; that is, before the world there was nothing (and, surely, the Bible is far from ignoring that nothing can come out of nothing). There is, in other words, no *before*. Space is the body of time, and time the soul of space. At an equal distance from all their interfaces (as hinted at in the biblical notion of ʿolam) stands God who, in the Christ, is equidistant from all humanity. This amounts to saying, in particular, that it is for one and the same reason that God creates the world and sends his only Son into it: namely, because he so loves it! Also, it is because this love is *realisable*, as all utopia is realisable, so long as it consists not so much in changing worlds as in changing the world.

Is it any wonder, then, that Israel throughout its history should cling to the Land, and receive it as a gift renewed on every Sabbath, in every sabbatical year and in every year of the jubilee?

5. Datum and mandatum: memory and hope

I have probably stretched the story of Genesis enough already to be allowed one further proposal. If the biblical notion of the creation is to be properly understood, one must not limit oneself to the Book of Genesis alone. One must take equal account of many other books of the Bible, such as Revelation, the Gospel of John or the wisdom literature. Indeed, the cosmology of wisdom literature, in particular, is somewhat akin to a theology of nature and, as such, differs from anything found in Genesis. Rather than a theology of nature, what is at stake in Genesis is a theology of the word or even a theology of language. God is thought of in terms of language, not in terms of nature. He is Word, and that is why he creates. He creates man and woman, and what makes them human is the way that they can speak and relate to God: to speak is to have faith. It is to break away: to break off with nature or with the past and, likewise, with all that comes *before* one's own advent to speech. It is to break off with all that comes before, and to be delivered from it: *Ecce homo*, without precedent! To be human is to be *without precedent*.

Related exclusively to God, we become conscious of evil as we become conscious of our sinfulness. We do what we do not want to do, and we do not do what we do want to do. No sooner do we obey the law and practice the commandments than we are guilty, if only because the very practice of what is commanded, regardless of whether it turns into ritual or not, displays more often than not all the characteristics of, and is tantamount to, a commemoration. The moorings of memory to the past are then more important than the remembering itself. And that kind of remembering is about as useless as the human venture is futile if it remains tied up in its past.

Only to the extent that she hopes, does Israel remember!

We hope, therefore, we remember. And we remember whence we come - Egypt or chaos, monkey or amoeba - only if we go to our rendez-vous with destiny, whether the Promised Land or New Jerusalem is the name of whither we go. Just as without the Exodus there would be no Genesis, so also without destiny - and Calvin took great pains to distinguish it from fate - there would be no beginning. And no end either. Not that - as some mystics are fond of asserting - my end is in my beginning. The source of a river is part of the river, but the meaning of a source lies in the river that reaches its estuary, and there it can only start *de novo*. No river runs twice in the same bed. To be sure, there is no origin that does not leave a trace. But no trace can ever lead back to the origin: the notion of creation is an eschatological one. Put differently, the God who creates is also the God who comes.

But if creation thus tips us from nature over into history, it is, however, the eschatological alone that is historical. The meaning is indeed given but it is never a datum: it is always a gift. Not a *datum*, but a *mandatum*, a commission. Not the preservation of a story, but the scenario of hope. It is a prolepsis: 'Do this in remembrance of me, *until I come*'. There is no experience of human reality except that of newness, that of grace. And that is why, in the biblical tradition, both natural man and the old man are assimilated to the sinner. There is no sinner, however, save before God and his grace, before the law as well as the gospel, *sub numine Dei verbi*.

Finally, in so far as it implies a theology of the word, the biblical notion of the creation also entails an ethic. Through the Sabbath. Remember, no sooner are we chased out of the Garden of Eden than we must eat our bread by the sweat of our brow. We must work. We must not, however, remain tied up in our work, but we must keep the Sabbath. This means that work, a desacralizing operation, is itself desacralized on the Sabbath. In the Jewish tradition, moreover, the Sabbath symbolizes the Kingdom of God and is, therefore, the day on which, as Paul puts it in keeping with the Old Testament, the rich have nothing much while the poor lack nothing. The lion and the lamb dwell together. The world starts *de novo*. God makes a new thing, as he does on each morning of the creation and Easter. In the Old Testament, the creation is accordingly geared to the Torah and, in the New, to the Christ - the word at once creative, redemptive and innovative.

Creative: in that the human, being human *first*, is not merely some by-product of nature alone at whatever degree of its evolution. Evolution will never reach such a point that God, in whose image we are created, will not be imageless and radically Other.

Redemptive: in that all human is all too human. Sinful as we may be, we will never be so alienated that we will cease deserving in Christ the future we do *not* deserve.

Innovative: in that, at last human, we come into our own and are at one with our selves, one body - and God is Spirit if the body then is, indeed, the temple of the Spirit, and, as such, rather than being a part of nature, partakes of the creation just as it partakes of the Body of Christ.

'Shall I bring to the birth and not cause to bring forth? says the Lord.' (Isaiah 66, 9)

What was man before man (a question that may be of scientific concern) or life before life, and man after man or life after life? Strange as such notions may appear by comparison with those of creation or redemption, they are perhaps not totally foreign to them. Something changes, of course, as we pass from traditional notions of life after death to the enticingly demythologized notion of life after life. A biological notion entirely, or almost, at that! But then, it does not follow either that, because creation or redemption cannot be reduced to physics or biology, theology must adhere to the cosmology of Antiquity or to its anthropology. Nor should theology be driven to accept sloppy patchwork in order to retrieve a Canaanite vision of the world through the use of an abused scientific jargon, or in order to retrieve conversely today's scientific vision of the world through the use of an abused theological jargon.

Must we choose between the Charybdis and Scylla of fundamentalism and concordism? The better way is still that of theology. The more so because science itself invites us more and more impressively to follow this way.

6. Ethic of the creation and theology of the word

On the origin of origins one can only speculate. Irreversible, it lies beyond the purview of science, as Bergson has already pointed out. Yet I am not sure whether NASA's Robert Jastrow is even more categorical. In *God and the Astronomers*, he concedes freely that, nowadays, science does not seem ever to be able to pierce through the mystery of creation. Rather laconically, he tells instead of the surprise that awaits the scientist who, about to conquer the highest peak, climbs over the last rock only to be welcomed by a band of theologians who had been there for centuries. Much too flattering, indeed, as far as theologians are concerned. Jastrow gives them the better role. And, by the same token, he evinces the same penchant for bad theology which is so characteristic of us all. I mean that he avoids rethinking theology from scratch, just as theologians refused previously to take due account of the impact of scientific discourse upon language.

Anyhow, one thing needs to be stressed at this point. If, today, science and theology must rival one another, they can do so only on the basis of mutual trust and confidence. The days of hostility are over. On the one hand, faced with a scientific method that opens on the question of religion, it is important that the theologian not merely renovate the façade of his house, but instead re-examine its structure and make the necessary changes, whether at the conceptual or the ecclesial level of faith. On the other hand, science, which, at one time, indulged itself by giving lessons on our mores, if not on morality outright, seems in this respect more circumspect nowadays. One might add, though not without noting a certain malaise in its stance, even to the point of shying away altogether from the moral question.

This explains perhaps why it seems more attracted to the question of origins than to questions of ultimate concern. But then, ever since the Sabbath was established, has there ever been anyone who did not really know that it was made for man, and not the other way round?

Science can, of course, upset the applecart of our values. But man is not made for applecarts. Nor will any scientific theory ever be able to withdraw God from the horizon of faith. Such a theory, however, might well widen it. For example, the theory of relativity eradicates all dualistic principles that cleave matter and energy. It also forbids all cleavage between space and time. And by the same token, it invests the ethical, and hence religious, question with no less prestigious a significance than is granted to it - somewhat after the event - by the theory of causality. Not that the scientists' Big Bang and the biblical notion of the creation must belong to the same mode of thinking, to the same mood of the verb. Yet, at another level we should not be surprised if we are dealing here with some kind of ultimate evidence of the fact that, as José Delgado puts it, thought is not reducible to the brain, although thought is produced by the brain.

It was, if I am not mistaken, one of the Cappadocian Fathers who used to say that man has a mouth because he speaks. The human is embodied through speech. Likewise, God creates through the word: the biblical understanding of the world as well as of human reality or, for that matter, of God has nothing to do either with cosmogony or with theogony; indeed, it is not so much Christocentric as *Christo-logical* throughout.

Not unlike the idol or history muzzled by 'the sound and the fury', nature is mute. At best it is capable of a cry - or a Big Bang. It is capable of an onomatopoeia. It can really burst forth only when it is taken over into the symbolic power of language. It bursts forth on that day when God speaks and the thing happens; when God speaks and the word becomes flesh, and it lasts - as long as the metaphor lasts: eternally, which is to say *once for all*.

Part II

Contributions in sectional meetings

Science and religion: a Ghanaian perspective

Johannes A. Mawuli Awudza

Man, created in the image of God, has been a co-creator with God since prehistoric times. Science and technology are tools that have been used for this purpose. These two disciplines have passed through several stages of development. The advanced stages of science and technology as we know them today originated from Europe some centuries ago. Subsequently, they have filtered to different parts of the world. Science and technology have had a great impact on man and on the whole of creation. It is only to be expected, therefore, that the courses of science and technology will continue to be influenced and shaped largely by those who have made them what they are today.

This contribution considers how the introduction of science and religion by European colonizers *and* the existence of certain religio-cultural practices in some parts of the African world have actually prevented people in these regions from being co-creators with God. Also, a passionate appeal is made to all scientists, theologians and men of goodwill to continue with the work of creation in a more humane manner, while at the same time maintaining a well-balanced ecosystem. Finally, it is proposed that science and technology should be used to foster better relationships both among people within the same region and between the north and the south.

Johannes A. Mawuli Awudza:
Department of Chemistry, University of Science and Technology, Kumasi, Ghana.

The mystical ideal and the humanistic ideal within the world of ideals in the sciences

Richard Becerra-Acevedo

Only in its deeper modes of thinking is the mind able to give birth to the humanistic ideal and to those convictions from which all progress springs, that is, progress with respect to any mode of human existence in which ethical concerns have been deepened. It is evident, however, that there is no way leading from the knowledge or cognition of what IS to the knowledge or cognition of what OUGHT TO BE. In fact, science can only be pursued by people who are wholly convinced of their aspirations to search for truth and understanding, because only commitment to real, profound aims and values confers an essential meaning to our existence and to our actions. Nevertheless, the knowledge obtained by natural science with its significant influence on the thinking of human beings and on practical life has weakened the religious sensibility of people. And, because of the traditionally close relation between religion and morality, this implies that the intensities of ethical sensibility and of ethical concern have likewise seriously decreased. In this connexion it should be emphasized that the ethical claim is not only a matter of religion, but rather the most important Good of humanity that has ever been transmitted.

Richard Becerra-Acevedo: Calí, Colombia

Scientific truth and religious truth

G. J. Béné

We show that the search for truth in religious faith proceeds along the same lines as in science. In both cases it is necessary to make use of the distinction, suggested by J. Ladrière, between the *rational* (which can be established by scientific procedures that are compelling) and the *reasonable* (which depends on judgment, on choice and wisdom). As a result, the confidence we have in religious truth can be shown to be of the same kind as that placed in scientific results, but at a different level of credibility. We have, in fact, in both cases three steps in the pursuit of truth:
- The setting of the philosophical axioms that are the foundations of knowledge, i. e. the fundamental postulates of science and the set of all religious dogmas.
- A rational and scientific analysis of human experience, allowing the improvement of scientific postulates as well as of religious dogmas. In the first case, the analysis gives a strong basis for such postulates and, in the second, the religious dogmas are at least not disproved.
- And finally a synthesis of the Theory of science and the Theology of religion.
Some examples illustrate these two aspects of the search for truth as the three steps are traced. In conclusion we express the conviction that it is the duty of each searcher, scientist and/or believer, to propagate the Truth.

Note:

The full text of the above communication has been published, in french language, in *Nouveau Dialogue*, Service Incroyance et Foi, 2930 Rue Lacombe, Montréal, H3T 1L4 Canada, no. 80, mai 1989, pp. 4-9.

G. J. Béné: DPMC Section de Physique de l'Université de Genève, Institut de Physique, Geneva, Switzerland.

Two approaches and one reality: on religion and the perception of the Cosmos

P. W. Böckman

Starting with Paul Tillich's concept of God as the Power of being in all reality, it is emphasized that, on the one hand, reality cannot be separated from God while, on the other hand, the empirical, rational and non-theistic character of science must be taken into account. How are these two apparently conflicting views to be reconciled?

Referring to the World Council of Churches conference in 1979 on 'Faith, Science and the Future', it is maintained that reality is *one*, although there are four different approaches (scientific, ethical, aesthetic and religious) to this one and only reality. Concentrating upon the distinction between the scientific approach and the religious one, it is emphasized that God cannot be listed as a supplementary factor or force in the understanding of reality perceived through science. Also, the scientific approach cannot provide a basis for any statements - negative or positive - about God as the Power of being 'in, cum et sub' reality as a whole. This, however, does not exclude the possibility of the scientific (or ethical or aesthetic) approach pointing beyond itself towards a transcendent foundation that can only be recognized through the religious approach.

An investigation of the predominance of science in Western culture indicates that all four approaches should be considered equally valid because, in fact, they give access to four *different dimensions* that cover the whole of reality. God is not just a 'viewpoint', but the Power of being in all reality perceived through the religious approach in the religious dimension in which all of reality exists.

The consequences of this understanding for the concepts of *creation* and *wonder* are discussed, and the concept of a *personal* God is asserted while maintaining the understanding of God as the Power of being. This concept makes the concepts of creation and wonder relevant.

P. W. Böckman: Department of Religion, University of Trondheim, Dragvoll, Norway

Man and the high-technology society

S. L. Bonting

High Technology is defined as the technical application of novel and emerging scientific concepts and knowledge for design, development, production and integration in the fields of computerization/automation, the aerospace industry and biotechnology. Computerized automation has the most *pervasive* effects, whereas the military aerospace sector poses the greatest *danger* to man's existence. Can High Technology be controlled? Man cannot opt out of his High Technology because, once having tasted 'the fruit of the tree of the knowledge of good and evil', he is doomed to continue his search for new knowledge and technical skills, for good or evil: that is, he has become part of his own technological system. Only by using his God-given intelligence and moral judgment can he try to abolish or to alleviate the undesirable effects of his technological activities, while benefitting from the positive effects. Control of technological development is very difficult. Yet it must be attempted. Concerted action is needed by concerned expert groups, labour unions, industrial and political leaders, and the churches. The focus of the Church's ministry should be to complete technology by infusing the spiritual dimension, and to renew our awareness of the sacramental nature of the universe.

S. L. Bonting: Sunnyvale CA., United States of America

On David Bohm's theory of wholeness and implicate order: provisional notes, some of which with special regard to the possible applications to the philosophy of religion

M. E. Carvallo

The relation between nature and cognition, which is taken to be metaphoric for the relation between religion and science, is described by three models: the model of *bifurcation* (subdivided into the Homeric, Platonic, and Cartesian variants), the model of *convenance* (subdivided into the conversational, vitalistic, and animistic variants), and the model of *fusion*. The model of fusion is further described in the light of David Bohm's philosophy of physics. (According to Bohm, the whole of existence, including inanimate matter, living organisms *and* mind, arises from a single ground in which these forms of existence are all *enfolded*, that is, contained implicitly.)

It is shown that much of the contemporary philosophy of religion is obsolete because, as far as the author knows, it is still predicated upon the model of bifurcation. The possible relevance for the philosophy of religion of the latter two models is indicated. Particular emphasis is given to the model of fusion and to David Bohm's philosophy of physics.

M. E. Carvallo: Department of Philosophy of Religion, State University of Groningen, Groningen, The Netherlands

A. Koyré and the metaphysics of modern science

Antonino Drago

In the past, many difficulties have arisen that affected the relation between science and religion because science claimed to be completely devoid of metaphysics and to be 'compelling', that is, without any intrinsic alternative. However, recent studies of the history of science offer a new appraisal of the nature of science.

Forty years ago, A. Koyré masterfully described the birth of modern science* . This birth was triggered by two ideas, namely, 'the dissolution of the finite cosmos' and 'the geometrization of space'. Although separately each of these phrases had an experimental meaning, their combination led to a distinct metaphysical level of discussion. In particular, it led to the conception of a cosmic space that was infinite and abstract rather than a (finite) sum of the concrete places of contiguous objects. In my opinion, the two crucial ideas mentioned above correspond to two basic choices in Newton's work: he developed a mathematical theory that included *actual* infinity, and he organized physical theory on the basis of self-evident principles. In the next development of science some theories were proposed that contrasted the choices made by Newton with alternative ones, and thus that introduced a different metaphysics: L. Carnot's mechanics, S. Carnot's thermodynamics, and classical chemistry chose a kind of mathematics that included, at most, *potential* infinity. Moreover, each of those theories was organized around a particular fundamental problem. In this way the notion of space involved in each was different from the Newtonian one, so that, for instance, in classical chemistry an explicit notion of space does not exist at all.

Such facts prove that any theory presupposes decisions taken with respect to basic options that constitute its very metaphysics. The latter may or may not agree with a given religion considered as a *theoretical system*. Conversely, religious thinking may give priority to those scientific theories that are most consonant with its basic tenets.

Antonino Drago: History of Physics Group, Department of Physical Sciences, University of Naples, Naples, Italy

---

* See e.g. Alexandre Koyré, *Du monde clos a l'univers infini*, Presses Universitaires de France, Paris 1962; original publication: *From the closed world to the infinite universe*, John Hopkins University Press, Baltimore 1957.

The unus mundus (One World) as meeting ground of science and religion

Herbert van Erkelens

A conceptual framework is sketched in which the search for a unified theory of the universe and the striving for human integrity are viewed as arising from a common ground. In consonance with the medieval concept denoting the pre-existent model of the cosmos in the mind of God, this common ground is called the *unus mundus* or *One World*. According to the depth psychologist Carl Gustav Jung, the One World is a unitary domain outside the human categories of space and time, and beyond our division of reality into matter and spirit. It is argued that a reconciliation of science, psychology and religion can be achieved, if the various partners in the interdisciplinary exchange acknowledge the following empirical manifestations of the One World:
- the unifying power of the self (this archetype of orientation and meaning can be called the inner God-image; mandala symbolism),
- the occurrence of meaningful coincidences in the world (synchronicity), and
- acausal order in the field of science (compare for instance the anthropic principle: a slight change in the values of fundamental constants and the properties of elementary particles rules out human life from the beginning).

Herbert van Erkelens: Unit for the history, philosophy and social aspects of science, Faculty of Physics and Astronomy, Free University, Amsterdam, The Netherlands

The play that is going on in the cosmic scenery

A.D. Fokker

Astrophysics tells us a story of extreme circumstances and violent processes that blindly take their course. Cosmic processes do not appear to serve any purpose; we do not perceive a Will-in-action. Yet complexification seems to be a mechanism that, under favourable circumstances, is at work in some corners of the universe. And so the emergence of life defies the endless monotony of apparently meaningless cosmic processes.

A metaphor is adopted in a quest to grasp the ultimate sense of it all. Astrophysics informs us about the pieces of scenery that are erected on a stage, but it reveals nothing about the play that is being performed. What the play is all about lies beyond the imaginative faculty of human beings. The more fantastic the play, the more precarious it is. The role assigned to human beings is one that is finely balanced on the edge between success and failure. Could it be that we humans, as creatures gifted with the power of reflection, with a sense of moral values and with a capacity to love, have in our hands the key to unravel, perhaps, a tiny part of the Secret of the universe?

A.D. Fokker: Bilthoven, The Netherlands

A report from the Reformed College of Debrecen

Botond Gaál

The Reformed College has many teachers who, as committed Christians, are engaged in the teaching of the various branches of the natural sciences. We try to implement our specific insights of Christian education in the instruction of every subject of our curriculum. Two examples are given:

- To us, history is not simply a process governed by the laws of economics and social life, but a manifestation of the providence and guidance of God. Hence we may work confidently for a just and happy future, being sure of the victory of life over death, this victory guaranteeing the ultimate triumph of good over evil. 'Our labour is not in vain in the Lord.' (1 Cor. 15:58)

- We are especially interested in the cultivation of the natural sciences. We have a great tradition concerning this matter. It is a joy for us to know, to discover, and to teach the laws of nature, of the material world, for all this may further the progress of man. However, this knowledge of the laws governing the world of nature does not lead us to devise theories of the origin of the world. We do not seek so-called 'final causes', that is, we do not turn our knowledge into a philosophical world-view. We confess that God created the world as it is with its laws and perspectives. The origin of creation is a mystery which faith accepts without being able to fathom it fully. Moreover, the cultivation of the natural sciences has its ethical aspects. Nature is not merely an object of knowledge. If this were so, one might presume to exploit nature mercilessly. The Scriptural injunction, however, is that man has 'to till the garden of Eden and care for it' (Gen. 2:15).

Botond Gaál: The Reformed College of Debrecen, Debrecen, Hungary

Interdisciplinary lectures at 6 o'clock

Gyula Gaizler

Since March 1983, we have had a six o'clock tea every first Monday of the month in our own flat. During the tea, at least one interdisciplinary lecture is delivered. About 60-100 friends gather in our home, sometimes more, e. g. when the former president of the Hungarian Scientific Academy, Prof. Szentágothay, gave a lecture, there were 150 people present, so some of them had to sit on the floor.

The subject of the lectures varies widely with the lecturers approaching theology and philosophy from their own particular directions. The one hour lecture is followed by a discussion that lasts for about two hours. Occasionally there are young people present (16-18 years); the vast majority of the guests are university graduates.

The 'New Deal' in Hungary made it possible to found a Christian Ecumenical Fellowship. We now have three series of lectures monthly at various places with 100-300 visitors. 'Our humanity and our nationality from a Christian point of view' is the title of the first series of lectures which addresses a very important question in Hungary today. 'Nationality and internationality in the perception of the natural scientist' and 'Morality and the lawyer' are two representative titles of this series which tackles urgent problems in our country. Ecumenical themes are discussed separately in a second series, and aspects of Hebraic-Judaic studies are dealt with in the third series.

In addition we have a section deeply concerned with the problems of the more than two million Hungarian people at present living in Transsylvania in Rumania. Their personal plights are not just theoretical puzzles for us, but raise very practical issues: e. g. How do you supply food and medicaments to them?

Gyula Gaizler: Budapest, Hungary.

Beyond the alternative: divorce or methodological chaos

Małgorzata Głódź

The divorce of science and religion in recent decades has reached the stage of a 'treaty' based on the peculiarity of the empirical method as compared with other methods of acquiring knowledge. It manifests itself in the form of mutual non-intervention. In my opinion this duality is unavoidable, at least at present, and it reflects the inadequacy of the cognitive tools we possess. But a believer-scientist (provided he acknowledges the existence of one Reality) may feel uneasy about this state of affairs. For, if there is no ontological duality, there should be no duality on epistemological grounds either.

On the one hand, the scientist-believer, who experiences this situation as an internal dissociation, may look for some symptoms of a possible future synthesis on observing successful attempts at convergence among various scientific disciplines.

On the other hand, issues that are 'forbidden' within science could be discussed in meta-scientific, and perhaps meta-religious, language. The most qualified grounds for a philosophical or theological approach is this area of *meta-science*, where the most fundamental regularities of cognitive processes and presuppositions are analysed.

Małgorzata Głódź: Warsaw, Poland

Neither divorce nor reconciliation: is there a gospel for the sciences?

Hermann Hafner

Some fundamental features of the relation between science and Christian faith are analysed. The thesis is that conflict together with the possibility of, and the desire for, a unifying association are deeply rooted in the predispositions visited upon this relation. Special attention is given to the fact that the Gospel (as the foundation of Christian faith) is not a system of knowledge or a world view, but a *message* giving a new foundation to human life as a whole and in every respect. Hence, the relation under consideration is between two things of very different natures, and the question is not simply one of 'divorce' or 'reconciliation', but: how does the Gospel as Gospel relate to science as science and *vice versa*?

If science is considered as the embodiment of the human endeavour to come to grips with reality, it is clearly challenged by the Gospel, and specific aspects of scientific understanding will be involved in the confrontation. Although it is a standing problem, how to assert convincingly the relevance of extra-scientific views and considerations in scientific practice, some hints concerning the relevance of the Gospel for science may be discussed. Finally, it will be explained that the expectations concerning the construction of a unity of science based on exclusive sets of methodological presuppositions and religious indifference are largely unfounded.

Hermann Hafner: Marburg, The Federal Republic of Germany

The experience of limits: new physics and new theology

Michael Heller

Logical positivism aimed at understanding the revolution that took place in the fundamentals of physics at the beginning of this century. However, the revolution in the sciences is still going on, and analyses carried out in the spirit of logical positivism have been left behind. It seems that the destination of every philosophy of science is to be a philosophy 'along the way'. Nevertheless, some trends can be discovered in this 'transitory chain' of progress that are likely to persist long into the future.

In the 'new physics' the mathematical structure of a given theory determines its own empirical content. The old dualistic philosophy of science, splitting physics into theories and experiments, has been definitely transcended by physics itself. I would say that it is exactly this *organic unity* of theory and experiment that makes the contemporary physics more experimental than the older classical physics. In the 'new physics' matter does not seem to exist unless as an aspect of a theoretical structure. This seems to corroborate the philosophical structuralist view. One of the most fascinating features of mathematical structures as models of the world is their apparent ability to justify themselves. These structures are so strictly connected with each other that they seem to be necessary and to be in no way open to arbitrary, speculative alterations. A theologian could be afraid that the totalitarian tendencies of science are being revived in their most exaggerated form. The following response, however, should be considered:

Mathematical structures that reflect the structure of the world are indeed able to provide a kind of ultimate understanding. In a theological perspective the ultimate rationality is that of God. The fact that it is a mathematical type of rationality is not a new factor in theology. The metaphor of 'God thinking the Universe' is well rooted in the history of theology.

Michael Heller: Faculty of Philosophy, The Pontifical Academy of Theology, Cracow, Poland, and The Vatican Astronomical Observatory, Vatican State.

Evolution and progressive revelation: the Bahá'i approach to a converging reality

Ingo Hofmann

In our attempt to reconcile science with religion, we are dealing in particular with the scientifically accepted concept of the world as a system that is open to the future. Essential ingredients of this openness are the increases of complexity and potentiality that imply evolution. According to the Bahá'i-Faith, the notion of evolution is not restricted to the scientifically explorable world. It has its counterpart also in religion, which is in fact the basis for 'One World' - as meant in the Conference title - and for a new understanding of reality. *Progressive revelation* means that divine guidance is not limited to one religion, but that there is an infinite progression of divine revelations through the different founders of religion. Their common source and purpose, however, make the essential *unity of religions.* According to Bahá'u'lláh (1817-1892), founder of the Bahá'i-Faith, mankind is a hidden treasure of gems of possibilities and opportunities, that are laid bare through knowledge and learning. And the recognition of the *organic oneness of mankind* in all essential human relationships is the challenging step of human evolution ahead of us.

Science and religion have complementary functions in the ways they deal with both the known and the unknown. The essence of God is the supreme unknown, yet God is known through his manifestations in his ordinances. Religion can be looked at as the art of dealing with this unknown day by day. This has significant implications for the unfolding of a new world order through learning and faith.

Ingo Hofmann: Dieburg, The Federal Republic of Germany

Beyond dogmatism: rationality in theology and science

J. Wentzel V. van Huyssteen

The justification of cognitive claims in theology can be dealt with adequately only if the epistemological issues of metaphorical reference, experiential adequacy and explanatory progress are seen as crucial issues for the more encompassing problem of rationality in theology. To claim some form of reality depiction the theologian will have to argue for a plausible theory of reference on the basis of interpreted religious experience. In this discussion important analogies between the rationality of theological theorizing and that of science are revealed. Thus explanatory progress in theology is shown to be a form of inference to the best explanation and, therefore, the rationalities of theology and science are determined by the specific epistemic values that they have in common.

J. Wentzel V. van Huyssteen: University of Port Elizabeth, Port Elizabeth, Republic of South Africa

Spirituality and science: summary of purpose and proceedings *

Richard Kirby

Participants discussed the relevance of systematic spirituality for conferences such as this one, and for scientists in general, especially those interested in religion and/or theology. Faiths represented in the discussion were the Bahá'i-Faith, Buddhism, Hinduism and Christianity. Participants agreed that the interaction of science and spirituality was of immense importance for true progress in science and technology. Prayer, for example, promotes scientific research and its integrity, and gives moral direction and insight to scientists. Meditation helps scientists to know God, and to observe and measure Nature with greater accuracy and resourcefulness.

This group recommends the appointment of a *Committee on Spirituality and Science* for future 'Euro Conferences on Science and Religion'. Such a committee could serve: to provide expositions of the meaning, methods and results of the varieties of meditation; to begin a 'Varieties of religious experience' project as a scientific arm of international scientific methodology; to arrange 'Quiet times' within the Conferences when participants can experiment in spiritual exercises as they relate to their own habits and occasions of scientific research; to begin a Data Base of Scientists' Religious Experiences; and to create a starting point for an intersection of scientific and theological method around an empirical phenomenology of both scientific observation and religious experience.

Those wishing to join such Committee should contact Rev. Richard Kirby, Victoria Terrace, Ealing Green, London W5 5QS, England; phone (44) (1) 5790059.

Richard Kirby: Ealing Green, London, England

---

*   Report of a Conference workshop.

The unchanged relationship of theology and science

P. P. Kirschenmann, M. A. Maurice and A. W. Musschenga

This epistemological contribution mainly points up invariants in the relationship of theology and science:

- The relationship is not symmetrical. A diversity of theologies confronts the unity of scientific progress. Although the belief in one reality has led to attempts at integration and dialogue, the questions and answers keep varying. The very question of the relationship itself remains a theological one. The answers to this question vary in dependence upon a number of central (philosophical and theological) concepts and their relations.

- There is the particular question: Has recent scientific knowledge drastically changed this relationship and led to new demarcations? Some of the central concepts and relations have indeed undergone changes. Yet, rather than leading to a revolution in this relationship, scientific knowledge has, above all, rendered certain formulations of theological assertions untenable.

- Many people have claimed that modern scientific theories imply novel demarcations or closer ties. Examples show that (philosophically) such claims are virtually indefensible.

*P. P. Kirschenmann, M. A. Maurice and A. W. Musschenga: Bezinningscentrum (Interdisciplinary
centre for the study of science, society and religion), Vrije Universiteit,
Amsterdam, The Netherlands*

The concept of evolution: its reception in philosophy and theology

Rainer Koltermann, S. J.

Ever since Darwin wrote his 'Origin of Species' there has been an almost continuous contest between scientists and theologians about the (in)compatibility of the concepts of creation and evolution. On the one hand, many scientists are convinced that the very concept of evolution excludes creation. For evolution means a gradual change, and creation, in the understanding of Darwin and of many scientists of today, is an instantaneous coming into existence. On the other hand, fundamentalist creationists, who tend to take the Bible as a scientific textbook, and who interpret the 'story' of creation (Gen. 1) literally, are convinced that Christian faith excludes evolution. The solution can be found in three steps:
- Science has nothing epistemological to say about creation because it is not a scientific concept.
- A new philosophical analysis of creation shows that one has to distinguish between *creatio directa* at the beginning of the world and *creatio continua* which is a continuous keeping in existence. This creatio continua is necessary because organisms are contingent beings. Living beings are able to evolve because God keeps them in existence.
- This 'creation in evolution' is the teaching of the Catholic Church and of most other Christian Churches. Thus there is no contradiction between the two concepts of evolution and creation.

Rainer Koltermann, S. J.: Frankfurt, The Federal Republic of Germany

Secularization of nature during the early Enlightenment: conceptions of water circulation as an impulse for secularization

Udo Krolzik

The seventeenth century view of water focused on the forces of erosion. Behind this was a pessimistic, conservative worldview which saw the world declining as the result of the fall of Adam. Man had to fight against the declining natural processes as they were conspicuously represented by the forces associated with water. In opposition to this view, the early Enlightenment saw water and water circulation as the expressions of God's providential love. It was driven by an optimistic and progressive worldview. Philosophers of the Enlightenment perceived the qualities of water that provide and sustain life; the leading figure was the German physico-theologian, Johann Albert Fabricius, who developed a theology of water.

Later generations could forget about these theological motivations and limitations. The idea of water circulation, which was quickly and widely accepted, led to the opinion that the supply of water was inexhaustible and was meant for man's use. A circulation without a centre, as found for the circulation of water, became the secure foundation of the cosiness and wealth of bourgeoisie life. And, according to Montesquieu, it was held to be generally true that increasing riches were the consequence of an ever increasing 'circulation'. Thereafter, many things began to circulate, not only water, blood, stars and matter, but also ideas, money and labour.

Udo Krolzik: Hamburg, The Federal Republic of Germany

The scientific mind and personal faith

Gérard Lepoutre

Faith is facilitated by a scientific mind when good use is made of many *analogies*. Four examples are selected for this summary.

- Community: physicists and chemists as well as theologians submit their research to the community of their peers for validation. Also, in physics and chemistry as in matters of Faith, nobody can verify everything: the community is trusted.

- Images: photons, electrons or the Kingdom of Heaven are not felt by our senses. They are described by abstract mathematical or theological concepts. In order to speak of them in ordinary language we need complementary images: wave and particle, or a set of parables.

- To know and to act: scientific knowledge invites technological actions that, by implying free will and values, pass beyond the realm of science. Theological knowledge invites the act of Faith involving free will and help from the Ultimate Value who is well beyond the realm of knowledge.

- Mysteries: in science, when leaving the domain of our senses, words are inadequate and pictures that are complementary are needed; in theology words are forever deficient in describing a mystery.

Gérard Lepoutre: Catholic University and Diocese of Lille, Haubourdin, France

The views of a Hungarian catholic scholar on evolution at the end of the nineteenth century

György Medgyesi

Ottokár Prohászka (1858-1927) was a prominent person of the Hungarian Catholic Church. As a priest, a professor and later a bishop, he wanted to promote a Christianity that could answer the challenges of time. He was convinced that a split between science and religion could only be a temporary phenomenon. In his great overview of natural theology, 'Earth and Heaven', and in an earlier essay on 'God and World', he expressed a positive response to the concept of evolution. Trying to explain the driving forces of evolutionary processes, he postulated an *inherent plasticity* of living organisms, that makes changes possible and, therefore, allows the generation of new species. Environmental conditions and the 'struggle for life' can act as pressures bringing about the manifestation of this plasticity. Prohászka preferred sudden evolution over gradual evolution, arguing that the latter would tend to dissolve the concept of 'species'. He emphasized that creation could work through evolution, and that the acceptance of evolutionary theory did *not* necessarily involve materialism. The generation of the human species posed a dilemma for him. He accepted that the human body, but not the full human nature, could have come into existence in an evolutionary way.

György Medgyesi: Budapest, Hungary

Traditional religion and Christianity

Charles Ouafo Moghomaye

Traditionally African Society has always been an integrated society. Thus, scientific truths and religious truths - and whatever other truths - come together in man himself. And human dignity provides the standard that must be applied in evaluating the relevant truths.

Because of its progress, the industrialized world regards science and technology more and more as the supreme expression of humanity which, however, has entailed a gradual weakening of basic human values. In fact, as we Africans perceive it, the world proves to be dominated by sophisticated power and to be commercialised under its aegis - for the benefit of the rich. African countries based on agriculture produce what they don't need themselves, and the prices of those products are fixed by the consumers in the industrialised world. In this way, no loan can ever really contribute to the development of poor countries. Indeed IMF intervention increases their debts, and the African peoples lose their dignity just to get a loaf of bread.

Consequently, in the present discussion between 'science' and 'religion', the crucial question to be asked concerns *human dignity*. If the world operates on the bases of business and war, if the present civilizations prove to have no feeling of a common humanity, and if peoples lose the things that are sacred, they will lose their civilizations too! And, since Christianity has taken the place of traditional religion, the fundamental question to be asked is whether Christ is still the foundation of our existence, that is, whether he is still regarded as the first born of all Creation.

Charles Ouafo Moghomaye: Douala/Garoua, Cameroun

A generalized principle of complementarity
- seen as a sign

Lucien Morren

A sign is a fact or an event that conveys meaning: it rests upon the factual, so generally praised in our scientific era, but it opens the mind to the sphere of meaning, presently too often forgotten. Knowledge obtained by observing signs is of prime importance for the grounding of Christian faith. Remarkably, some recent scientific advances take a paradoxical form: they produce the sign that the reality they investigate transcends the finitude of our mind. We shall concentrate our attention on one example of such transcendence, one that we may call a generalized principle of complementarity drawn from a major scientific advance.

The complementarity of the corpuscular and undulatory aspects of elementary entities is well known in physics. It implies the conjunction of antinomic aspects in a single entity: this is really the basis of the principle. Now, we may discern in any being a similar dichotomy. We may distinguish in any being, at all levels, an aspect of *substratum* and an aspect of *information* but without grasping how they work together (e. g. in ourselves, our body including the brain and our reflexive conscience). The lesson, thus taught by science, reminds us of a structural similitude to major Christian mysteries; in particular, to what we hold true when confessing the Trinity and the Incarnation, both of which unite antinomies. Here we are, of course, in the realm of signs. In this way, moreover, new light is thrown upon the old theme of the Image, that is, the creation reflecting the Creator.

In summary: the awareness of signs helps us to overcome the divorce between science and religion if we remain alert to the analogy between the mysteries found by means of natural science and the mysteries experienced in religion.

Lucien Morren: Louvain-la-Neuve, Belgium

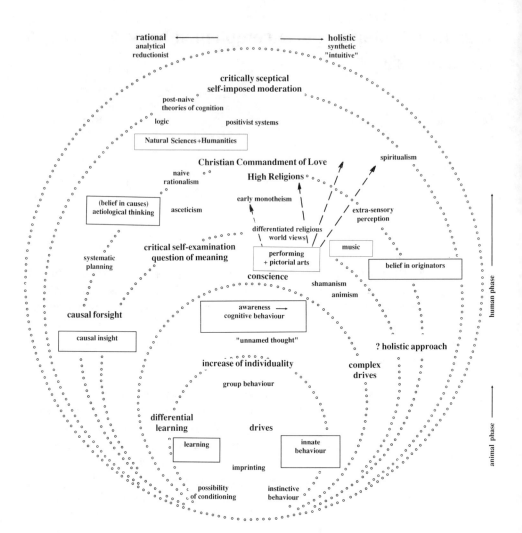

rational ← → holistic
analytical synthetic
reductionist "intuitive"

critically sceptical
self-imposed moderation

post-naive
theories of cognition

logic   positivist systems

Natural Sciences+Humanities

Christian Commandment of Love

naive   High Religions   spiritualism
rationalism

early monotheism

(belief in causes)   asceticism   extra-sensory
aetiological thinking   perception

differentiated religious
world views

critical self-examination   music
systematic   question of meaning   performing
planning   + pictorial arts   belief in originators

conscience

shamanism
animism

causal forsight   awareness →
cognitive behaviour

causal insight   ? holistic approach
"unnamed thought"

increase of individuality   complex
drives

group behaviour

differential
learning   drives

learning   innate
behaviour

imprinting

possibility   instinctive
of conditioning   behaviour

human phase

animal phase

Evolution and future of human possibilities of gaining knowledge

Wolfram Noodt

Palaeontology, ethology and psychology, on the one hand, and comparative theology, on the other, have gathered together so much information and speculation on the path of human-kind that an attempt to summarize all this seems justified. This is done with the help of a scheme (see preceding page) that clearly distinguishes between the two known types of human cognition:
- synthetic-intuitive, 'holistic' cognition, and
- analytic-rational cognition.
The roots of both approaches can be traced back far into the animal kingdom, but perhaps the origins of intuitive insight and cognition appear to be more obscure than the equally revolutionary advent of causative perception. Humankind became 'human' largely through the gift of 'conscience', which can be seen as the cornerstone as well as the driving force of everything that has evolved as part of cultural evolution.

Within this framework the term 'culture' is examined and the question of where cultural evolution will lead us seems quite legitimate. Should humankind enter successfully - and this is by no means certain - a truly 'post-naive-phase' of existence following the withdrawal from present-day cul-de-sac situations, then, faced with our limited possibilities, we will need to organize ourselves in the hopefully stabilizing condition of critical and sceptical self-restraint. If this is to happen, the essence of our *entire cultural history* must undoubtedly continue to provide, as indeed it already does, the most pressing answers.

Wolfram Noodt: Zoological Institute, The University of Kiel, Kiel, The Federal Republic of Germany

The relation between science and theology: the case for complementarity revisited

K. H. Reich

In contrast to D. M. MacKay's cautious suggestion that 'we need the logical concept of complementarity in scientific and theological thinking if we want to avoid logical blunders', none of the eight relationships between science and theology considered by A. R. Peacocke is labelled 'complementarity'. Thinking in terms of complementarity has now been explored further, both from a psychological perspective and from an epistemological one: for a genuine understanding, certain explananda require pairs of descriptions that refer to different situations/conditions together with pairs of interpretations that are non-compatible. Four distinct types of case are described that command different degrees of consensus, and a definition is given that covers all of them. After presenting adolescents' 'complementary' views on Creation and on their corresponding scientific accounts, such views are assessed with respect to the pertinent definitions and compared with the statements of experts. Broadly speaking, certain criteria for complementarity are met and the adolescents' views are confirmed by the experts, professionals of the different sciences and theologians. These findings suggest that, under the conditions discussed, the assumption of the complementarity of science and theology is reasonable and useful, both in research and in teaching.

Note:

Adolescents' complementary views referred to above are characterized by a coordination of the biblical and scientific belief systems in such a way that both contribute to an understanding of the matter in question, e. g. 'God made the laws of nature and then let events take their course' (cf. R.L. Fetz and K.H. Reich, 'Interaction of world-views and religious development: Five empirical case studies', to appear in the *Journal of Empirical Theology*).
The other publications referred to are: D. M. Mackay, 'Complementarity in scientific and theological thinking', *Zygon (Journal of Religion and Science)*, 9(1974), p. 225f and A. R. Peacocke (ed.), *The Sciences and Theology in the Twentieth Century*, Oriel Press Ltd, Stocksfield 1981.

K. H. Reich: Institut de Pédagogie de l'Université de Fribourg, Fribourg, Switzerland

Base the science-religion dialogue on facts, not on doctrines!

Jens Scheer

The aim of the present communication is to point to some developments within physics that are contrary to the doctrines of the interpretation of quantum theory that have been in vogue now for more than six decades. In short, the whole edifice of the 'orthodox' interpretation, characterized by concepts like uncertainty, complementarity, non-causality, intrinsic limits of cognition and non-objectivity, is unfounded for two reasons:
- The known phenomena can be explained by visualizable models. From these models the usual formalism can be derived, so that it should no longer be accepted as a collection of formulae that are contradictory and basically inexplicable.
- There are phenomena that cannot be described by the usual formalism. Therefore its incompleteness and lack of generality have been proven.

All this does *not* mean a return to classical physics, rather there are genuine new features like superluminal correlations, or wholeness of spatially separated objects, that in their turn can be understood within the framework of the model. Thus one can no longer claim that certain religious teaching can be 'derived' from physics, as has been asserted, e.g. by P. Jordan and Pope Pius XII for Christianity, and, equally, by F. Capra and G. Zukav for Eastern religions.

Jens Scheer: Physics Department, University of Bremen, Bremen, The Federal Republic of Germany

The reconciliation of social science and theology - is it still not possible?

Michał Siciński

The conflict between natural science and theology arose when the two disciplines started to talk about the same reality in different ways, and it was only resolved when they understood that each had a different cognitive status. Reconciliation came with the acceptance that they were not rivals but rather complementary approaches to the one reality. It was their full autonomy, the independence of natural science from theological concepts and *vice versa*, along with their distinct relations to social praxis that secured true reconciliation.

The conflict between social science and theology has a different history. The close connection of both, social science and theological thought regarding social questions, to the practical social contexts, and the need for both disciplines to articulate the same social problems made them rivals rather than complements. As a matter of fact the need for a new metaphysics appeared long after the old metaphysics had been eliminated from natural science, and a more modern theology helped in the search for this sensibility when natural science and theology had already become independent. Social science, however, was never fully liberated from its theological kinship and, therefore, there was neither a place nor a need for it to accommodate any entirely new form of theological impact in its view on reality.

A radical separation of social science and theology would severely cripple both. But, even if the integrity of each discipline is respected, both being virtually inseparable from their practical contexts, tension will inevitably persist. The highly specialized theoretical status of natural science allowed natural science and theology to be initially separated and subsequently reconciled. As long as the status of social science remains different, it cannot be expected to exhibit the same kind of development.

Michał Siciński: University of Mining and Metallurgy, Cracow, Poland, and University of Oslo, Blindern, Norway

A new perspective on reality

G. J. Stavenga

By an investigation of the structure of revelation as elaborated by Karl Barth, it is shown that the thesis at the beginning of his *Church Dogmatics** is correct: ALL SCIENCES AT THEIR ACME CAN BE AND FINALLY WILL BE THEOLOGY. A special theology will then become superfluous. Analysis of modern experimental physics shows that the principal records of recent research, for instance, those of the tracks of elementary particles, exhibit exactly the same structure as revelation. Thus revelation shows no irrational or authoritarian characteristics when it is recognized as a kind of cognition with an exceptional but definite structure. Physics and the other sciences, in fact, can attune themselves to the most fundamental structure of reality, that is, to the reality of revelation. For their own sake the sciences should become conscious, therefore, of this fundamental breakthrough. Indeed, Barth's theological research programme directs the attention of science to its conceptual limitations and to a new perspective on reality, that may be of great importance to the acute crises of our days.

G. J. Stavenga: Department of Philosophy, State University of Groningen, Groningen, The Netherlands

---

*   See Karl Barth, *Kirchliche Dogmatik Band 1-1* , p. 5.

Humanitas oecologica

János Szél

Ecology and polemology belong together. That environmental problems and the questions of peace and war cannot be solved separately is more than just an obvious truth. A discussion of this is presented on the basis of Isaiah's chapter 11 and Virgil's Fourth Ecloge. Both texts, in which rustic and even bucolic elements abound, contain the description of a utopia that has a critical function, though in different ways, particularly with respect to the role of power. Where Isaiah clearly discerned the necessity of a rupture with the conditions existing at the time of writing, Virgil attempted to legitimate them. However, the authors of both texts share the common vision that hostility must be overcome by mutual acceptance, in other words, by the abolishment of force and the peaceful coexistence of those who once were litigious partners. Mankind will be genuinely human only if it is truly 'ecological', that is, if man is an integrating factor in nature as well as an integrated one. Hence, Isaiah and Virgil teach us that antagonisms and dichotomies are not to be resolved by powerful confrontations, that lead to annihilation, but by the profession and actualization of attitudes that acknowledge the possibility of a plurality of viewpoints, and that create an atmosphere of conviviality. (eds.)

János Szél: Budapest, Hungary

On a relativistic structure in theology

Christoph Wassermann

First, the principal abstractive elements that are effective in physical applications of the principle of relativity are analysed. These elements are the controlled coordination of two apparently conflicting representations of a physical situation (mechanics or electrodynamics), their unification on a higher level of abstraction (relativistic field theory) and the polycontextual conception of the underlying descriptive infrastructure (invariance to transformation).

We then go on to examine theological scenarios in which the same abstractive elements are operative. Special attention is given to the concept of atonement in the sacrificial laws of the pentateuch. It shows that the priestly theology of atonement can be seen as the higher level of abstraction that controllably coordinates two apparently conflicting representations of human existence: the framework of sin and death with that of forgiveness and life.

On the basis of this study we argue that a common relational structure is at work in both theoretical approaches. We refer to it as a 'relativistic' structure, and finally compare it with both the structure of complementarity in physics and the dialectic structure of philosophy. A critical evaluation of the significance of these findings for the physics-theology interface then points out the difficulty of coordinating directly physical and theological representations of the respective relevant situations. It also makes clear that, on higher levels of abstraction, the use of identical abstractive elements may contribute to a theory that controllably coordinates the two disciplines.

Christoph Wassermann: Interdisciplinary Research Group on Theology and Physics, Faculté Autonome de Théologie Protestante, Université de Genève, Geneva, Switzerland

The Academy of Research of the Evangelical Church of the Union, German Democratic Republic, a research report

H. J. Winkler

The Academy has its office in Berlin, Auguststrasse 80, was founded immediately after the Second World War, and is an interdisciplinary community of Christian scientists and academicians who, through dialogue between the natural and human sciences, pose again and again the question of responsible action in teaching and research. Traditional contacts have been kept for years with friends in The Netherlands.

As a contribution to this conference a survey is presented of the symposium on genetics and genetechnology that was organised by the Academy in January 1988. Some points may be highlighted here. According to evangelical understanding, responsibility cannot be delegated. Everybody is responsible - and to know is better than not to know. A new aspect of life today, in particular as regards genetechnology, is that it is *not* always clear what humanity means in science. And the question, 'Does this type of research enhance or disfigure human dignity?', has no clear-cut answer. In point of fact, scientific expectations - science fiction included - already colour everyday language. For instance, a sick person should simply be called a 'sick person', and not be alienated from his condition by (dis)qualifying him or her as a 'particular (genetic) mutant'.

Thus, because of the development of the sciences, the concept of Creation has to be understood better and to be 'implemented' in new ways. A slow transition to active natural selection, however, should not be excluded apriori.

H. J. Winkler: Berlin, German Democratic Republic

The split between science and religion and the doctrine of God's immanence in nature

Joseph Życiński

New discoveries in relativistic cosmology lead to a new philosophical perspective and result in a new cognitive attitude of scientific *Homo spiritualis*. Compared with this attitude, traditional scientific naturalism seems 'shallow and destitute'. An analogous regularity appears in many other disciplines. New cognitive patterns are implied by B. Mandelbrot's description of chaos in terms of fractal mathematics and by I. Prigogine's thermodynamics of dissipative structures, both of which prompt essential revisions of earlier philosophical comments on the biological theory of evolution*.

All those discoveries create a new scientific basis to counteract the present intellectual split between the natural sciences and Christianity. To develop such a basis, and to avoid the many philosophical simplifications that were accepted in the past, we need a new philosophy of nature. It seems that the doctrine of God's immanence in nature and, in particular, the philosophy of *panentheism* provide such a philosophy. It was A. N. Whitehead who, in his system of metaphysics, presented God as the immanent 'Poet of the World'** in order to accentuate his role in creating cosmic harmony. This vision of an immanent divine Logos, who is manifested in the ordered structure of cosmic evolution, remains much closer to the biblical perspective than the philosophical vision of the immovable Mover implied by the cosmological arguments of the past.

Joseph Życiński: The Pontifical Academy of Cracow, Cracow, Poland

---

*   See e.g. Ilya Prigogine, *From being to becoming*, W.H. Freeman and Company, San Francisco 1980.

**   See his *Process and Reality, Part V, Section 4*.

Part III

List of names and addresses

Alaie, L.
P.O. Box 155, IL - 31001 HAIFA

Allert, G.
Höllhäuserweg 43, D - 7570 BADEN-BADEN

Andersen, S.
Institut for Etik og Religionsfilosofi, Aarhus Universitet
(Hovedbygningen, Nrd Ringgade), DK- 8000 AARHUS C

Ariëns, H.
p/a KU-Nieuws, Comeniuslaan 4, NL- 6525 HP NIJMEGEN

Awudza, Mawuli, J.A.
Dept. of Chemistry, University of Science and Technology, GHANA - KUMASI

Becerra-Acevedo, R.
Avenida 2A, Norte, No. 44-185 (Vípasa), COLOMBIA - CALI (Valle)

Becker, Th.
Goethe-Strasse 40, D - 7800 FREIBURG i. Br

Béné, G. J.
DPMC Section de Physique de l'Université de Genève, Institut de Physique,
24 Quai E.-Ansermet, CH - 1211 GENEVE 4

Bennema, P.
Faculteit der Wiskunde en Natuurwetenschappen,
Afdeling Vastestofchemie en Kristalgroei,
Universiteit Nijmegen, Toernooiveld, NL- 6525 ED NIJMEGEN

Bickel, W.
Taubenstrasse 3, D - 4400 MÜNSTER

Bloemendal, M.
Vakgroep Algemene en Analytische Chemie, Subfac. Scheikunde, Vrije Universiteit,
De Boelelaan 1083, NL - 1081 HV AMSTERDAM

Böckmann, P.W.
Religionsvitenskapelig Institutt, Universitetet i Trondheim,
N- 7055 DRAGVOLL

Bokhout, H.
Anemonenweg 32, NL - 2241 XL WASSENAAR

Bonting, S.L.
1006 E. Evelyn Ave., USA - 94086 SUNNY VALE, CA

Bosch, M.W.
Iepenlaan 47, NL - 2061 GJ BLOEMENDAAL

Bourgeois, F.
Plein Vogelzang 13, NL - 3722 AT BILTHOVEN

Brinkman, M.E.
Interuniversitair Instituut voor Missiologie en Oecumenica, Heidelberglaan 2,
NL - 3584 CS UTRECHT

Brom, L.J. van den
Faculteit der Godgeleerdheid, Rijksuniversiteit Utrecht, Postbus 80105,
NL - 3508 TC UTRECHT

Brzeski, M.W.
22 Lipca 1/3, PL- 96-100 SKIERNIEWICE

Carvallo, M.E.
Faculteit der Godgeleerdheid, Rijksuniversiteit Groningen,
Nieuwe Kijk in 't Jatstraat 104, NL - 9712 SL GRONINGEN

Chalmers, B.
Keynes College, University of Kent, GB - CT2 7LR CANTERBURY, KENT

Corbally SJ, C.J.
Vatican Observatory Research Group, Steward Observatory, University of Arizona,
USA - 85721 TUCSON, AZ

Curtin, M.
c/o Religious Programs, RTE, EIRE - DUBLIN 4

Daecke, S.
Flandrische Strasse 36, D - 5100 AACHEN

Derkse, W.F.
Postbus 37, NL - 5260 AA VUGHT

Diekerhof, C.H.
Wilgenweg 13, NL - 7556 HD HENGELO, OV

Dierick, G.
Katholiek Studiecentrum, Katholieke Universiteit Nijmegen, Erasmuslaan 36,
NL - 6525 GG NIJMEGEN

Dijk, P. van
Faculteit der Wijsbegeerte en Maatschappijwetenschappen, Universiteit Twente,
Postbus 217, NL - 7500 AE ENSCHEDE

Dinis SJ, A.
St. Edmund's College, GB - CB3 0BN CAMBRIDGE

Drago, A.
Università di Napoli, Dipartimento di Fisica, Mostra d'Oltremare, Pad. 19-20,
I - 80125 NAPOLI

Drees, W.B.
Hertog Hendriklaan 11, NL - 3743 DL BAARN

Durant, J.R.
The Science Museum, Exhibition Road, GB - SW7 2DD LONDON

Duyn, P. van
Jacob van Maerlantlaan 3, NL - 2343 JX OEGSTGEEST

Engström, P.G.
Mansfield College, Mansfield Road, GB - OX1 3TF OXFORD

Erkelens, H. van
Unit for the history, philosophy and social aspects of science,
Faculty of Physics and Astronomy, Free University, De Boelelaan 1083,
NL- 1081 HV AMSTERDAM

Feil, D.
Faculteit der Chemische Technologie, Universiteit Twente, Postbus 217,
NL - 7500 AE ENSCHEDE

Fennema, J.W.R.
Faculteit der Wijsbegeerte en Maatschappijwetenschappen, Universiteit Twente,
Postbus 217, NL - 7500 AE ENSCHEDE

Fokker, A.D.
Kruislaan 17, NL - 3721 AL BILTHOVEN

Gaál, B.
A Magyarországi Református Egyház, Debreceni Kollégiuma, Kálvin tér 16,
H - 4044 DEBRECEN

Gaizler, G.
Népköztársaság útja 132, H - 1062 BUDAPEST VI

Gierer, A.
Max Planck Institut für Entwicklungsbiologie, Spemannstrasse 35 IV,
D - 7400 TÜBINGEN

Głódź, M.
ul. Mokotowska 51/53 M.12, PL - 00-542 WARSZAWA

Golshani, M.
Department of Physics, Sharif University of Technology, P.O. Box 11356 - 8639,
IRAN - TEHRAN

Görman, U.
Lunds Universitet, Teologiska Institutionen, Sandgatan 1, S - 22350 LUND

Gradussen, W.J.
Breegraven 51, NL - 7231 JB WARNSVELD

Gregersen, N.H.
Institute for Dogmatics, University of Aarhus (Hovedbygningen), DK- 8000 AARHUS

Gust, E.C.
Steinweg 40, D - 3550 MARBURG

Hafner, H.
Unter den Eichen 13, D - 3550 MARBURG

Hageman, M.J.M.
Katholiek Studiecentrum, Katholieke Universiteit Nijmegen, Erasmuslaan 36,
NL- 6525 GG NIJMEGEN

Haikola, L.
Teologiska Institutionen, Lunds Universitet, Sandgatan 1, S - 22350 LUND

Hall, M. van
Ministerie van Onderwijs en Wetenschappen, Postbus 25000,
NL - 2700 LZ ZOETERMEER

Halkes, C.J.M.
Vossenlaan 13, NL- 6531 SB NIJMEGEN

Heijerman, E.
Internationale School voor Wijsbegeerte 'De Queeste', Dodeweg 8,
NL - 3832 RD LEUSDEN

Heller, M.
ul. Powstancόw Warszawy 13/94, PL - 33-110 TARNOW

Hemminger, H.
Evangelische Zentralstelle für Weltanschauungsfragen, Hölderlinplatz 2a,
D - 7000 STUTTGART 1

Hofmann, I.
Am Schloss Stockau 15, D - 6110 DIEBURG

Hübner, J.
Forschungsstätte der Evangelischen Studiengemeinschaft (FEST), Schmeilweg 5,
D - 6900 HEIDELBERG 1

Huisman, W.
Minister Loudonlaan 41, NL- 7521 BA ENSCHEDE

Huyssteen, J., Wentzel V. van
Department of Religion, University of Port Elizabeth, P.O. Box 1600,
RSA - 6000 PORT ELIZABETH

Isak, R.
Arbeitsbereich Dogmatik im Institut für Systematische Theologie,
Universität Freiburg, Werthmannplatz 3,
D - 7800 FREIBURG i. BR

Jackelén, A.
Prästgaarden Högseröd, S - 24033 LÖBERÖD

Jalali, A.
c/o St. John's College, GB - OXFORD

Jong, H.M.E. de
De Bazelstraat 22, NL- 2321 EH LEIDEN

Jongh, J. de
Studentenpastoraat, Universiteit Twente, Postbus 217, NL - 7500 AE ENSCHEDE

Kärkölä, A.
Kotimäen Katu 29 A 1, SF - 20540 TURKU

Kiesow, E.R.
Sektion Theologie der Wilhelm-Pieck-Universität Rostock,
Lehrstuhl für praktische Theologie, Universitätsplatz 5,
DDR - 2500 ROSTOCK

Kirby, R.
3 Victoria Terrace, GB - W5 5QS EALING GREEN, LONDON

Kirschenmann, P.P.
Faculteit der Wijsbegeerte, Vrije Universiteit, Postbus 7161,
NL - 1007 MC AMSTERDAM

Kjöllerström, B.
Department of Theoretical Physics, Sölvegatan 14 a, S - 22362 LUND

Knijff, H.W. de
Faculteit der Theologie, Rijksuniversiteit Utrecht, Heidelberglaan 2,
NL - 3584 CS UTRECHT

Koch, G.K.
Colinslandsedijk 47, NL - 3234 KA TINTE

Koltermann SJ, R.
Philosophisch-Theologische Hochschule Sankt Georgen,
Offenbacher Landstrasse 224,
D - 6000 FRANKFURT/M. 70

Koole, B.
De Grutto 154, NL - 3972 PE DRIEBERGEN

Kooten Niekerk, K. van
Skovgaardsvaenget 634, DK - 8310 TRANBJERG J

Köstler, C.M.
Fichtenweg 11/111, D - 7400 TÜBINGEN

Krolzik, U.
Poppenbüttler Stieg 29, D - 2000 HAMBURG 63

Laarse, P. van de
Veenbesstraat 598, NL - 3765 BS SOEST

Lam, H.
Funch Thomsens Gade 1,1.tv, DK - 8200 AARHUS N

Lange, H.M. de
Frankenslag 81, NL - 2582 HE 's-GRAVENHAGE

Laurikainen, K.V.
Kelotie 4, SF - 01820 KLAUKKALA 2

Lenferink, H.J.M.
Tas 8, NL - 6852 EN HUISSEN

Lepoutre, G.
19 Rue du Bourg, Ennetières-en-Weppes, F - 59320 HAUBOURDIN

Lof, D.
Europaweg 141, NL - 7761 AC SCHOONEBEEK

Manenschijn, G.
Parmentierlaan 29, NL - 1185 CV AMSTELVEEN

Martin, D.
'Cygnetbank', Clydestreet, GB - ML8 5BA CARLUKE, LANARKSHIRE

Maurice, M.A.
Faculteit der Wiskunde en Informatica, Vrije Universiteit, De Boelelaan 1081
NL - 1081 HV AMSTERDAM

May, H.
Evangelische Akademie Loccum, D - 3056 REHBURG-LOCCUM

Medgyesi, G.
Szamóca utca 3, H - 1125 BUDAPEST

Meijknecht, T.
A. Duyckstraat 4, NL - 2613 GZ DELFT

Melsen, A.G.M. van
Adrianaweg 29, NL - 6523 MV NIJMEGEN

Moghomaye, Ouafo, C.
Sonel B.P. 263, CAMEROUN - GAROUA

Mooij, J.
Abel Tasmanlaan 12, NL - 3603 GB MAARSSEN

Morel, B.
16 Rue de l'École-de-Médecine, CH - 1205 GENEVE

Morren, L.
Avenue du Grand Cortil 15A, B - 1348 LOUVAIN-LA-NEUVE

Mortensen, V.
'Forum Teologi Naturvidenskab', Institut for Etik og Religionsfilosofi,
Aarhus Universitet (Hovedbygningen), DK - 8000 AARHUS C

Munk, H.
Latiumpad 2, NL - 5631 JS EINDHOVEN

Musschenga, A.W.
Bezinningscentrum, Vrije Universiteit, Postbus 7161,
NL - 1007 MC AMSTERDAM

Nebelsick, H.P.
deceased March 1989
in life: Center of Theological Inquiry, PRINCETON, N.J.

Neubauer, T.
Viktor-Renner-Strasse 17, D - 7400 TÜBINGEN

Neut, B. van der
A. Toscaninistraat 20, NL - 7558 DX HENGELO, OV

Nijenhuis, E.N.
Chopinstraat 18, NL - 1901 VH CASTRICUM

Noodt, W.
Zoologisches Institut der Universität, Olshausenstrasse 40, D - 2300 KIEL

Nuchelmans, J.C.F.
Katholiek Studiecentrum, Katholieke Universiteit Nijmegen, Erasmuslaan 36
NL - 6525 GG NIJMEGEN

Oosterwegel, G.G.
Von Weberlaan 5, NL - 7522 KB ENSCHEDE

Opitz, H.
Kopernikusstrasse 3, DDR - 4050 HALLE/SAALE

Opočensky, M.
Nepomucká 1025, CS - 15000 PRAHA 5

Oster, M.
15 Victoria road, Summertown, GB - OXFORD

Parsons, M.W.S.
St. Augustine's Vicarage, 155 Almond Street, GB - DE3 6LY DERBY

Paul, I.
100 Glen Road, GB - ML2 7NP WISHAW, LANARKSHIRE

Peacocke, A.R.
55 St. John street, GB - OX1 2LQ OXFORD

Pedersen, O.
Institut for Videnskabshistori, Aarhus Universitet, Ny Munkegade,
DK - 8000 AARHUS

Pękała, M.
Department of Chemistry, University of Warsaw, Al. Zwirki i Wigury 101,
PL - 02-089 WARSZAWA

Petri, C.
Boslaan 16, NL - 7231 DH WARNSVELD

Polkinghorne FRS, J.C.
The President's Lodge, Queens' College, GB - CB3 9ET CAMBRIDGE

Quapp, E.
Philipps-Universität Marburg, Fachbereich Evang. Theologie, Pommernweg 18,
D - 3550 MARBURG 1

Reich, K.H.
Pädagogisches Institut, Rte des Fougères, CH - 1700 FRIBOURG

Reitsma, H.
Patrijslaan 17, NL - 2566 XL 's-GRAVENHAGE

Rivier, D.
Chemin de l'Oche, CH - 1008 JOUXTENS

Rodrigues da Cruz, E.
Pontifícia Universidade Católica de São Paulo, departamento de Teología,
Rua Monte Alegre 984, BRASIL - 05014 SÃO PAULO, SP

Roes, J.H.
Katholiek Documentatiecentrum, Erasmuslaan 36, NL - 6525 GG NIJMEGEN

Scheer, J.
Fachbereich Physik der Universität Bremen, Postfach 330440,
D - 2800 BREMEN 33

Schiffer, E.
13 Chemin de la Montagne, CH -1224 CHENE BOUGERIES, GE

Schipper, F.
p/a Faculteit der Wijsbegeerte, Vrije Universiteit, Postbus 7161,
NL- 1007 MC AMSTERDAM

Schmitz-Moormann, K.
Im Ostholz 160, D - 4630 BOCHUM-LINDEN

Schneider, H.G.
c/o St. Cross College, GB - OX1 3LZ OXFORD

Schocher, A.J.
Voa Baselgia, CH - 7078 LENZERHEIDE

Schoonen, W.
p/a Dagblad TROUW, Postbus 859, NL - 1000 AW AMSTERDAM

Schotman-Veldman, J.L.
Oranje Nassaulaan 41, NL - 3708 GC ZEIST

Sevenhoven, J.C.A.M.
W. Barentszstraat 59, NL - 3572 PD UTRECHT

Shahidi, S.
305 Ave. Matahari, IRAN - TEHRAN

Siciński, M.
c/o Institutt for filosofi, Universitetet i Oslo, Postboks 1024, Blindern,
N - 0315 OSLO 3

Stavenga, G.J.
Johan Frisostraat 15, NL - 9285 TS BUITENPOST

STEGON
Kon. Sophiestraat 124, NL - 2595 TM 's-GRAVENHAGE

Striegnitz, M.
Evangelische Akademie Loccum, D - 3056 REHBURG-LOCCUM

Struikmans, R.
Brahmslaan 103, NL - 2625 BT DELFT

Szél, J.
Ady Endre utca 57, H - 1196 BUDAPEST IX

Thomas, G.
Stauffenbergstrasse 100, D - 7400 TÜBINGEN

Thomson, A.
31 Highburgh Drive, Rutherglen, GB - G73 3RR GLASGOW

Thung, M.A.
Multidisciplinair Centrum voor Kerk en Samenleving, Postbus 19
NL - 3970 AA DRIEBERGEN-RIJSENBURG

Tijmes, P.
Faculteit der Wijsbegeerte en Maatschappijwetenschappen, Universiteit Twente,
Postbus 217, NL - 7500 AE ENSCHEDE

Torrance, T.F.
37 Braidfarm Road, GB - EH10 6LE EDINBURGH

Treumann, A.
Neue Strasse 55, D - 7402 KIRCHENTELLINSFURT

Trigg, R.H.
Department of Philosophy, University of Warwick, GB - CV4 7AL COVENTRY

Vahanian, G.
Faculté de Théologie Protestante, Université des Sciences Humaines,
Place de l'Université 9, F - 67084 STRASBOURG CEDEX

Van der Veken, J.
Predikherenstraat 11, B - 3000 LEUVEN

Vernhout, P.P.
ul. Mikhnevskaya 11-80, SU - 115547 MOSKVA

Verveen, A.A.
Faculteit der Geneeskunde, afdeling Fysiologie, Rijksuniversiteit Leiden,
Wassenaarseweg 62, NL - 2333 AL LEIDEN

Voorhoeve, M.W.
Prinses Marijkelaan 16 II, NL - 3708 DD ZEIST

Waringa, C.G.
Groningerstraatweg 211, NL - 8922 GG LEEUWARDEN

Wassermann, C.
Faculté Autonome de Théologie Protestante, Place de l'Université 3,
CH - 1211 GENEVE 4

Weidlich, W.
Institut für theoretische Physik der Universität Stuttgart, Pfaffenwaldring 57/III,
D - 7000 STUTTGART 80

Wiltsher, C.D.
55 The Avenue, GB - DH1 4EB DURHAM

Winkler, H.J.
Eginhardstrasse 19, DDR - 1157 BERLIN

Wintermans, J.F.G.M.
Grameystraat 4, NL - 6525 DP NIJMEGEN

Woerden, H. van
Kapteyn Laboratorium, Rijksuniversiteit Groningen, Postbus 800,
NL - 9700 AV GRONINGEN

Woestijne, J. van de
p/a Redactie KU-nieuws, Comeniuslaan 4, NL - 6525 HP NIJMEGEN

Zangger, C.
Am Wettinger Tobel 38, CH - 8049 ZÜRICH

Zyciński, J.
Bernardynska 3, PL - 31-069 KRAKOW